The Historic Landscape of Devon

A study in change and continuity

Lucy Ryder

WIND*gather* PRESS

Windgather Press
is an imprint of
Oxbow Books, Oxford, UK

ISBN 978-1-905119-38-7

A CIP record for this book is available from the British Library

This book is available direct from:

Oxbow Books, Oxford, UK
(Phone: 01865-241249; Fax: 01865-794449)

and

The David Brown Book Company
PO Box 511, Oakville, CT 06779, USA
(Phone: 860-945-9329; Fax: 860-945-9468)

or from our website

www.oxbowbooks.com

Cover: Photo of Combe Martin by Andrew Warran

Printed in Great Britain by
Short Run Press, Exeter

Contents

Abstract

Methodologically, the aims of this book are simple; to discuss the nineteenth-century historic landscape of Devon though the creation, manipulation, and querying of a Geographical Information Systems (GIS) database. My intention is not only to look at the physical evidence of change and development in the historic landscape through field and settlement patterns, but also to discuss the relationship between field and settlement morphologies and patterns of nineteenth-century Tithe Surveys landholding. The investigation is undertaken through the examination of field and settlement morphology, but also Tithe Survey landholdings, field-names and associated documentary evidence, for three case-study areas in Devon. Key issues of the research include: how far back patterns of nineteenth-century landholding can be traced or projected back into the medieval period; the occurrence and extent of open field farming in Devon; and the spread of nucleated and dispersed settlements. However, it is also my intention to look beyond the physical aspects of landscapes and discuss the idea of landscape *pays* and the identification of regional differences in the study of the historic landscape.

Acknowledgments

This book has grown from my doctorate thesis undertaken at the University of Exeter and from the work carried out during the Community Landscape Project. In light of this my thanks go to my supervisors Prof. Steve Rippon and Prof. Tony Brown; Dr. Ollie Creighton; Sean Hawken and the volunteers of the Community Landscapes Project, in particular, Ken Wakeling and the Clayhidon History Society for access to their archive; Brian and Liz Tusten for lending me their private Family Faces volumes; Steve Hobbs from the Hartland Town Trust for his help and digital archive; Roger Grimley for the loan of his Bigbury Tithe Apportionment workbook; Lorinda Legge for digitising the fields of Clayhidon; Joy Smerdon and Jane Young for typing up the Tithe Apportionments for Churchstow and Clayhidon; Doug Hislop and Grahame Smith.

My thanks must also go to Frances Griffith, Bill Horner, and the staff of the Devon HER for their help, the use of the Landline digital data, and the much appreciated coffee and biscuits; Dr. Sam Turner for the useful conversations and the access to the Devon Historic Landscape Characterisation before its completion; Dr. Mark Riley and Dr. David Harvey for the use of the Nymet Rowlands material and copies of unpublished journal articles; Dr. Phil Hull and Steve Clarke at Rolle Campus of Plymouth University for access to the Sam Richards Archive; Dr. Mark Gillings for his support and advice, particularly in all things GIS; Mary Reece, Peter Smith, and the staff at the Exeter University Disability Resource Centre; Prof. Tom Williamson for encouraging me to write up my research; and Dr. Joe Franklin for help with motivation (!).

This book is dedicated to Neil and Elowen Ryder and Pete and Sue Franklin for their unwavering and constant support throughout.

List of Illustrations and Tables

Figures

Charts

Tables

Appendix 1 (Tables 1–11)

Appendix 2

Abbreviations

AR2/727/1	in Woolgar 1999
CLHG	Clayhidon Local History Group
DB	Domesday Book.
DRO	Devon Record Office
FA	Feudal Aids. The Deputy Keeper of Records, 1879.
FamF	Family Faces series.
FF	Feet of Fines
GS	Geological Survey of Great Britain (England and Wales) Drift 1:50,000 Sheets 326 and 340; 311
IPM	*Inquisitiones post mortem*
Leland 1535–1543	The Itinerary of John Leland in or about the Years 1535–1543. Toulmin-Smith, L. (ed.) 1907.
NMR	National Monument Record
PND	Place Names of Devon
PRO	Public Record Office
RH	*Rotuli Hundredorum* Record Commission 1812–1818, 2 vols. i pp. 73b, 89b
SMR <ref>	Sites and Monument Record <record number>
SRA	Sam Richards Archive. Plymouth University Rolle Campus Exmouth
TdN	*Testa de Nevill*

CHAPTER ONE

Introduction

'Roads and lanes wind and twist abruptly in apparent confusion all over the landscape … So many farmsteads in Devon lie alone at the end of a deep-sunken lane thick with mud in winter, stony and rutted in summer. Each lane has its own history: it is not there by accident: and every twist it makes once had some historical meaning …'

(Hoskins 1954, 4)

Introduction: seeking the origins of the historic landscape

The introductory quotation comes from W. G. Hoskins' 1954 book *Devon*, a study which still forms one of the most in-depth analyses of the county. Within this single paragraph Hoskins neatly summarises the complexities of the Devon landscape, by describing the interlocking nature of roads, settlements, and fields. Hoskins knew that the landscape of Devon had a time depth in which it was created; a sequence of evolution and change which spans back into the Mesolithic and beyond (Fig. 1.1).

FIGURE 1.1. The complexities of Devon's landscape. Above the Grimspound, Dartmoor

The work of Hoskins, both in Devon and the rest of the country, has inspired and influenced a succession of historians and, latterly, archaeologists, and it is within this rich inheritance that this research is set.

By focusing on three different areas of Devon, chosen to represent the different characteristics of the county, the overall theme of this book is to understand the origins and, in particular, development of the nineteenth-century historic landscape; the landscape recorded and mapped through parish Tithe Surveys of 1839 to 1845. However, a landscape study is not merely about identifying the physical entities, such as field patterns and settlements interconnected by routeways, or understanding their origin through assigning their characteristics to particular morphological models. The aim of this study is to look at not only the physical evidence of landscape change and development but also the relationship between the morphologies of field and settlement evolution and patterns of nineteenth-century landholding as recorded in the Tithe Survey, and, by use of this methodology, add greater depth to our understanding of the historic landscape. Crucial to this is the development of a holistic approach in which different strands of information are collated, expanded, and explained. This is undertaken through the examination of field morphology and settlement patterns, Tithe Survey landholdings, field-names, and associated documentary evidence, such as the eleventh-century Domesday Survey and medieval *Inquisitions Post Mortem* (IPM), but also by looking at more 'perceptual' evidence, such as folklore and storytelling. This will be discussed in greater depth shortly.

Taking all these factors into account, a new morphological approach is needed to assimilate and manage the different types of information which make up a study of Devon's historic landscape. The use of Geographical Information Systems (GIS) in understanding the historic landscape is paramount, and allows questions such as the relationship between morphology and landownership to be asked. This will be discussed in greater detail later in this chapter.

The use of GIS is fundamental to establishing how far back patterns of nineteenth-century landholding can be traced or projected into the medieval period, and this is important particularly from a methodological point of view. Opinion is divided regarding back projection of landscape features into the past, particularly using sources such as the Tithe Survey. Despite this, Roberts and Wrathmell's work is perhaps the largest scale use of nineteenth-century sources for categorising the landscape of England. Roberts and Wrathmell (2002, 27) used nineteenth-century Tithe Surveys as analytical tools to try and understand the pre-industrial landscape from which, they argue, traces of earlier landscape can be seen. Studying the nineteenth-century historic landscape in this way allows for other information (such as population densities and the past extent of woodland) to be considered; building up layers of information which can inform about the development of past landscapes.

The collation of information, namely the different layers of the historic landscape, relies on the identification of the morphological patterns. This is inextricably linked to the back projection of landscapes. The morphologies identified through field and settlement patterns can be linked with other strands of information to corroborate the suggested development of particular landscape features. For example, long, narrow strip-like fields form a distinct morphological type and combined with field-names could be used to confirm the presence of now enclosed open field regimes. These distinct types of landscape patterns can then be used to make informed suppositions or predictions about the origins and development of other areas where the same combination of morphology and documentary evidence occurs.

Interest in the existence and extent of open field farming in Devon has seen a resurgence in in recent years, with recent landscape studies suggesting that open fields were more widespread in Devon than first thought. The logical extension of this is to establish the actual extent of the spread of nucleated and dispersed settlements within the county, and of where Devon reflects the landscape trends throughout not only the South-west[1] but also the whole of England. Discussion will particularly focus on the idea that the north and north eastern regions of Devon experienced a nucleation of settlement related to manorial control, compared with the development of nucleated settlement in other parts of the county.

The relationship between field and settlement morphology and patterns of Tithe Survey landholding are perhaps the most significant. A number of studies have mapped patterns of landownership on a hamlet or parish scale, however, through the use of a GIS database a far larger area can be investigated and this allows previously unsuspected clarity to be revealed.

Finally, in light of using a GIS database, another important theme is the idea of landscape *pays* and the identification of regional differences in the study of the historic landscape. It is important to establish what causes these differences and whether these *pays* can also occur at a more local parish or settlement level.

Approaching a new methodology to study Devon's historic landscape

As alluded to in the previous section, despite the importance of these themes, it is the methodological approach and the use of GIS which is fundamental to how the historic landscape is researched. Therefore, in order to answer the questions regarding the relationship between landholding practices and field morphology and the issues relating to the extent of open field systems within the Devon landscape, this research will use a new morphological approach created for this study.

The methodology developed builds upon the work of Williamson (1987) and will be discussed in more detail in the next chapter. It is important to highlight that Williamson used retrogressive analysis in order to understand the past; treating the landscape as layers to be stripped away. The primary aim here is to create a more regressive approach, looking at the landscape in a more philosophical way. This approach differs from Williamson's retrogressive analysis in a number of ways. Perhaps the most obvious difference is the way in which the historic landscape, as an object in the archaeological record, is treated. Williamson removed the modern features of the landscape and used archaeological features, such as Roman roads, to work out which parts were laid out before or after the known monuments. Once this was established, Williamson retrogressively peels away layers to end up with the earliest landscapes. This methodology results in a number of time slices, explaining the landscapes evolution. In this study, rather than stripping away layers of information to recreate the medieval landscape, the methodology used focuses on key elements of the historic landscape, and seeks to understand the processes which acted upon it. An important tool in the creation of this methodology is the Geographical Information Systems (GIS) database.

The applications of GIS are discussed in more detail in later chapters, but it is important to highlight that without the use of such a database this study of Devon's historic landscape could not have been conducted on the scale and depth attempted here. GIS enables a forum for multi-disciplinary studies to be created, which in turn assists interpretation (Chapman 2006, 21). As such, the use of GIS in landscape studies is nothing new. However, the approaches which investigate the medieval or historic landscape have been hitherto achieved with varying success, and one methodological example will be discussed here.

English Heritage's national programme of the Historic Landscape Character-isation (HLC), undertaken on a local government level, is a GIS-based method for defining the historic and archaeological dimensions of the present day landscape (Fairclough *et al.* 2002, 69). The new methodology which HLC undertakes is, they suggest, new to archaeology but not to other fields such as landscape assessment (Fairclough *et al.* 2002, 70). The method works under the assumption that the historic landscape is first and foremost the product of change, and crucial to it is the scale and broad-brush approach, treating landscapes as material culture (*ibid.* 2002, 70–1).

Due to the depth of scale at which HLC is carried out, its overall archaeological validity can be questioned, although Turner (2006) states that 'valuing the landscape as historic on a broad scale will not necessarily mean the attenuation of other interests: instead, it might help foster a more balanced, wide-ranging and democratic debate about what we really value and why'. This is discussed more in Chapter Six with reference to the Devon HLC, but it must be noted that in the broadest sense HLCs provide a wealth of information about changes to the present day landscape which would not otherwise be visible.

To understand the patterns of change and continuity occurring with Devon's past landscapes, the earliest known consistently available map source for the three study areas is the nineteenth-century Tithe Survey. This source is available for all parishes in all three areas, although the coverage varies considerably in some places (see Chapter Three regarding the discussion of Dunkeswell Parish in the Blackdown Hills), and some surveys are damaged (such as Hemyock in the Blackdown Hills and Hartland in the Hartland Moors area) causing gaps.

Despite these problems, this survey provides an excellent base for the study of Devon's historic landscape. An information layer is created within the GIS database which combines a number of individual Tithe Surveys. Each Tithe Survey field is given the Tithe Survey field number which identifies it within the Tithe Apportionment. The map layer created within the GIS is then linked to a dbf file which contains the Apportionment data via the field number. Each entry within this database, such as the individual landowner with the landownership class, is given a unique colour ID, so that any distribution patterns can be identified not only on a parish level but also across the study areas. Each field is coded with seven pieces of standard information; field number, field name or description, land owner, land occupier, land use, and the estate the field belongs to (if available). Other information such as rent, acreage, and Tithe information from other sources (for example, information from William Braddick 1839 *Working Book for Clayhidon*) is also added to the database if available. The coding of the Tithe Survey information in this way allows for the historic landscape to have more depth; moving beyond the recording of field and settlement morphology, providing information over a wide area on material such as field-names, and for more information, such as post-dissolution landholdings, to be compared with the nineteenth-century landscape. In addition to the Tithe Survey information, further documentary information is also added to the GIS database, for example, Domesday Holdings, the location of monastic estates, TdN records, and physical features such as geology, topography, and drainage.

With the creation of this GIS database, the presence and location of morphological features, such as ring-fenced enclosures, relic open field systems, and nucleated settlements, can be discussed in relation to the addition information added from the Tithe Apportionment and other documentary sources. Perhaps more importantly, the occurrence of patterns within the historic landscape which 'fit' with known models of agricultural processes, such as convertible husbandry, or particular events, and can be seen throughout a study area, can be identified as landscape signatures. The occurrence of these signatures can then be discussed within the wider context of the historic landscape of Devon, and whether they can be transferred between study areas.

The creation of this methodology relies on a number of factors, firstly the use of a consistently available source, secondly, the identification of known methodological features, and thirdly, the recognition of landscape features and signatures which mirror the evidence presented though documentary sources. Due to the nature of the archaeological record in the three areas of Devon considered in this study, there is no firm dating evidence to confidently confirm any suggested chronology. However, by the regressive approach devised for this research, a timeline of events can be suggested (see Chapter 6). Within this timeline, episodes such as the formation of open field systems, or the enclosure of wasteland though Acts of Parliament can be given more precise dates, due to what is known about them from other areas, or from the associated documentary evidence. From these 'fixed' points other events can be added to the timeline sequentially. By creating this methodology, the complexities of the Devon landscape can be addressed.

Addressing the issues of Devon's landscapes

The short quotation at the start of this chapter reinforces the argument that Devon provides an interesting case-study for landscape researchers. However, despite interest from historians and cultural geographers (such as H. G Hoskins and Harold Fox), little research has been conducted from an archaeological perspective outside of Dartmoor and Exmoor. Interest which has occurred in Devon's landscape has drawn attention because of its complexity and apparent juxtaposition with the academically 'familiar' landscapes of the lowland 'Midlands Zone', which comprised large arable fields, neat hedgerows, and nucleated villages.

Much of the archaeological and historical research previously undertaken within Devon focuses upon the upland regions of the county. Research has most notably concentrated on Dartmoor, which has a long tradition of study. This fascination with Dartmoor began in earnest in 1862, when, reflecting the fascination for all things Druidical, it was singled out as a 'natural Druid temple' (Timms 1994, 7). Subsequently the Dartmoor Exploration Society was established, and excavations focused primarily on prehistoric monuments. Of particular interest were the monuments at Grimspound, and the first 'systematic' excavation by the Dartmoor Exploration Society was conducted in 1894 (*ibid*. 1994, 1).

The wealth of historical narratives for the county which have resulted from the archaeological investigations of Dartmoor has provided a valuable insight into Devon's historical past. However, as a consequence, there has been less archaeological investigation outside these uplands. This is particularly true of the lowland areas of Devon which have been relatively neglected archaeologically in relation to the upland moors, and therefore the nature of past human activity here is little understood. Areas such as the 'upland fringes' and areas seen as economically and socially marginal have also been overlooked; these include the coastal areas of north Devon, and the Greensand Belt of the Blackdown Hills. The term marginality within this book refers to a perceived agricultural inferiority, and an upland aspect as consisting of moorland or unenclosed rough pasture. Marginality is also used to refer to regions socially divided from surrounding areas though topography or cultural reasons (including fear or illness).

The distinctive landscape of the South-west must be seen within its wider context; Devon and the South-west are frequently compared with the large scale arable producing regions of the Midlands Zone. Therefore, various schemes characterising the historic landscape have been created, many of which have been informed by the agricultural potential of land, and defined by topography.

Regional divisions are particularly affected by settlement nucleation or dispersion. Before discussing field patterns and the agricultural practices which shaped the landscape within Devon it is important to define the key differences which divide the county and the South-west from the rest of England. The first key difference is the preconception that much of the south-west had a dispersed settlement pattern. This then informs ideas about agricultural cooperation and estate structures.

Village or hamlet? A question of nucleation and dispersal

Roberts and Wrathmell (2000) comprehensively mapped nineteenth-century rural settlement patterns for the whole of England. Figure 1.2 illustrates the difference in nucleated settlement density between Cornwall and Devon and neighbouring Somerset. Roberts and Wrathmell's mapping has become crucial in any discussion of the distribution of settlements. Using nineteenth-century sources, they divide the county into three provinces: the nucleated central province, the northern and western province (in which Devon lies), and the south-eastern province. These provinces are then divided into a number of sub-provinces and smaller local regions based upon the presence, absence, and variation in the intensity of nucleation or dispersion (Roberts and Wrathmell 2000, 3, 16).

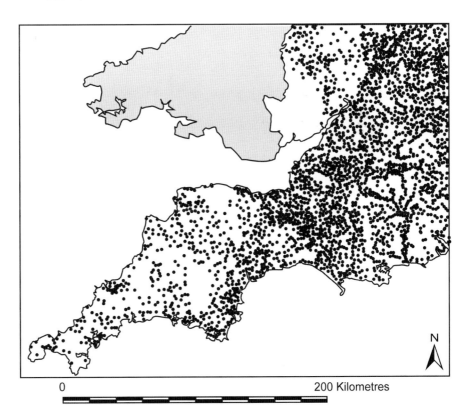

FIGURE 1.2. Distribution of nucleated settlements defining the dispersed 'Ancient Countryside' of the South-west from the concentrated 'Midlands zone' (Redrawing after Roberts and Wrathmell 2000, 7)

N

0   200 Kilometres

Key to this analysis is the definition of what is a nucleated settlement, as this categorisation underpins the characterisation of the historic landscape. Previous research in medieval settlements has suggested alternative explanations to explain nucleation; manorial influences created villages for efficient management of estates, with population density used to suggest people were forced into nucleation for co-operative farming. Cultural changes in the shape of the Anglo-Saxons, Vikings, and Normans has also been cited as a determining factor as to whether a settlement became nucleated or not (Lewis *et al.* 2001, 23).

As mentioned above, the Midlands Zone landscape tends to represent the 'norm' from which everywhere else deviates (see Rackham, 1986). This area has seen the greatest concentration of research into the origins and development of settlement and in particular the emergence of nucleated villages. Figure 1.3, taken from Roberts (1996, 30) and based on Slicher van Bath's 1967 scheme (discussed in Chapter Two), is a schematic model of a 'typical' nucleated settlement and its associated resources.

The central circle of the model illustrated in figure 1.3 contains the dwellings of the settlement and the church/chapel or manorial house. Each dwelling had an associated plot of land. The second ring illustrates land directly associated with the habitation. Present here are tree crops and orchards (a land use of particular relevance in the South-west) and associated meadow land and

FIGURE 1.3. Schematic model of a nucleated settlement and its associated resources (Redrawing after Roberts 1996, 30)

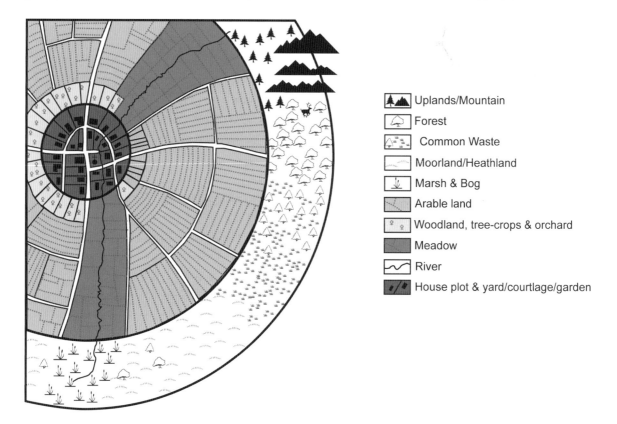

Uplands/Mountain

Forest

Common Waste

Moorland/Heathland

Marsh & Bog

Arable land

Woodland, tree-crops & orchard

Meadow

River

House plot & yard/courtlage/garden

unenclosed strip fields managed through co-operation, and controlled by the manor (Astill 1988b, 64). Beyond these strips and orchards, there is more arable and meadow land, this time divided into parcel blocks as the open field became enclosed. The final ring represents the upland moorlands, commons, and marsh land. This land can be taken for arable production when demand is great, but is generally used for grazing of stock.

In comparison to this neat model of nucleation, Devon was characterised by a combination of scattered hamlets and farms and nucleated villages during the Middle Ages (Williamson 2002, 115). These nucleated settlements are particularly prevalent in the Devon lowlands to the east and south of the county (Roberts and Wrathmell 2000, 57). Hoskins (1952a, 290), however, suggests that there was a 'big village setup' in some parishes in north Devon which were affected by the presence of the powerful Dynham family.

To illustrate the point further, figure 1.4 demonstrates the differences in medieval settlements and field morphology between the classic 'Midlands' landscape and the varying types of settlement seen in the South-west (Roberts and Wrathmell 2002, 65–7).

Example 1 is the 'classic' nucleated settlement. The central village encompassed by fields of arable and meadow, divided into strips with multiple ownership. This is surrounded by woodland and common pasture which may be held by

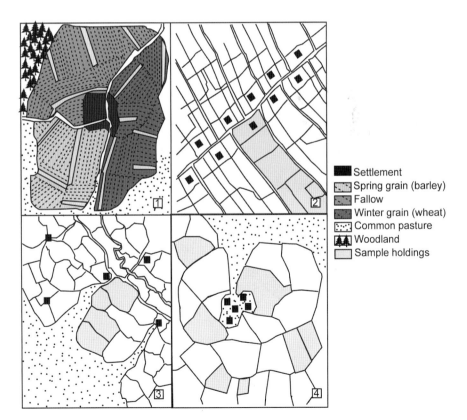

■ Settlement
░ Spring grain (barley)
▒ Fallow
▓ Winter grain (wheat)
⋯ Common pasture
▲ Woodland
☐ Sample holdings

FIGURE 1.4. Models of settlement and related fields systems (Redrawing after Roberts and Wrathmell 2000, 65–7)

a single farmer. This is the pattern described in figure 1.3. Example 2 shows the 'co-axial' systems which generally occur in upland areas, and shows parallels to the prehistoric reaves found on Dartmoor. In comparison, Example 3 illustrates morphology of settlement and field systems for upland valleys; the areas of open rough pasture common in the South-west, north of England and the Welsh borders. Within this model there are successive head dykes (boundaries between the enclosed land and the commons) creating droveways (Roberts and Wrathmell 2002, 67). Example 4 relates to the plan of upland hamlets, which are common in the South-west and North-west of England. These may have developed from temporary or squatter occupation sites, creating a hamlet with a ring-fenced enclosure with land held either as blocks or strips (Roberts and Wrathmell 2002, 67). This type of layout can be seen throughout England, and corresponds with the pattern of fields seen in diagram 9 of figure 2.1 discussed in later chapters.

The creation of such models is useful, but can be misleading. Astill (1988a, 36) states that in the past the definition of village was easily defined 'as the epitome of rural settlement in the lowland areas of England', and dispersed settlements were 'solitary building groups or hamlets…typical only of the highland zone'. This polarisation simply does not work, and archaeologists and historians cannot be so clear-cut in their descriptions of settlement (Astill 1988a, 36).

What makes a nucleated hamlet and what constitutes a 'village', is still a point of interpretation. In the South-west much of the research and excavation of medieval settlements during the 1960s and 70s focused on post-twelfth-century 'typical' settlements in areas now deemed economically marginal (Astill 1988a, 41–3). For example, in Somerset the survival of irregular (agglomerations of unequal plots) and polyfocal villages within the archaeological record may indicate earlier, Saxon, scattered hamlets and farmsteads (Ellison 1983, 7). In Devon, the excavation of longhouses formed the foundation of discussion into medieval vernacular building practice. Work completed at Okehampton (see Austin 1978) has become an archetype for settlement in the county. Subsequent excavations have provided information leading to the establishment of a homogeneous tradition. Although little is known about their origin, longhouses were thought to have had a life span of 150 to 200 years (Austin and Thomas 1990, 55). The demise of the longhouse is less discussed, but Fox (1989, 43–4) states that with the decline of the smallholder in the early Middle Ages an important transformation manifested itself within the south-western landscape. Muir (2001, 107) suggests that increased bureaucracy of the later medieval period and the growth in farms attributed to a break of manorial control and the change to copyholder tenants could explain the number of individual holdings within this period.

Despite this research, the problem of defining settlement type arises from the 'vague application of "village"' to the surviving archaeology (Austin 1985, 75). The survival of stone-built sites on Dartmoor creates a distorted chronology and typology of settlements that cannot related to Devon's lowland areas (Austin

1985, 71). Where research has focused on the dispersed low lying settlements of the South-west, a different social structure can be seen. Dispersed settlement functioned as communities through sharing use of land and amenities over a wide area, forming strong common boundaries (Sawyer 1985, 6; Fox 1999, 279). Over time these dispersed farmsteads and hamlets formed *vills*, or townships. These are considered to have been 'the most ancient and stable of the units of local administration', consisting of a group of farmers sharing a defined area (Winchester 1997, 6). Within these dispersed settlements were a high number of free tenants, who were generally considered as being of a higher status, and who could, theoretically, quit their tenancies at any time (Fox and Padel 2000, liii–lvii). This can be compared with the social structure associated with the settlement evidence of areas such as Dartmoor, which were thought to be a more servile population (Lewis *et al.* 2001, 24).

It must be noted that, with the decline of the Devon longhouse, little work has concentrated on the shrinkage or abandonment of lowland settlements, be that farmstead or village, within Devon and the South-west (see Fox 1989, 49). This valid point needs to be considered with reference to what classes as a nucleated settlement in the first place. The categorisation of villages, or indeed what classes as nucleation, is particularly subjective. Roberts and Wrathmell (2000, 9) suggest that nucleated settlements are definable as discreet entities despite variations in physical size, degree of building intensity, and the extent to which elements like open spaces are concentrated. A village can also be defined by its relationship with the wider landscape. For example, its position as the sole settlement within a parish, its relationship with open fields, and the co-operative management of resources, such as metal working.

Within Devon it is clear that the little evidence available for upland and lowland areas indicates that nucleated settlements which could be classed as villages (due to open fields, service provision such as churches, and shared resources) are present alongside isolated farmsteads, or plots with one or two dwellings in landscapes generally defined as dispersed. I argue that the relationship between nucleated and dispersed settlements is more complex than first thought, and that the presence of villages related to a number of factors relating to the landscape as a whole.

The characterisation of the rural landscape

So far I have discussed that the categorisation of settlement distribution defines other landscape classifications. Of these various schemes, drawing on the work of Fox and others, Oliver Rackham's is one of the simplest. Rackham (1986, 1–4), classed much of Devon as part of the Highland Zone of England, with the county sharing physical similarities to the northern counties, like the western part Yorkshire. Put simply, the Highland zone refers to upland areas, but Rackham (1986, 4) also states that it defines a landscape of moors, dales, ancient oakwoods, and a mountain way of life'. The remaining area of the county, along the Devon/Somerset border, formed part of the Ancient Countryside classification, which also included the Welsh Marches, and south-eastern England including Sussex, Essex, Suffolk, and Kent (Rackham 1986, 1–5). The Ancient Countryside consisted of hamlets and small towns rather than villages; isolated farms; irregular mixed species hedges with much of the land enclosed before 1700; many sunken winding roads and footpaths; and small wooded areas of mixed antiquity, with some isolated pollarding, and abundant heathland.

The categorisations of the landscape into the zones are defined predominantly by agricultural production. The Highland Zone and Ancient Countryside regions are in direct comparison to the Midland Zone or 'Champion' landscape. The Midlands landscape is deemed to be most favourable zone for arable production characterised by nucleated settlements and open fields.

In the Midlands landscape the open field systems were generally organised through the manorial court as a method to ensure the resources were distributed amongst the inhabitants (Hall 1982, 22; Astill 1988b, 64). The open fields necessitated co-operation and, therefore, are associated with nucleated settlements (Astill 1988b, 64). The changes in the blocks of furlongs give an idea how these fields systems were laid out in the fourteenth and fifteenth centuries (Hall 1982, 46). Furlongs were a number of furrows grouped together in one section, referring to an area of land (Hall 1982, 6). The land attached to a holding or virgate, varied in size from region to region, with small acreage typical for intensively cultivated areas with little marginal land (Hall 1982, 17).

Williamson (2002, 11) states that although this category of Ancient Countryside is a broad generalisation (which Rackham himself acknowledges) the classification has a sound basis. Moreover, Rackham's division importantly highlights a separation between east Devon and the rest of the county. This is of interest and suggests that when discussing regional variation and the development of the historic landscape, it should not be assumed that the county should be treated as one complete unchanging entity.

Williamson (2003, 22) also notes that historians and archaeologists have long known open field systems were present in every English county. In Devon, this was highlighted by the work of W. G. Hoskins and H. P. R. Finberg who during the fifties and sixties defined landscape studies for the county. As a Devonian Hoskins focused much of his academic energies on the study of Devon's landscape history, and his internal perspective of Devon provides an interesting interpretation of past landscapes in the county. As Everitt (2004, 6) states 'in Hoskins' vision of the landscape, as in his own nature, there was a deep vein of poetry, yet nothing in the least mystical or unreal'. Hoskins had the ability of relating visual evidence to the structure of landscape, the evolution of the economy, and society behind it (Everitt 2004, 7). His lack of interest in the mystical or unreal may go some way to explaining why much of his landscape studies began in the early medieval period and virtually excluded prehistoric material. Despite this, Hoskins (1954, 14; 1955, 82) saw Devon as a complex entity divided by streams and valleys, and he drew parallels between the west and north of England, due to the occurrence of scattered hamlets and farmsteads in remote clearings. Comparison is also made between Devon and Kent, as both counties underwent enclosure of open fields during the thirteenth and fourteenth centuries (Hoskins 1955, 85). Therefore, the lands that Hoskins classed as ancient enclosure covered the 'peripheral counties of England'; areas such as Devon, Sussex, and Kent (Hoskins 1955, 184).

In 1948 Hoskins set up and held the chair of the Department of English Local History based at the University of Leicester, and was later succeeded by Finberg. It was the latter's studies on the medieval field systems in Devon that suggested that open fields, previously the characteristic of the 'Midlands' zone, were present within the county. Using documentary sources Finberg confirmed the existence of individually named strips dividing larger enclosures, and used the documentary sources to examine the early tendency of enclosure developing from strip fields (Finberg 1952b, 267–8, 277).

The work of both Hoskins and Finberg was based on systematic regional comparisons and in-depth studies of the historic environments (Phythian-Adams 1998). Many landscape scholars working in England and particularly those researching within Devon have developed this early work, and provided a sound historical narrative for the county. From this antecedence, there is a well defined historical narrative of Devon in the medieval period providing information for the archaeologically neglected areas.

The agricultural landscape: some examples

It is important to consider the processes which shaped Devon's historic landscape. Homans (1941, 16) states that in the medieval period Devon was an old-enclosed woodland county with fenced infields, and yet, the country is associated with the moors of Dartmoor and Exmoor. Homans argues that areas under plough in the medieval and post-medieval period tended to be enclosed, and G. J. Turner, a nineteenth-century traveller, described '…small, squarish fields and big walls…' (Homans 1941, 16). Neither Homan's nor Turner's accounts of Devon can be seen as impartial records, for as Fox (1975, 182) notes, these accounts came from visitors who were travelling well-worn routes across the county. Nevertheless, they provide an interesting contrast with the work of Hoskins, whose view of the Devon landscape was defined by the familiarity of a native Devonian.

The relative extent of open and enclosed fields in Devon is unclear. Nevertheless, it is known that during the early medieval period parts of the Devon landscape was divided into intermixed strips and subdivided open fields. These strips and open fields became enclosed between the thirteenth and sixteenth centuries. It is thought that most hamlets did not 'have the communal form of agriculture necessary for an open field system; instead there was an infield-outfield system' (Astill 1988b, 63). The type of cultivation practiced in medieval Devon was also different to the Midlands. Jewell (1981, 95), an agricultural historian based in

Devon, suggests that ley farming, a rotation between tillage crops and 'ley' or grassland, was the basic field husbandry of Devon and Cornwall from the sixteenth century. The successful establishment of grassland was due to the relatively mild climate and well-distributed rainfall, providing a system which worked under varying intensities of cropping or animal stocking. Jewell argues that this form of agriculture differs from convertible husbandry, a system which he describes as being 'more English…where reversion was generally from arable to "permanent" grass' (*ibid*. 1981, 95–6).

This division is hard to justify, and it is suggested that Jewell may just be pedantic. Nevertheless, Fox and Padel's (2000) work in the South-west on patterns of agriculture during the fourteenth century describes a model of ley or convertible husbandry. Farms laid out in numerous small closes were ideal for crop rotation and intensive livestock farming.

The common configuration worked on the idea that a farm of 30 acres would have seen around eight enclosed compartments of three to four acres. Crops were grown in the enclosed infields, those nearest the settlement, followed by grass for up to five years. The outfields, that is the land beyond the infield usually above the settlement, consisted of moorland and furze that was divided up at specific times and cropped for two or three years. It was then left to revert back to heath over a period of at least eight years (Tonkin 1811, 63 cited by Fox 1973, 22; Finberg 1951, 32; Dyer 1982, 21; Fox and Padel 2000, lxx–lxxi). Crops would vary, for example in west Devon the crop consisted of wheat, barley and oats which were predominantly for livestock (Havinden 1969, 8). Therefore, even when under cultivation, Havinden (1969, 8) suggests that the crop for human consumption was only produced two years out of ten. This indicates the predominance of animal husbandry within the rural economy.

An example of how such a regime worked can be seen at Holne Moor on Dartmoor. The work undertaken by Fleming and Ralph (1982) at Holne Moor illustrates that access to moorland was gained from tracks leading through a series of fields. These fields are dated to around the tenth century, and were enclosed in a lobe and divided into three parts. This suggests these fields may have been used for crop rotation (Astill 1988b, 82). In the thirteenth century, small scale field extensions were created, followed by a large enclosure and new access routes onto the moorland. Around 1300 it is thought that a larger extension was created, which was briefly cultivated before being returned to moorland. In this later period the other extensions and some of the original fields also reverted to pasture, a state in which they remained (Fleming and Ralph 1982, 125–6; 130–132).

Land for convertible husbandry was generally converted from existing cleared land. However it is suggested that in some parts of the county land for ley or convertible husbandry came from assarting into woodland, particularly during the medieval period. Taken from the Old French word *essarter*, 'to grub up trees', assarting is the clearance of wood and scrubland on common land (Hoskins 1955, 86). Evidence of this encroachment can be seen on Dartmoor, which under the jurisdiction of the Duchy of Cornwall had become heavily wooded. Assarting is known to have occurred from the middle of the thirteenth century, and can be seen though the number of small irregularly shaped fields, or intakes, cut into the woods (Hey 2000, 194; Hoskins 1955, 103). Jewell also suggests that the conversion from grassland to arable for cultivation was a labour-intensive process that involved paring (removal of the ground surface) and beat-burning to clear weeds before cropping. It is estimated that one person could reclaim about an acre a week (Jewell 1981, 98–9). Between the seventeenth and the nineteenth century horses were introduced to pull ploughs for *velling* (where all the turf is pared) and *skirting* (where alternative furrows are pared leaving strips) (Jewell 1981, 100).

Oral history provides an insight in to this type of agricultural land management. The work undertaken by Mark Riley on World War Two plough-up campaigns has elucidated a number of interesting analogies. The following excerpt is from a farmer in Nymet Rowlands, and discusses the process involved in the rotation the use of fields (Riley *pers comm.*).[2]

> A: *They got the certain fields that they knew would grow good wheat, good barley, good oats (pause) and it was all done on a seven year system. You knew that, din't 'ee?*
> Q: I knew it was on a rotation.
> A: *Yeah. Yeah. It was done on a seven years.*
> Q: Seven years, so how would that work, say for one field? What sort of thing would be in it?
> A: *Well, for, if you said you was gonna plough a certain field on your farm, the winter, starting, I should say, from October, whatever wood was on the edges and stuff would be cut and used as firing. The edge would be reinstated as a Devon bank, because there would be grass, you know, turf in the field, wouldn't there. And you was allowed to use any turf that you wanted out of that field because it was gonna be ploughed, see. And you reinstated your banks. Well, that one would be, the field would be ploughed before Boxing Day of that autumn, and in January if they wanted spring wheat it was tilled in January, if not it was tilled late February, early March for oats and barley. And then the following year 'ee would go into winter wheat, which would be tilled in November, see, that's a one year gone. Winter wheat second year, and then the second year winter wheat would come off early July, but then 'ee would be re-ploughed then and put into what used to call sheep's meat, which is kale, swedes, turnips, for the sheep. And then you'd have two years of barley, which that's five year gone, innit. The sixth year would be oats and the last year again would be barley with grass seeds, under-sown with grass seeds. In that seven year the hedge would have chance to re-grow from where 'ee was layered and that, 'eed be nice and thick, wouldn't it and you'd get a nice stock-proof hedge out of that. You'd also had your crop of firing, because there was nothing burnt and even the [spray wood?] was all tied into what they used to call faggots for burning in the bread ovens and that in the big houses, and the other stuff was, you know, the harder wood was used in the fireplaces and that. There was nothing wasted when I started work. Whatever you cut off a hedge was all, you never had a bonfire, you know like you see it today.*

Despite discussing farming practices from the last 50 years, this excerpt illustrates the type of landscape management occurring in Devon. It is thought that such processes had their origins in much earlier agricultural practices, as

Fox and Padel (2000) suggest. Through the use of palaeoenvironmental evidence Fyfe *et al.* (2003, 231) argue that the practice of convertible husbandry had a pre-Conquest origin.

Different farming practices occurred beyond the neat closes used for convertible husbandry, and particular to Devon, Cornwall, and parts of western Somerset was the cultivation of steep hillsides for arable and grass crop rotation, as this land was often relatively fertile and well drained. However, the cultivated soils were prone to slippage, and the ploughs could only work 'lairee'; down slope in one direction (Jewell 1981, 101).

The creation of lynchets and ploughing transversely across the slope, so that half the furrows would turn uphill and half down, could overcome the problem of slippage. Another technique local to Devon during the eighteenth and nineteenth centuries was the use of a one-way plough. To stop slippage on hilly ground the plough followed the contours of the land pushing furrows uphill, creating banking-up of the soil (Jewell 1981, 102).

Oxen were used to plough the steep ridges but are less manoeuvrable than horses. The use of oxen for pulling ploughs is thought to account in part for the curved or 'S' shaped ridges found in field boundaries (Langdon 1982, 40; Astill 1988b, 71). 'S' shaped fields in Devon are less defined than the types visible in the 'Midlands' landscapes, and are not directly comparable. It is known through oral history that oxen were used for ploughing in Devon during both World Wars due to the shortage of horses (Riley *pers comm.*). As a result caution must be taken when using 'S' shaped fields on their own as an indicator of medieval ploughing.

The creation of these distinct field shapes corresponds with the process of enclosure developing a greater impetus during the later Middle Ages (Astill 1988b, 81). However, it is important that the pre-medieval landscape is not seen as something blank and featureless. It is clear that there are many cases where prehistoric boundaries have been incorporated into later medieval fields. Lambourne's (2004) study of Dartmoor argues that this is rarely the case, and suggests that field systems were ultimately a product of the medieval period. This undeniably is true for many field systems within Devon. However, attention must be drawn to the Historic Landscape Characterisation (HLC) carried out for the county. As I will go on to discuss, the study of the nineteenth century historic landscape does indicate that prehistoric elements survive into the modern era.

Nevertheless, even if prehistoric fields have not survived in use into the medieval period, the landscape would still not have been created on an empty backdrop, and this can be seen in Devon's upland areas, in particular Dartmoor. Most of the archaeological investigations into medieval field systems have focused on Dartmoor, and this has, as a consequence, affected the interpretation of other medieval sites in Devon. Despite this, the work of H. S. A. Fox (1972a) on historical documents of east Devon, and particularly Axminster, has added much to what is known about the medieval field systems in low-lying areas. In east Devon there was relatively little meadow due to the low-lying well-watered ground, but significant amounts of waste (Fox 1972a, 91, 97–99). Fox (1972a, 97–99) proposes that the waste was broken up and used for arable for a few years then reverted back to rough pasture. Apart from meadow, which due to its scarcity was highly priced, arable was the most greatly valued in economic terms (Fox 1972a, 93, 101). Fertile areas like east Devon, and also the South Hams, meant that arable fields of individual farmers were often held in subdivided fields subject to some communal regulations (Astill 1988b, 81).

Devon in the sixteenth and seventeenth centuries became predominantly pastoral, particularly in the northern half of the county, with pockets of fielden, corn, and fruit growing, and wood pasture towards the south and east (Thirsk 1967, 71–72). The final major transformation of the historic landscape occurred through the Acts of Parliamentary Enclosure during the nineteenth century. Parliamentary Enclosure is the last large-scale, one phased change within the landscape and in many cases it resulted in the removal of land from common access and into private hands. Unlike the counties of the Midland zone, Devon did not experience sweeping Parliamentary Enclosure. Rather Parliamentary Enclosure was confined to uplands which had not been encroached upon or enclosed during the medieval period, such as along the Devon/Somerset border.

Summary

It can be seen that the preservation of relics of the medieval settlements and field systems on Dartmoor, and the survival and interpretation of historical documentation within Devon, has allowed for the construction of an uneven picture of the medieval rural landscape. The narrative created by archaeological and historical research illustrates a landscape which is very different from what is seen in the classic Midland zone, but also differs from the northern counties with which the region is compared with in Rackham's Highland zone categorisation. The growing opinion that the occurrence of open fields within Devon was more substantial than previously thought coincides with a landscape of easy access to high slopes and moorland that creates little pressure for pasture and allows for areas of temporary cultivation and a mixed farming regime (Astill 1988b, 81).

The differences that can be identified in the historic landscape between regions presents an idea of cultural identity. This identity varies depending on factors such as agricultural practices, and the extent of nucleation or dispersal in settlements. The following pages explore the idea of identity occurring within Devon, and the notion of *pays* regions; unique cultural regions.

Regional trends: Devon's place within the South-west's archaeological heritage

Phythian-Adams (2000, 240) states that the provinces which make up Rackham's Ancient Countryside region (or what he classes as the South British Sea zone), comprise a range of cultural regions or *pays*, which can overlap each other. The idea that landscapes can be classified by cultural difference as well as economic is interesting. The term *pays* derives from the Gallo-Roman *pagus* and is used to identify distinct French regions (Braudel 1988, 37; 409)

The identification and division of regions into these discrete cultural provinces or *pays* can occur on a national, regional, or, as shown here, a local (parish or settlement) level. According to Vidal de la Blache's *Tableau de la géographies de la France* (1903), *pays* are: 'an area with its own identity derived, not only from divisions imposed of physical geography, but also from ethnic and linguistic divisions imposed by a region by its history' (Graham 2000, 88). Although derived from French scholarship, the concept of *pay* regions has been increasingly applied to English historic landscape studies.

Identification and discussion of pays *in Devon*

Within landscape studies, the term *pays* is used in the context of economic regional specialisations, and describes the way in which agricultural resources are managed (Fox 1989, 63–4). 'English' *pays* relate to the physical and social elements of the landscapes, in Devon being particularly defined by topography.

Within Devon topography is an obvious physical factor in creating regions, with the ridges of high ground creating plateaus and valleys, making access difficult, and preventing outside influences for many centuries (Todd 1987, 3). The coast and estuarine areas also create delimitation which control access and create natural borders allowing for pockets of uniquely different landscape to be created. As a consequence, the upland expanses of Dartmoor and Exmoor are considered as discrete regional *pays* in many landscape studies.

Wealth and industry have been employed as an indicator of social units, a means of making the *pays* divisions more cultural than functional. Using the 1086 Domesday record and the lay subsidies of 1334 and 1525, Darby *et al.* (1979) discuss the distribution of wealth in relation to geographical regions. Because of the lowest ratios of recorded lay subsidies in the country, this study portrayed the whole of Devon as experiencing little change until the sixteenth century (*ibid.* 1979, 259). After this date, it was thought there was a dramatic change in the land-use and management, coinciding with similar activity in Cornwall and Somerset.

Darby *et al.* (1979) create areas within Devon which experienced different degrees of land management, wealth and population increase. These categories also highlight different cultural identities; the growth in economic fortunes was thought to have been in part stimulated by the diversity in employment, creating regional differences (Darby *et al.* 1979, 259). In estuarine and coastal regions, fishing was a form of by-employment alongside farming, and on Dartmoor, by-industries included the mining of tin and other metals (Thirsk 1967, 73). The main cloth-manufacturing centres were located in north and east Devon, and the western side of Dartmoor. Tavistock was the centre for 'kersey' (a coarse woolen cloth), and the vale of Exeter and the Exe Valley were important locations for the finer 'kerseys' (Hoskins 1954, 124–5). As a consequence, there was variation in the distribution of wealth around the county. These economic groupings created by the diversity in employment caused not only physical divisions based on resources but also social *pays* relating to the types of people within the region: for example, miners, fishers, or textile workers.

In comparison, Shorter focuses on the putative decline in small country towns from the 1840s, a result of this division by economic location, as a key factor in creating *pays* in Devon. Accelerated by agricultural depression and the effect of the railways on trading markets and local industry, mid- and west Devon suffered the greatest decrease in rural population. This decline in population has also been attributed to poor communications, amenities and housing and limited employment within this area (Shorter *et al.* 1969, 191).

Although he based his classification of Devon on geographically and geologically determined districts, Vancouver (1808) also uses nineteenth-century population densities to define a region. Vancouver identified seven, but excludes Exeter and Dartmoor. He states that the district of the South Hams may have had the greatest population (121, 139 inhabitants or 309 people per 1000 acres), but the area covered by 'red sandy loam' (corresponding to Exeter hinterlands and the Clyst Valley) was the most densely populated with 456 people per 1000 acres (*ibid.* 1808, 423). The area of 'granite gravels', to the east of Dartmoor, has the lowest population, but experiences one of the highest percentages of inhabitants engaged in agriculture.

Similarly, Weldon Finn (1967, 255) calculates Domesday population densities by dividing Devon into 31 units, based upon the physical and geological features, and corresponding with parish boundaries. At the time of Domesday, the most densely populated areas appear to be the lower Taw and Torridge basins, the lower and middle part of the Exe basin, and the coastal districts of south Devon between the Teign and the Avon (Weldon Finn 1967, 255). From the 31 units, seven eleventh-century regions are then identified. These seven divisions are: the Exmoor Border; the Taw and Torridge lowlands, the Culm Measures Belt, Red Devon [mid Devon], East Devon, South Devon, and Dartmoor and its borders (Weldon Finn 1967, 290).

Both Vancouver and Weldon Finn indicate seven similar broad categories for Devon, and this can be compared with the study conducted Roberts and Wrathmell (2000, 69, Appendix 1) who map and characterise 'subprovinces' within the nineteenth-century historical landscape of their western and south-western peninsula province. These subprovinces are defined through using river systems, major topographical features and traditional names. In many ways these subprovinces mirror the categorisation used by Weldon Finn and others. Hence the county was divided into Moorland (which includes Dartmoor, Exmoor, the Axe Valley, and the Blackdown Hills), the Lowlands (including the north Dartmoor slopes), north-west Devon and the South Hams regions encompassing the south Devon coast and southern hinterlands of Dartmoor (*ibid.* 2000, 69, Appendix 1).

The identification of subprovinces by Roberts and Wrathmell can be related to what I describe as 'micro *pays*': parish or settlement-based cultural units as opposed to the larger regional designations. Although in practice the subprovinces of Roberts and Wrathmell still identify regions rather than communities, they are the first authorities to recognise that *pays* function on a series of levels.

Roberts and Wrathmell's use of what they class as 'traditional' names can also be considered as good indicators of *pays* regions. Shorter *et al.* (1969, 97–98), for example, also considered the distribution of 'celtic'[3] place-names in relation to their topography and altitude. They identified that a significant percentage of so-called 'celtic settlements' (also identified as 'native') could be found at an altitude of between 401 and 450 feet, with many located on valley heads or on spurs. Shorter *et al.* (1969, 98) also discussed the distribution of Domesday manors in the same way, concluding that there was a gradual increase in the number that occurred from sea-level to a maximum altitude of 300 to 500 feet. It was concluded that farming was being practised as high as 1,200 feet by the end of the eleventh century with, they suggest, a movement out from the lowlands occurring over three or four centuries (*ibid.* 1969, 98).

Padel (1999, 88), in contrast, suggests that it is impossible to establish how many existing settlements acquired new 'celtic' names, or to identify any population shift or assimilation of established and incoming settlers within Devon. However it can be seen that western Devon has a higher percentage of place-names with the Old English *tun* suffix (Padel 1999, 91), suggesting, at the very least, a differential survival of the linguistic traits in Devon. Pearce (1978, 19) contradicts this and suggests that the distribution of surviving British place-names is not particularly significant, as there is only a small concentration in the north-west of the county, with a generally evenly dispersal throughout Devon. However, she does indicate that there is a noticeable gap in this distribution corresponding with the uplands of Dartmoor (*ibid.* 1978, 19).

The identification of specific pays *in Devon*

Having discussed the use of *pays* by previous landscape historians, it is important to examine in more detail the areas highlighted by these studies. The collective research suggests that six regions can be identified within Devon: the South Hams, North-east Devon, The Blackdown Hills, East Devon, Mid-Devon, and the moors, which encompasses both Dartmoor and Exmoor (Fig. 1.5).

Within the collective literature, the clearest defined *pays* region is the South

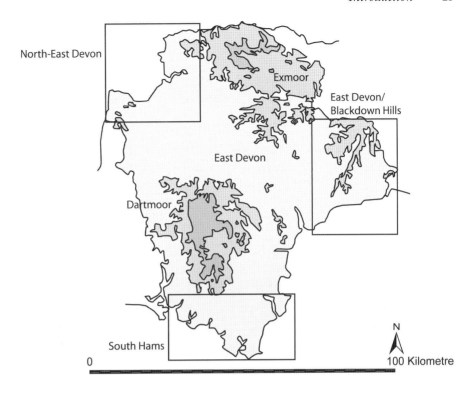

FIGURE 1.5. Location of *pays* regions defined through the literature

Hams in the south of Devon. The name of the South Hams traditionally relates to the area lying between the lower Dart and the Erme, which was the 'land of enclosed pastures south of Dartmoor' (Shorter *et al.* 1969, 253). Vancouver (1808, 9) bases part of his decision to identify the South Hams on the climate, as he suggests that this area is much milder than elsewhere in Devon.

The region was subject to relatively widespread human occupation from the Neolithic period (Todd 1984, 79). The settlement pattern within this area comprises a scattering of nucleated villages and farmsteads (Roberts and Wrathmell 2000, 57), and as discussed earlier in the introduction, this has been identified as unusual compared with other parts of Devon, which are usually classified by dispersed settlements.

The establishments of ports, and later of the naval base 2 miles to the west of Plymouth, served as a magnet for settlement. Within 70 years the population that grew up around the docks was equal to the older towns of the Sutton Pool region (Shorter *et al.* 1969, 191).

The northern coastal district has been identified as a historic *pays* because of the difference in climate and topography, especially in comparison to the coastline of the South Hams, but also in the nature of the medieval and post-medieval industry that was based in the area. Using Padel's example, within this region there are relatively large numbers of 'worthy' and 'ford' place-names, suggesting separation from other parts of Devon. Moreover, the distribution

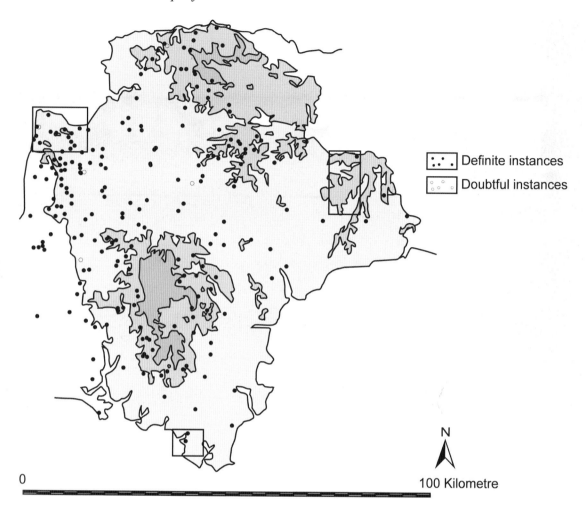

Definite instances

Doubtful instances

N

0   100 Kilometre

of Old English place-names in this area is perhaps more telling. As figure 1.6 illustrates, there is a distinct concentration of 'worthy' place-names occurring along the north-eastern boundary of Devon, and also the eastern half of Dartmoor and across Exmoor.

FIGURE 1.6. Distribution of -worthy place-names (Redrawing after Padel 1999, 88)

The Blackdown Hills are a range of hills, flat plateaus and river cut valleys that appear to have experienced isolation from other parts of east Devon, due to the topography. The key character of the landscape here is determined by its underlying geology, an outcrop of Upper Greensand capped by Keuper Marls and chert, making it unique within the South-west. This geology serves as an important factor in the development of an ironworking industry (Todd 1984, 4; Griffith and Weddell 1996, 27). Iron ore can be found on the upper levels of the Greensand, a plateau which is divided by the rivers Sid, Otter and Axe (Griffith and Weddell 1996, 27). The extraction of the iron ore, which is thought to date back to the second half of the first century AD (*ibid.* 1996, 33), means

FIGURE 1.7. Use of available building material, Houndtor, Dartmoor (© Neil Ryder)

that such a cultural division may have made through the types of people who lived and worked in the Blackdown Hills.

The region of east Devon is sometimes incorporated with the Blackdown Hills, but because the physical differences in aspect and geology it is frequently divided into a discrete region of its own. This broad region is sometimes divided into geological sub-groups (see Vancouver, 1808), but essentially comprises the areas which do not fit into any of the other regions. Fox (1996b, 65) suggests that during the sixteenth century the fishing villages of Devon's coastline used building materials designated through local *pays*. For example, the shores of the Exe saw building out of cob, whereas other areas to the west had a tradition of dwellings constructed from horizontally laid slatestone (*ibid.* 1996b, 65). This exemplifies the idea of smaller *pays* within larger regions.

Despite being very different, Exmoor and Dartmoor are classed by all the authors cited above as one *pays* region. This designation is based on topographical constructs alone. The differences found in, for example, Dartmoor settlement types (see Fig. 1.7 for an example) are seen as merely indicators of resources (stone rather than wood) rather than a cultural manifestation. This is short-sighted and disregards crucial indicators for seemingly easy categorisation.

Summary

The previous research into the cultural regions of Devon focuses primarily on the physical aspects of the landscape, with economic or population dynamics used to infer social attributes to the *pays*. These are undeniably important factors in the way we assess the historical landscape, but *pays* are supposed to be physical *and* cultural indicators. Therefore, further examination is required to build on this framework. The categorisation of Devon makes broad *pay* boundaries, and I argue that there is a need for internal divisions within these defined regions. These broad units ('macro *pays*' which encompass regions), can be analysed further by the identification of smaller zones on a more local parish or settlement scale (the idea of 'micro *pays*').

Important to the categorisation is how the landscape is viewed. Do we always look at landscapes in terms of what Higuchi (1983, 90) describes as potential habitats; logically seeking out advantageous (and thus aesthetically pleasing) places in which to create a living? Is this the only basis on which people decide where within a landscape they occupy or is there also something which reflects the culture of these communities which provokes reactions in the way people think about themselves, and affects how others perceived them?

This leads to further questions about how the physical landscape was seen and perceived by those who dwelt within it. Within medieval and post-medieval archaeology little consideration has been given to the ways in which people visualised and understood their environment. Due to the types of evidence available, namely historical documents, conventional medieval landscape studies are generally concerned with the physical traces of people's occupation and livelihood such as food production and so on. The notion of 'mental' landscapes, relating to the 'superstructures of meanings and values' attached to these material remains are not explored, although common place in prehistoric studies (Bradley 2000, 2; Altenberg 2003, 3).

Examples of this type of approach can be seen in the following examples based within the South-west region. As mentioned above, Altenberg (2003) discusses the medieval landscape through phenomenology. Focusing on Dartmoor and Bodmin Moor, the experience of landscapes and the expressions of superstition, ritual and folklore usually associated with prehistory are explored. From this starting point the perceptions of these marginal environments held by the Catholic Church, the secular landowners, and their tenants are explored to create a more holistic landscape study (Altenberg 2001, 98–100). Also working within the South-west, Harvey (2000) approaches medieval landscapes from a geographer's perspective. He addresses territoriality and the role of hagiographical legends within west Cornwall and argues that during the medieval period the 'hero-saints' were used not only to legitimise elite authority and prestige, but also by communities as part of their identity; a form of 'early Cornish "Patriotism"' (Harvey 2000, 205, 208). In terms of landownership and manorial structure, this type of information is useful, and the use of such factors is key within the discussion of the Blackdown Hills and Hartland Moors areas. The ideas of perception and folklore and their relevance to medieval Devon will be dealt with again in Chapter Six.

To take these issues into account, it is perhaps of benefit to look at areas on a parish or settlement scale (in a sense the idea of 'micro *pays*'). Of relevance to landscape studies is how individual regions co-existed and worked as holistic units within a larger region.

Identifying areas of study

To discuss the origins and development of the nineteenth-century historic landscape and the subsequent relationship between morphology and patterns of Tithe Survey landholding, I focus on three of the more archaeologically overlooked areas of Devon (Fig. 1.8). Five overlooked regions were originally highlighted for study by the Heritage Lottery Funded Community Landscapes Project (CLP), undertaken by the School of Geography, Archaeology, and Earth Resources at the University of Exeter. The aim of the CLP was to increase community participation within the county in terms of scientific, archaeological and historical resources. The five regions selected by the CLP were selected for

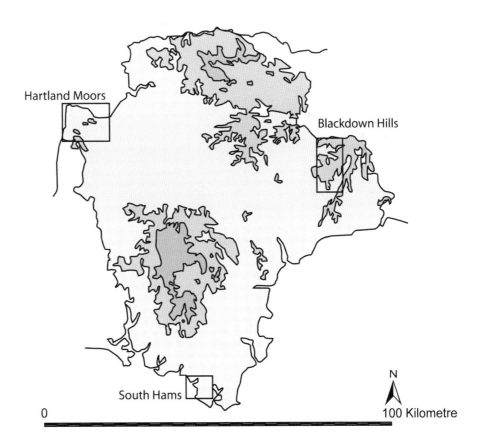

FIGURE 1.8. The three study areas highlighted for analysis

their suitability for palaeoenvironmental research because of the occurrence of spring mires or bogs, and to readdress the archaeological bias towards Dartmoor (Brown 2001, 9). Furthermore, he work conducted by the CLP within the Blackdown Hills would build upon the important work of the Blackdown Hills Ironwork Project (see Griffith and Weddell, 1995; 1996).

The three areas, the Blackdown Hills which span the Devon/Somerset border in east Devon, Hartland Moors in north Devon, and the South Hams region on Devon's south coast, are representative of the Blackdown Hills, North-east Devon, and South Hams *pays* described above. Two of these areas, the Blackdown Hills and Hartland Moors, have been highlighted for in-depth study, with smaller representative sample areas identified within these regions. The further third case-study, within the South Hams area, will also be discussed to provide a comparison between the more upland Blackdown Hills and Hartland Moors as its location on Devon's south coast has meant that it has been considered less marginal in terms of agricultural production.

The Blackdown Hills can be categorised as upland fringe, and by modern perceptions are deemed marginal, particularly by external communities, despite their location in the relatively fertile region of east Devon. By contrast, the Hartland Moors region consists of coastal uplands containing large tracts of moorland and is marginal in terms of modern agriculture. The third smaller case-study area of the South Hams, however, consists of coastal/estuarine lowland. The distinctly different physical locations of the three study areas will allow regional variations (or indeed similarities) in the historic landscape, and also those in the social and cultural structures, to be identified and discussed.

It has been demonstrated in other landscape studies that it is possible to recognise regional variations within social structures by looking at the landscapes of particular regions on a more local scale (Rippon 2000, 48). Therefore, within the three study areas, smaller subsections have been highlighted for in-depth analysis. This subdivision enables variations in field morphology, settlement plan and landholding patterns within the historic landscape to be identified on a field-by-field basis. Therefore, by looking at the regions in microcosm, a picture of how past landscapes evolved and how they were manipulated can be seen. Moreover, it is proposed that the siting of settlements, the creation of field systems, and the interaction between them are central to an understanding of how the landscape of the Blackdown Hills, Hartland Moors, and the South Hams were used, managed, and understood, throughout the medieval and post-medieval period.

Moving away from previous studies, I propose a new, more holistic, method in order to establish the history of Devon's historic landscape. I will discuss this methodology further in Chapter Two. The first study area discussed will be the Blackdown Hills. This study area covers 151.27 square km of east Devon and is divided into seven parishes. Six are discussed in depth, but the seventh, Dunkeswell, is discussed in less detail as it was not surveyed much in the nineteenth century Tithe Survey. As the Tithe Survey forms the basis for this study, it would be impossible to discuss Dunkeswell in the same detail as the other parishes. The Blackdown Hills receives the greatest coverage due to the degree of fragmentation and complexity of patterns of landownership and field morphology within this study area. The second study area, discussed in Chapter Five, is Hartland Moors. This study area is similar in size to the Blackdown Hills (175.51 square km), but is divided into four unequally sized parishes. This presents a different level of material and complexity. Within the Hartland Moors study area there are two influential bodies at work during the medieval period; the Dynham family who held the manor of Harton (Hartland), and the Abbey of Hartland. This pattern of compact ownership provides a contrast to the fragmentation occurring in the Blackdown Hills.

A 56 square km area around the [Devon] Avon Estuary (also known as the river Aune) in the South Hams makes the final case study, and this is presented as a comparison where the hypotheses raised in the other study areas can be tested. Three sample areas are highlighted to test patterns of settlement and field morphology, informed and chosen by the evidence and patterns of morphology identified in the Blackdown Hills and Hartland Moors area. The distribution of landholding and field-names identified in the other two case studies are also considered in these sample areas. Four parishes have been highlighted for research within the South Hams study area, with two, Bigbury and Thurlestone, divided into sample areas for field-by-field analysis.

The relationship between field and settlement morphology and patterns of landholding, and their related field-names, are also examined within the study areas, on a field-by-field basis over 13 parishes.

Summary

The aim of this chapter was to introduce the complex nature of Devon's landscape and introduce the primary aims and sub-themes which make up the investigation of the historic landscape in this study. The key aim is to understand the origins and development of Devon's complex historic landscape through the investigation of field and settlement morphology, landownership patterns and field-name evidence on a field-by-field basis over a wide area. The relationship between field and settlement morphology and patterns of nineteenth-century landholding gained from the Tithe Survey are crucial in adding greater historical depth to the landscape.

It can be seen that the South-west in general, and Devon in particular, are more complex then the broad models identified by Roberts and Wrathmell and Rackham. Furthermore, the identification of different physical and cultural regions within Devon is important in trying to understand how the landscape developed over time, and where specific trends or signatures arise. How this information can be gained and developed is discussed in the next chapter.

Notes

1   Within this study the South-west is defined as being Devon, Cornwall, and Somerset.
2   'Landscape Archaeology and the Community in Devon; An Oral History Approach' AHRB Innovation Award: R15611.
3   A lower case 'c' has been deliberately used for the spelling of celtic, as the term can have numerous meanings, which are beyond the remit of this study.

CHAPTER TWO

Discussing Sources and Methodologies for Studying the Historic Landscape

In the previous chapter the regional and national debates in the study of the historic landscape were introduced, focusing on the issues regarding the nucleation and dispersal of settlement, the agricultural processes involved in shaping the landscape, and the identification of *pays* regions within Devon. Chapter One also identified the key themes and issues which are addressed within this study through the accumulation of mappable sources in a Geographical Information Systems (GIS) database.

This GIS database allows large amounts of data to be manipulated, queried, and compared across the three study areas. As discussed in the previous chapter, such a comparison requires the use of consistent sources for all three study areas. These sources comprise of information that is available for all areas, such as Tithe Surveys, Domesday record, and lay subsidies, which all have the ability to be mapped systematically. Additional sources, such as early medieval charters or antiquarian accounts, IPMs, and court rolls, which are only available for one or parts of regions, are employed to gain add greater understanding of particular locations. These sources are used after the consistent sources have been analysed. As is the case in many landscape studies, large amounts of documentary sources were investigated for all three study areas, but much rendered little information valid to the study of the historic landscape.

The primary layer of information in the database is the nineteenth-century Tithe Surveys. These maps provide the first in-depth record we have of the landscape on a field-by-field, settlement-by-settlement basis. Associated with these maps are the Tithe Appointments, which list, for each individual field, its landowners, tenants, land use, name and description, and in many cases acreage and price. Combining the two sources together within the GIS provides an important foundation for study.

The creation of the GIS database in its simplest form (layers of historical map information and survey) allows for the 'building blocks' of landscapes to be considered. The information gained from the different historical sources using the methodology adopted by this research, allows for a greater understanding of growth, abandonment, and change.

Because of non-tithable areas on the nineteenth-century Tithe Surveys (such as in Dunkeswell in the Blackdown Hills) and poor preservation of the maps (Hartland parish in the Hartland Moors study area and Hemyock parish in the Blackdown Hills), there are gaps within the GIS database. Nevertheless,

6479 fields have been digitised for the Blackdown Hills study area, 5977 fields in Hartland Moors, and 734 in the smaller sample areas within the South Hams.

For each of the digitised fields an associated database has been created consisting of Tithe Survey landownership and occupier information, land use and field-names. Overlaying the digitised fields is a layer consisting of each individual dwelling marked on the Tithe Survey, and corresponding to each point is a database containing the name if known, the settlement it is part of (left blank if isolated), and the parish. Any associated buildings such as churches, chapels, or castles were also added as a point to the GIS.

Sources

In order to compare the Blackdown Hills, Hartland Moors, and South Hams, consistency is needed between the main sources for each study area. Therefore, the consistent sources (those which are available for all three study areas) need to be identified. Each element of the GIS database, for example topography, settlement, or individual fields, is derived from a consistent source. A number of non-consistent sources are also used to add further information to the database, enhance our understanding of the historic landscape. This extra data can provide additional information regarding the individual region, and can be used to confirm observations identified in the database through the consistent sources. The non-consistent sources are generally not mappable consistently, if at all, and where they are used their inconsistencies will be made clear.

Discussion of sources

For clarity, table 2.1 lists the primary and secondary sources used within this study divided into the following four subgroups: cartographic layers and aerial photographs, linguistic elements (mapped on a field-by-field/settlement-by-settlement level), documentary sources (like the IPM and Domesday records), and topographical writings. The final two subgroups are not directly mappable but can be added to the database in order to gain a clearer understanding of the historic landscape.

The main sources within this subgroup are the nineteenth-century Tithe Surveys and modern digital Ordnance Survey landline maps. The Tithe Surveys provide the earliest mapping evidence for the areas, but do not give total coverage of the study areas. This is because the Tithe Surveys are not available for all parishes, for example, Dunkeswell has large areas of non-titheable land, meaning that only approximately 200 fields could be digitised for the parish. These nineteenth-century documents allow access to a pre-industrialised landscape, giving place- and field-name evidence. Furthermore, the Tithe Surveys also give access to patterns of landownership, tenure, and land use for each individual field.

Geo-referenced digital Ordnance Survey and aerial photographs are used in collaboration with the Tithe Surveys, allowing for abandoned field boundaries, settlements, and other evidence (for example industry in the form of mills) to be identified. All digital information is rectified to the Ordnance Survey grid so that spatial comparisons can be made.

The area covered by the South Hams study area benefits from two early charter boundaries which provide information into the regional arrangement of the landscape, and can be compared to the later boundaries, aiding discussion into continuity within certain areas. However this information is not available for the other two study areas and therefore cannot be considered as a theme.

Linguistic sources include place-names and field-names and regional dialect. The use of place- and field-names is widely accepted as indicators of

TABLE 2.1. Table of sources that allow comparison of the Blackdown Hills and Hartland Moors study areas, listed chronologically

A Mappable layers	B Linguistic	C Demographic relating to manorial, settlement, and population structure	D Agricultural Treaties
Primary Cartographic	Field-names 19th century Tithe Survey Apportionment/ Field 1993	Domesday Book (and Exon) 1086 (Thorn & Thorn 1980)	Risdon *c.* 17th century
Tithe Survey and Apportionment	Place-names PND, 1932 Gellings 1984 Mills 1998	IPM various dates from 13th to 16th century	Polwhele 1793–1806
1880 First Edition Ordnance Survey	Devon Dialect Downes, 1998	Feet of Fines 1190–1272	Vancouver 1808
1961–2 1:25,000 Ordnance Survey	Oral History Mark Riley/Sam Richards Archive Exmouth	Crown Pleas of the Devon Eyre of 1238 (Summerson 1985)	
1962–3 1:10,560 Ordnance Survey		Feet of Fines 1272–1369	
Landline Digital OS		13th to 14th century Tax Rolls, and the Tax Roll of 'Testa de Nevill' 1234–42 (L'Estrange Ewen 1939)	
Photographic		Feudal Aids 1303 (Deputy Keeper of Records, 1879)	
1945 RAF Aerial Photographs		Lay Subsidies 1334/1544–45 (Erskine 1969; Stoate 1986)	
ECW digital Aerial Photographs		Devon Monastic Lands: Calendar of Particulars for Grants 1536–58 (Youing 1955)	
Interpretive			
Historic Landscape Characterisation. DCC/Sam Turner			

past land use, ownership, and topographic variations. Dialect sources are also useful in explaining elements of field-names which are distinctly rooted in the local area. These dialect names are particularly important when discussing agricultural practices, as they frequently fossilised forgotten vernacular terms used in agriculture. Field-names can be added to the GIS database via the Tithe Apportionment and can be mapped in relation to other, physical, elements of the historic landscape. The use of field-names indicates not only former land use types, such as areas of meadow or seasonal grazing, but also aid the chronology of the enclosure of the landscape. This chronology, gained through the survival of particular types of field-names is particularly useful as dating phases and sequences of activity in historic landscape studies is difficult because of the lack of tangible chronologically fixed evidence.

Documentary information is difficult to map; this is particularly true of earlier sources where locations of named places are uncertain in the modern day study areas. However, the information these sources can add in terms of tenurial and settlement structure is important to the regression of the historic landscape. Some of the sources used are transcribed copies of manuscripts, and it is noted that inaccuracies may be present in the transcription. However, this should not inhibit the inclusion of such documents, as the value as a source outweighs the risk of possible errors. Despite an uneven distribution, the three study areas are fortunate as they have information available from the 1086 Domesday Survey, which provides an indication of early estate structure, and lists pre- and post-Conquest landholders and wide range of other data. *Calendar of Inquisitiones post mortem* (IPM) lists the areas of manors and their land use, and where the extents are available the source helps to establish whether estate size has remained consistent throughout the medieval period. *Testa de Nevill* (TdN), the thirteenth-century tax roll records landowners and estates; transcribed *court rolls* provide both cartographic and demographic information, listing tenements, estates, field-names and people; and *Lay Subsidies and Feudal Aids,* which discuss broad population details and also help to establish the origins of some place-names through their inclusion as surnames. These help identify whether manors (and subsequently parishes) were fragmented throughout the landscape with tithing held within other hundreds.

Other documentary sources, such as the heath tax and muster rolls, were investigated in the creation of the GIS database but were discounted as they did not provide information which would have enhanced the study.

A final invaluable source comprises the descriptions by the local antiquarians and 'gentlemen travellers' of the seventeenth, eighteenth and nineteenth centuries which provide a unique snapshot into the landscape, and management during this time. Drawing on their perspectives, these sources can add information which is not usually accessible from other documents. Therefore, the work of Vancouver (1808), Polwhele (1798–1806), and Risdon (1811), for example, is invaluable.

Methods

The methodology formulated here presents a number of key questions:

1. Can different patterns of landownership be identified within the study areas and how do these relate back to documented earlier landscapes?

The Tithe Apportionments can be used to map the distribution of particular landowners within the parish and their tenants. Such large-scale mapping of landholding has not been attempted within the South-west (or elsewhere, see below), and therefore can provide information which will help explain the management of the medieval and post-medieval landscapes. Documentary evidence can be examined of known manorial sites, place- and field-names, and the areas defined through the patterns of landownership and field patterns to try and piece together estate boundaries. The aim is to integrate a study of field system and settlement patterns.

2. Identification of the extent of open field systems within the study area: does Devon experience open field practices in particular regions, or is it widespread and common throughout the county?

The use of Tithe Survey field morphology and patterns of landholding will enable the identification of areas of former open field that are now enclosed. Comparisons can then be made between the study areas (and looking outside of the designated areas to gain a fuller and truer picture) in order to determine the extent of open fields and whether they occur in similar conditions.

Through patterns of landownership, former areas of open field which have not been preserved in the historic landscape can also be seen, adding to the understanding of where these field systems were used.

3. Is there a singular typology of field patterns relating to similar settlement types; are they the same in all three study areas and does topography make a difference in the forms of settlement and field systems that occur?

By using nineteenth-century Tithe Surveys, typologies can be identified. This information can then be compared across the study areas. If there is not a single typology relating to different settlement types, then there is a need to identify how many variations occur, and whether they are duplicated across regions. Furthermore, layering physical features over field and settlement patterns can confirm or disprove the presence of any environmental factors which may affect the type holdings and fields occurring in a particular area.

4. How commonly is arable recorded within sources such as Domesday and the Tithe Surveys and is the picture gained from these sources a true reflection of land use at this time, or is it showing other forms of farming practices such as the regionally distinctive ley or convertible husbandry?

The practice of convertible husbandry in Devon (discussed in Chapter One) provides a picture which is very different from that given within documentary sources. The Tithe Apportionment record of land use is used as a guide, alongside field patterns, to suggest the extent of convertible husbandry and other agricultural practices. Key to this is the definition of arable. Within the

Devon Tithe Surveys it is thought to mean plough-able, land which could be made suitable for crops, but not necessarily used for them.

5. How do field-names gained from the Tithe Apportionment add to the interpretation of previous land uses?

By plotting names which indicate land use, such as woodland indicators or evidence of droveways, against suggestive field pattern morphologies, whether field-names act as an indicator of poorer soils, farming regimes, or other elements which effect the historic landscape.

The landscape in the South-west and Devon in particular is classically thought of as having a dispersed settlement pattern:

6. Is Hoskins' 'big village' idea affected by manorial intervention (as suggested by Fox, see Chapter Five) and applicable outside of the northern regions of Devon, and is village even the right word to use?

Hoskins (1952a, 290) describes the settlements in Hartland as belonging to a 'big village'. The 'big village' suggests that the type of settlement associated with the midlands zone (nucleated villages with associated open fields and controlled by a central lord) can be found in Hartland. In turn, Fox (1983, 40) argues that the manor of Harton influenced settlement patterns in the area, causing nucleation in the parish. To answer this theme there is a need to assess known manorial centres and their estates, and their relationship with the surrounding holdings. This will be easier for Hartland (where the big village idea was developed) because of the influence of the abbey and the Dynham family. Within the Blackdown Hills, this idea can be tested at the Mohun family's manor of Mohun's Ottery and other estates which belonged to Dunkeswell Abbey.

The discussion of what classes as a village outside of the 'Midlands' landscapes is useful here, and by comparing the Tithe Survey settlement distribution and also the pattern of landholdings, land use and field composition this can be tested. These elements shape how a community sees itself (the organisation of the landscape is influenced by the degree of cooperation between groups) and the input of manorial and monastic landowners.

7. How far is this true in the study areas under investigation, and do we get a mix of isolated farmsteads and more nucleated settlements at study area and parish level?

Creating and querying the Tithe Survey settlements theme, which plots every holding, will allow a picture of pre-industrialised[1] settlement to be gleaned for the study areas. Comparisons with physical factors such as topography and drainage can also be made in order to assess whether there is any correlation between these features and settlement placing. Again, the Tithe Survey settlement plan will be used to discuss this by focusing on a parish scale.

Morphology and regressive approaches

As has been discussed, the morphology of settlements and field systems in Devon, in comparison with the rest of England, is not as straightforward as first thought. This section discusses in more detail the complexities of morphology within England, the South-west, and Devon in particular, and how these can be accessed from historic landscape studies.

Field morphology

The form in which landscape elements such as boundaries and roads appear on the earliest maps is the result of centuries of gradual, piecemeal change (Williamson 1987, 420). Therefore, as Williamson (1987, 420) notes, it is hardly surprising that the best evidence of such change comes from the areas of Rackham's 'Ancient Countryside'. The shapes and patterns which occur within the landscape result from definable processes and specific events, and from this it is possible to place landscape features into a relative chronological order, creating a landscape stratigraphy (Austin 1985, 202; Williamson 1987, 240). These stratigraphies can be described through the medium of morphology, and in a medieval context, patterns of field systems have frequently been used to test documentary records (Chrystall and McCullagh 2000, 117). As mentioned above, common indicators are the reversed s-shaped fields caused through ploughing with oxen, and generally associated with medieval arable.

As highlighted in Chapter One, Roberts and Wrathmell (2002, 63) draw attention to the work by Slicher van Bath (1963, 54–8) who created a schematic diagram of the four basic types of settlement/field relationships which can be historically identified. These correspond to the following types:

1. Square or block fields generally with length to breath proportions of 1:1/1:2 associated with either hamlets or scatter dwellings.
2. Strip fields, generally with the proportions of 1:10/1:20 associated with scattered dwellings or chains of farmsteads.
3. Strip fields with later subdivisions of holdings and the development of street villages and subdivided holdings with associated settlements, which are largely open or lacking formal enclosed boundaries, fences, hedges, banks and ditches *etc.*
4. 'Enclosed' fields, each parcel defined by a carefully constructed bounding feature.

Slicher van Bath (1963, 55) also suggests that the square fields described in type 1 may also occur in England without any habitation, and belong to the pre-Conquest period.

Slicher van Bath's work was a European model which was transferable across the continent. A parallel can be made with Havis and Brooks' (2004) scheme for the Essex landscape. In order to identify common characteristics of field types, this model uses the nineteenth-century Tithe Surveys and the first edition six inch Ordnance Survey as its basis (Havis and Brooks 2004, 418). Despite

Area of Field System

Woodland or Waste

N

Not to Scale

FIGURE 2.1. Model
of suggested field
morphology for the
Stansted area (Redrawing
after Harris and Brooks
2004, 48)

being devised for the south-eastern landscape, many of the features within the suggested models can also be identified in Devon.

The diagrams can be divided into two categories (Fig. 2.1). The first category of field types, numbered 1 to 5, encompasses the types commonly associated with 'Midland' or lowland landscapes. The second category, numbered 6 to 10 are associated with woodland clearance (Havis and Brooks 2004, 418).

Type 1 identifies large groups of fields with slightly curving or straight boundaries which would have been demesne fields under the ownership of the manor. The curved boundary indicates that the fields were once ploughed but held in severalty (a tenant would hold the land in their own right without any interest from other people).

Type 2 shows the pattern of fields associated with surviving or recently enclosed [open] fields. The recently enclosed fields have identifiable straight boundaries and inter-mixed large and small plots. The smaller plots with parallel boundaries are relic strips, and the presence of fields containing 'pan-handles' illustrate where a neighbouring furlong was added to a block of strips.

The fields in Type 3 represent tofts associated with individual dwellings. These small plots back away in regular blocks from a street in a village or hamlet.

Type 4 demonstrates the patterns created by meadows, particularly in relation to rivers and streams. Where common grazing rights have been expunged some individuals enclosed their land into small fields, creating a pattern of small fields with inter-mixed ownership.

Type 5 illustrates patterns of small and medium sized irregular fields which are the result of hedgerow removal. These fields may also belong to a single, smaller, landowner who has a need to accommodate crop rotation and the rearing of livestock within their land.

Types 6 to 10 show patterns associated with possible woodland or waste clearance (Havis and Brooks 2004, 419). Model 6 illustrates the most recent phase of clearance. Here the fields have straight parallel boundaries adjoining existing wood or waste. The enclosure shown in Type 7 is also recent, with straight regular and parallel field boundaries cut into areas of woodland.

The irregular ring boundary shown in Type 8 is associated with sections of surviving or recently cleared woodland or waste, with straight sided internal divisions. This particular pattern of fields can, in some cases, represent 'ghost woods' (areas which are no longer wooded, but still show a morphology indicative of its former use) with its external boundary.

Type 9 demonstrates fields with sinuous parallel boundaries surrounded by woodland or waste. This ring-fenced enclosure is suggestive of single ownership and/or one phase of development.

Type 10 shows small fields lying between a parish boundary and a parallel road, with a straight dividing hedge, and is associated with small tenements. These fields were formally covered by woodland and have been reclaimed by individual families or groups.

Distinctive curvilinear or ring-fenced enclosures have been identified in

Devon as representing the taking in of 'better land' with the least effort, or, in an upland context, may be for pastoral farming and stock production (Roberts and Wrathmell 2002, 152–3). These enclosures may be of considerable antiquity, dating to the medieval or pre-medieval period (*ibid*. 2002, 152). Roberts and Wrathmell's Type 2 illustrated in figure 1.3 shows the suggested development of this type of field pattern from its origin as the product of clearance, through use and subdivision to the type of patterns seen in the historic landscape (Roberts and Wrathmell 2002, 154–5). The models suggested by Roberts and Wrathmell are of particular interest because of their use of nineteenth-century Tithe Survey information in order to create their hypotheses (as discussed in Chapter One).

In summary, these three topological schemes (Slicher van Bath, Havis and Brook and Roberts and Wrathmell) work on a local, national and international level, and illustrate the various levels in which the historic landscape can be studied. The models provide distinct morphological types for field patterns and these are interchangeable between regions. The models, particularly the Roberts and Wrathmell and Slicher van Bath schemes, show how the development of landscapes can alter within relatively small areas. The idea that landscapes which are physically close to one another can experience very different forms of development is important to the three study areas within this research. This can also be related to the argument that *pays* can occur not only at a regional level, but also at local parish or settlement level.

Debates about morphology

Many models explaining the elements of the historic landscape view each component in isolation. However, it is generally acknowledged that settlement and field patterns evolve in relation to each other, and should not be discussed in isolation. The models discussed above show the use of morphology to understand the development of the landscape, but in recent years the validity of such an approach has been questioned

Where particular patterns of settlement, fields, enclosures, and boundaries are explained through morphology interpretational difficulties can emerge (Chrystall and McCullagh 2000, 117). As a consequence, many morphological models are based upon assumptions rather than archaeological and historical facts (Roberts and Wrathmell 2002, 155). Austin (1985, 203) argues that there are three problems with the use of morphology in reconstructing medieval landscapes:

1. It is easy to reconstruct simple patterns from complex landscapes, but it is almost impossible to reconstruct complex ones;
2. The processes of change are seldom explored methodically and critically;
3. Dating is difficult to achieve, since it cannot be applied from the particular to the general on the grounds of morphological similarity, and it cannot be sustained by the typology alone.

Rippon's (1991, 46) work in Essex adds a fourth problem to this list; the failure to consider large-scale landscape reorganisation. Despite these reservations, well-applied morphology can enhance the study of the historic landscape. Like any technique used to undertake landscape studies, morphology is 'only one tool in a complete kit' (Austin 1985, 206). The inclusion of documentary sources, place- and field-name studies, archaeological research, and, if possible, palaeoenvironmental analysis should be combined with morphological analysis in order to gain a more complete picture of early landscapes (Rippon 1991, 58).

The isolation of distinct morphological elements within landscape studies creates questions as to the origins of that landscape which can, in theory, be reached through the process of retrogressive analysis and regressive approaches. The use of the nineteenth-century landscape in this way has also come into question, particularly relating to the work of Roberts and Wrathmell.

Regressive approaches

Regressive approaches to landscape studies are the processes of mapping all the field boundaries for an area from the earliest cartographic sources, in many cases the nineteenth-century Tithe Surveys, and removing those elements which post-date the laying-out of the medieval landscape (Rippon 1991, 46). Essentially retrogressive analysis allows the landscape to be treated as a series of layers that can be removed one by one (Rippon 1997, 24), and thus, this approach lends itself well to being incorporated into a GIS database (see below).

Williamson (1987) used retrogressive analysis to reconstruct early patterns of land division in Scole-Dickleburgh in southern Norfolk. Using the nineteenth-century Tithe Surveys, Williamson (1987, 421) illustrated that it is possible to regress back to a pre-medieval landscape. Rippon's (1996) research in the Gwent Levels uses the ideas started by Williamson to show that the historic landscape of this area could also be regressed. This study analysed field forms, settlement and road patterns, in conjunction with documentary sources to regress back to the landscape of the medieval period (Rippon 1996, 10). Within the South-west, Gillard (2000; 2002) used the same process to study Exmoor, noting that the historic landscape contained evidence of distinctive enclosures located through extant field-boundaries. This is the exception, as regression of historic landscapes in the South-west to the pre- and early medieval period is extremely difficult. This is because of a lack of documentary and archaeological evidence and therefore little dating evidence for this period.

This research uses a regressive approach rather than a retrogressive analysis, and considers the data in a more philosophical way to the technique that Williamson undertook for Scole-Dickleburgh. The Blackdown Hills and Hartland Moors study areas both have good documentary evidence to support elements identified which will allow a picture of medieval landscapes to be elucidated. However, although it can be speculated that there are traces of an early medieval landscape present, this cannot be substantiated.

In order to undertake such a regressive approach within Devon's historic landscape, collation and interpretation of the constant and mappable sources must be undertaken. The regression of the historic landscape can be queried within a GIS database to create a picture of the structures involved in its creation. Use of a GIS database for management and manipulation of such large quantities of information is vital for the success of this study and builds upon a growing body of research within archaeology.

The use of Geographical Information Systems within landscape studies

GIS has been implemented proactively within archaeology for over 20 years, with the first applications being regional landscape studies (Gillings and Wise 1999, 7). However, it has been only recently that the position of computer modelling has moved on from simply replicating the paper maps on screen (Fischer 1999, 7). Essentially, what separates this complex database from packages such as Computer Aided Design (CAD), or illustration packages, is its ability to undertake analysis and query. GIS has the potential and the means to present, interpret, and de-construct spatial patterns from different datasets (Lock and Harris 1996, 215–216). Thus, the role of GIS in this research is to manipulate and order the vast amount of information that presents itself during analysis of a landscape. This is particularly so in the case of the Tithe Survey map and apportionment data discussed below.

For landscape archaeology maps, such as the Tithe Surveys, aid the creation of ideas of spatial awareness, especially in relation to the location of particular sites or artefacts, but convey specific notions of space which are 'subjective emotions and sensuous experience into pseudo-scientific interpretations of reality' (Witcher 1999, 14). Moreover, flat paper maps give no impression of topography; the contours are purely illustrative, presenting a view of landscapes and the archaeological material within them, which is seen from an intrinsically 'God-like' perspective. They give an idea of the gradient, and show a definition of steepness, but it is hard to demonstrate the geography of the areas represented intelligibly. Thus, the very notion of what we are studying as landscape archaeology is perhaps poorly represented on flat two dimensional paper maps. As Gerrard (2003, 228) notes, 'there must be applications here for GIS and DTM [Digital Terrain Model] modelling, which can convey a better impression of landscapes experienced on the ground than map or air photographs'.

It is not my intention to describe in detail the working of GIS, or catalogue developments and applications. Detailed discussions have been published elsewhere and interested readers are referred to them (for example Wheatley and Gillings 2002; Allen *et al.* 1990, Lock and Stančič 1995, Brandon and Westcott 2000). However, focus will be given to the seeming lack of applications of GIS to medieval and post-medieval landscape studies.

Few medieval studies within the UK have used GIS as part of their research structure. In America, the tradition of GIS-based research for the historical period is more common, for example Ray's (2002) mapping of the political and social elements occurring during the Salaam witch-trials. In British medieval studies, GIS databases tend to be used to map GPS surveys, plot population densities, or, as in the case of the Whittlewood Project (Jones and Page 2003), to plot fieldwalking densities. Unfortunately, in many cases the application of the GIS databases was not conducted as thoroughly as it may have been. But a good exception to this trend is Gregory and Southall's (2002, 120) mapping of population history, which aimed to use GIS to gain fluidness of administrative boundaries, and move away from the 'anachronistic frames available in printed maps'.

This use of GIS shows its worth as a complex database. However, the medieval studies which have utilised GIS have done so with varying degrees of success, and this must be because of the fact that most of the studies using GIS undertaken within archaeology either use it to create illustrations that merely replicate traditional mapping in glossy form, or, as in the case of prehistoric examples, use functions of the database irrelevant to the medieval period. This can be seen in the case of the Whittlewood project's use of GIS, although this is by no means the worst.

A rare example of the application of GIS in a medieval context is the work of the Cotswold Medieval Settlement Project (CMSP) undertaken by the Cotswold Archaeological Trust (Wilkinson 1996). This English Heritage funded project was supported by the Gloucestershire SMR and the NMR, and used the NMR data as a background to which documentary evidence was added. This evidence included Domesday, Anglo-Saxon Charters, lay subsidies, Tithe Surveys, and the Victoria County History, although this only covered half of the study area (Wilkinson 1996, 271). From this, the project was able to suggest the location of Hideage 'boundaries' and their relationship with the present parish boundaries, and deserted or modern-day settlements (*ibid.* 1996, 277).

However, the use of GIS within this project raises two concerns. Firstly the use of inconsistent sources means that comparisons in terms of landscape and settlement structure cannot confidently be made. Secondly, and perhaps most crucially, the CMSP used a CAD-based GIS system which means that the functionality of the GIS could not be exploited. This project was simply a mapping exercise, and the results gained from this study could have been equally reached, with perhaps less effort, by using an illustration package, or on hard map copies, and a good database program (something which, to his credit, Wilkinson (1996, 280) readily admits). This case study illustrates the problem: there is a trend within current archaeological research to use GIS as a buzzword and a 'magic box' which needs to be used to legitimise a study, and is used as a 'must-be-seen' element of research rather than a simple tool to aid it. There is a genuine use for GIS within medieval landscape studies when it is used for what it is, a spatial database which can manage and query large amounts of data. This is the only benefit of the CMSP, as it shows what could be done within medieval landscape studies, and the amount of information that can be manipulated.

Unfortunately, we must turn to prehistory in order to find a landscape study that has successfully incorporated GIS. Gaffney and Stančič's (1991) research undertaken on the island of Hvar off the former Yugoslavian coast provides a model for creating spatial databases for landscape studies, and still provides one of the best examples of its use. Gaffney and Stančič (1991, 36) created a spatial database with five 'thematic layers', topography, soils, lithology, microclimate, and archaeological site-location. The use of these five layers allowed for a more holistic study to be undertaken, and allowed for the database to be queried in order to further the understanding of the prehistoric landscape of Hvar.

Summary

The aim of this short section was to highlight the hitherto untapped potential of using GIS databases in studies of medieval landscapes. Used as a tool rather than as a product, the GIS when correctly applied can, as discussed above, aid study. Gillard (2002, 77) states that the use of GIS for this type of study leads to a case of 'hunt the variable', leading to the 'subtle and multi-faceted nature of settlement and landscape' to be missed. He has a point, as it is easy for researchers to be dazzled by the bright lights of the GIS's capabilities and miss the ultimate goal, although this is not the program's fault. The use of GIS regimes as a tool should make accessing the intricacies of landscapes easier, rather than detracting from it.

Acquisition of data: formation of GIS themes

With this in mind, in order to create a database within the GIS, it is important to identify the information components that will create the themes created within the GIS package.[2] A theme is fundamentally one individual element of the map; in effect, layers of tracing paper which get built up to create a complete image. This is important, as the GIS does not conceptualise, store, and manage spatial information in a holistic form. Rather, it relies on the concept of 'thematic mapping'; a collection of individual map sheets each themed to a particular facet of study (Wheatley and Gillings 2002, 25).

The themes identified are the primary elements in the enquiry that will be undertaken for the Hartland Moors and Blackdown Hills areas, allowing for the fundamental principles of the landscape to be considered and assessed using the capabilities of the GIS. Interpretation of this data within the GIS in the manner suggested obviously does not use the packages to their full extent.

To create themes, Wheatley and Gillings (2002, 26) suggest that we have to combine and overlay individual sources within the database whilst maintaining the original spatial relationships: the idea of geo-referencing. This is registering the spatial location of features within the individual themes to correlate with the surface of the earth (*ibid*. 2002, 26). This study benefits from using Landline digital Ordnance Survey maps, and digital aerial photographs, and therefore, all the GIS themes are tied to the National Grid, which helps to maintain spatial integrity.

Physical background

A number of themes relate to the physical aspects of the study areas. Soil and geology information can be used to establish whether particular field patterns occurred consistently on particular geological types. Drainage is also important in understanding how the physical landscape was shaped and how it is manipulated and worked. Thus, when comparing the different areas, it is important that this type of information is considered. It is crucial that the analysis does not become environmentally deterministic, but because of the nature of the study areas, it is important to the understanding of land use and settlement found within the archaeological record.

When looking at the physical elements of the historic landscape, aerial photographic evidence provides a useful comparison to the nineteenth-century Tithe Survey map data. Cropmarks and earthworks visible on aerial photographs can help to piece together what the landscape looked like where there are gaps in the Tithe Surveys, because of non-titheable areas or preservation issues. The aerial photographs produced for the study areas also provide an invaluable source of information for a regressive approach to historic landscape studies. Such photographs allow the earlier patterns of landscape organisation to be gleaned. By overlying the modern Ordnance Survey and nineteenth-century Tithe Survey information over the photographs within the GIS, former boundaries visible through crop- and soil-marks can be highlighted, and earlier agricultural practices potentially isolated. Therefore, aerial photographs allow for patterns in the landscape to be elucidated from a perspective unavailable using other means.

The creation of Digital Elevation Models (DEM) for the study areas allow for the topography of each study area to be considered in three dimensions, so that changes in landscape can be seen clearly within the layer. Interpolation between contours allows height categories to be developed, and provides a theme to which the other sources of information can be related. This information will then aid the analysis of the drainage and water catchments within the study areas. Although not a problem directly related to studies of the medieval period, caution must be taken when creating any type of map, and those produced within GIS are no exception. The fundamental assumption is that the modern observable landscape form and its related dynamics are comparable to those of the past, and obviously, this is not true (Gillings 1995, 67). In that respect, the Digital Elevation Models (DEMs) created are going to be reflecting today's landscape (Ruggles *et al.* 1993, 131). This is important to accept and note, but it should not deter research using such tools. These physical elements can provide a background onto which other information can be placed.

Land use

The descriptions regarding the state of cultivation provide an insight into how the landscape was used and manipulated, although caution must be taken when discussing the extent of arable land, as this may simply mean land that had been ploughed in the years before the survey was taken (Kain 1984, 68). The debate about the use of arable as a land use indicator will be discussed further in later chapters, in particular with reference to agricultural management strategies such as ley or convertible husbandry. Aside from this, the large-scale mapping of these elements will allow patterns to be highlighted which may occur across parish boundaries, and this will give an indication of the pre-administrative landscape. Combining this information with the morphology of fields, such as reversed S-shaped fields, strip fields, and other distinct field systems as highlighted from the Tithe Surveys, can aid understanding into the complexities of medieval and post-medieval land management.

This process is very much based upon individual interpretation of field shape and typology, and it is important that it is considered that there is no such thing as a dispassionate and non-biased map. Nevertheless, this is still a valid approach which can highlight historic elements fossilised within the modern landscape. This kind of characterisation greatly benefits from the use of GIS.

Field-names

Carrying on from this, access to the field-names recorded in the Apportionment of the Tithe Survey is also an important part of this interpretation. Field-names can be indicators of a number of things, including past land use and landholding. The occurrence of family names (as seen through documents) also helps with identification of land belonging to particular estates, or as stable elements in regression of landownership patterns. Field-names can also present an image of how the field was viewed, both in agricultural terms (field-names referring to good or poor soil such as Hunger-Lands or Starve-Acre) and social terms (recalling legendary people or events in history, for example Nelson's Plot).

Of particular importance are field- and place-names which suggest former waste land (for example "breach" names that occur in areas of formerly uncultivated land). These linguistic traits can be spatially plotted within the GIS database in a way which would have been virtually impossible by other means. The information gained from field- and place-names can also act as an indicator of chronology through the identification of different types of name (Old English derivatives *etc.*). Laing and Laing's (1996, 76) suggestion that the majority of these derive from later or post-medieval periods must also be considered, although this is an argument which applies more to the 'Midlands' landscape. Within the South-west, field-name sources can give a clearer indication of previous land use, thus aiding our enquiry into periods where documentary records are less frequent. Using the query function within the GIS, the occurrence of particular indicative names can be mapped, and their relationship to other features such as topography, landownership, and location defined.

Mapping patterns of landholding

The final element of the nineteenth-century Tithe Apportionments to be discussed is landholding. Previously, Tithe Survey mapping of landownership has occurred for single parishes. By mapping a series of adjacent parishes and then linking this spatial data to the Tithe Survey Apportionments (which list information such as landowner, land use, field-name *etc.*) further layers can be created within the GIS which provide a wealth of data that can be used and manipulated. Crucially, the information gained from the Tithe Apportionment can be represented in individual layers but viewed as a whole, allowing for larger scale patterns to be identified. This allows blocks of ownership and the concentration of specific land uses to emerge.

However, perhaps the most significant part of this research is the wholesale mapping of the nineteenth-century patterns of Tithe Survey landownership. In previous cases where there has been some application of this type of mapping they have been small scale, either settlement, or, at most, parish wide.

Aston (1998) uses the 1772 map of Codsend in Cutcombe Somerset to plot landownership around five small farmsteads. This showed some holdings scattered over several fields and divided from the commons by large field banks, which, he suggests, may have antecedents in the sixth to eighth century AD (*ibid.* 1998, 94–5). This small scale sample highlights the type of information which can be gained by combining archaeological features and patterns of landownership. Aston's mapping of the eighteenth-century landownership patterns at Codsend is important as it indicates the potential of studying the distribution of landholding against the physical evidence of field boundaries and settlement. The relationship between the holdings and the division of the common land is of particular interest.

Drawing on earlier sources, Ransom (2004) attempts to map the extent of the eleventh century Domesday manors of Ilsington parish in Teignbridge, east Devon using the method set out by Reichel (1894a). Reichel's method (1894a, *passim*) equates the area holdings listed in Domesday with the landscape surrounding the modern settlements bearing the same name. From Reichel's model, Ransom (2004, 10–12) states that the ecclesiastical parish boundary was largely determined before 1187 and suggests the possible boundaries of manorial centres in the eleventh century. This method is highly speculative, and Ransom himself states that the outcome of the study is merely conjecture (*ibid.* 2004, 10).

A second parish-based study also based in the South-west comes from

Williams' (1963) work on the settlement of Ashworthy in Devon, where landownership and tenancy were both mapped. This is useful for the larger estates, and elucidates information including the fact that a quarter of the households contained kin other than direct nucleated family (Lord 1993, 164), but it does not consider the intricacies of patterns of smaller landholders. This is more successful than Ransom's study, and the use of the Tithe Apportionment landownership patterns is especially useful to this research.

West and McLaughlin (1998) mapped the tenant holdings derived from 1581 and 1577 *Terratorium* for Walsham le Willows in Suffolk. The *Terratorium* is a sixteenth century estate document listing the holdings and information such as freeholders. This study created a hypothetical medieval map of Walsham using the *Terratorium*, and used this in conjunction with archaeological fieldwork which included fieldwalking (West and McLaughlin 1998, vii). At Walsham much of the land held from the manor was either free or copyhold, with the free-land dispersed liberally through the parish, usually in strips (West and McLaughlin 1998, 108). By mapping the *Terratorium* an image of the pre-1577 landscape can be gleaned, and from this it can be seen that there were a large number of strip fields which had been amalgamated by the time the survey was produced (West and McLaughlin 1998, 109). This parish-based study informs us about the nature of medieval archaeology within this area, and also the formation and processes involved in the creation of the historic landscape. The information gained about landownership will help to elucidate former estate structure, especially when comparing this with documentary evidence.

As previous cases of landholding mapping have been small scale, there is a need to assess whether nineteenth-century patterns of landholdings can be traced further back. By using blocks of Tithe Survey landholding and comparing their acreage to accounts in historical documents such as the *Inquisitiones Post Mortem* (IPM), landownership can then be traced back. It is clear that such a regression can go no further back than the late medieval period, but through historical sources it may be possible to infer continuity between the nineteenth-century historic landscape and earlier landholdings.

The IPM lists the acreage for the estates of the larger landowners within the Blackdown Hills and Hartland Moors study areas. This can be then compared to the nineteenth-century estates in order to establish whether there is any consistency between estate sizes. One example is the area known as Simon's Burrow in Hemyock, a parish on the Devon/Somerset border in the Blackdown Hills. There is reference to Simon's Burrow as *Simundesbergha* in a Cartulary of Buckland Priory circa 1190 (PND 1932, 617), and by the IPM dated to 1465 for Philippa Dynham (wife of John Dynham of Hartland and holder of the manor of Hemyock and Hydon [Clayhidon]); the area of Symondsesburgh was listed as covering 'three messuages and 200 acres'. The Tithe Survey dating to 1843 for Hemyock shows two farmsteads, Little Simonsburrow and Great Simonsburrow, suggesting that the three dwellings had been reduced to two. The Tithe Survey apportionments show 32 fields held as part of the Great

Simonsburrow estate all located around the two dwellings (Fig. 2.2a). The landownership records from the Tithe show all these fields are exclusively held by one man, William Land, and he owned no other land within Hemyock other than these fields. The fields held by William Land were located to the west of the farms, and were bounded to the south by an area held by the neighbouring parish of Clayhidon. In total these fields covered an area of 164.25 acres, short of the 200 acres discussed in the IPM. However, the Tithe lists 17 fields held as the Little Simonsburrow estate. These fields were owned by John Blackmore Senior and lie to the east of the farms. Interestingly, although being part of one of the larger landowning families in the Blackdown Hills and holding land in neighbouring Clayhidon, John Blackmore Senior only holds and occupies the 17 fields of the Little Simonburrow estate in Hemyock. Combining this area of land with the fields held as part of Great Simonsburrow brings the total acreage to just over 223 acres (Fig. 2.2b). It could be suggested from this evidence that at some point in the 378 years between 1465 and 1843 the Symondsesburgh manor was divided into two holdings, Great and Little Simonsburrow, as indicated by the Tithe Survey landownership patterns.

It is clear that the use of such early documentation, and the problem as to what was meant by the measurement 'acre', means that such a suggestion can only be speculation, just as Ransom could only speculate for Ilsington. However, the example seen at Simonsburrow indicates the potential of using such information. Crucial to this is the idea of customary and statute acres. The Tithe Surveys would have used statutory acres, whereas the earlier documents most likely used customary acres defined locally.

The selling-off of former monastic lands during the Reformation in the sixteenth century can, in some cases, allow for past landownership patterns to be explored. The manor of Stoke in Hartland provides an interesting example as the calendar of monastic grants gives an insight into the earlier landscape of this estate (Youings 1955, 75 m.4). In the grant, the names of the fields associated with the manor are listed. This is unusual, and although some of the names have subsequently changed, by querying the Tithe Survey dataset in the GIS many of these fields can be identified. Combining this with the Tithe Survey landownership, it can be seen that these fields were all held by William Lewis Buck, as was much of the land around Stoke St. Nectan and the former Abbey. Thus it may be fair to suggest that here, at least some continuity between that late medieval estate and that shown on the Tithe Survey occurs.

Further information about landownership patterns can be gained from individual estate records. Hoskins (1952a, 103) discusses the holdings of the Galsworthy family, with particular reference to Moors Farm in Hartland parish. He notes that in 1566 Moors Farm was 46 acres in size, and that the family continued to farm here until 1848 (*ibid.* 1952, 103; Pearse Chope 1940, 153). The Tithe Survey landownership pattern confirms this, and it can be seen that the area around Moors Farm held by John Galsworthy covered an area of approximately 55 acres. This continuation of ownership and size of holdings

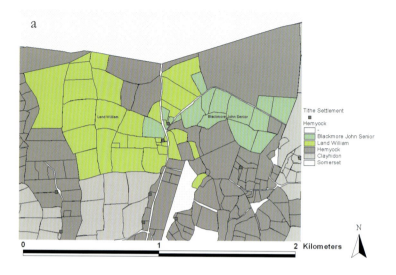

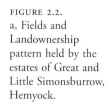

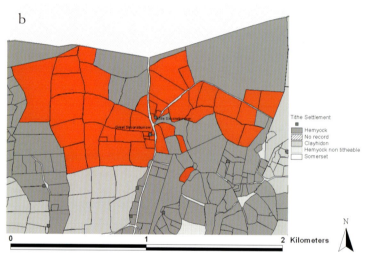

shows the importance of visible patterns within the nineteenth-century historic landscape. At Galsworthy a direct correlation between the nineteenth-century Tithe Survey landownership and the sixteenth century landscape can be made.

It can be suggested that Tithe Landownership patterns can, in some instances, provide a reference to earlier manorial holdings. This is particularly so in the case of the holding at Moors Farm in Hartland, where the ownership of the Galsworthy family could be traced back from the Tithe Surveys to the sixteenth century. This will be raised in more detail in subsequent chapters and discussed in Chapter Seven.

Summary

The data collated during the investigation of the structure of historical and cultural landscapes provides an insight into the use, regulation and division of the landscape within the medieval and post-medieval periods. These elements provide the basis for furthering the study into the cultural landscapes of a particular region, providing the link between the physical structures on the ground and the people who created, used and lived amidst them.

Testing the hypothesis

Through the large-scale mapping of the Tithe Surveys for the parishes within the study areas and the documentary evidence which supports it, a number of avenues of investigation should become apparent. Information regarding particular types of land use and field boundaries, types of settlement, and the nature of landownership in relation to these structures should form coherent and recognisable forms within the study areas, and also between them. Therefore, having complete areas of field and settlement arrangements, and their associated land use and ownership, allows hypotheses regarding the presence of particular patterns within the landscape to be made about the third study area. Comparing the elements mapped for the Blackdown Hills and for Hartland Moor, target areas within the South Hams can be highlighted for small scale investigation. Suppositions can then be made in regard to the form and nature of the historic landscape within these targeted small areas of the South Hams study area, which can go on to be tested. In this way, the landscape of the third study area can be 'cherry picked', focusing on characteristic traits in order to answer specific questions.

Summary

This chapter has introduced the sources which are to be incorporated into the study of the historic landscape in Devon, and highlighted how the GIS database is to be used.

The following three chapters focus on distinct study areas. Chapters Three and Four will discuss the Blackdown Hills in east Devon and Hartland Moors in the north-west of the county in field-by-field depth in order to understand the complexities of the historic landscape in these two different regions. Chapter Five will discuss the landscape of the South Hams, and use a number of sample areas within that study area to answer key questions raised by the examination of the other two regions.

Notes

1   The three study areas did not see the levels of industrialization that other areas of England experienced. However, this statement refers to the landscape before agricultural mechanisation and the cloth and lace industries which developed in east Devon.

2   Within the GIS software used in this study (ArcView 3.2 with additional 3D elevation mapping created through ArcMap 8.3) the themes are placed in a framework known as a layer, which constructs the resultant images.

CHAPTER THREE

'A Wild and Untamed Landscape' – The Blackdown Hills

Introduction to the Blackdown Hills

The Blackdown Hills are a range of hills along the eastern side of Devon and the south-western corner of Somerset. Although the designated area of research is focused on the Devon half of the Blackdown Hills, it is important to discuss the region as a whole in order to place the study area in to its wider context and explain why particular decisions were made.

The Blackdown Hills were designated as an Area of Outstanding Natural Beauty (AoNB) in 1989, and as an Environmentally Sensitive Area (ESA) in 1993 following surveys carried out by English Heritage and Devon and Somerset County Councils (Griffith and Waddell 1996, 27). As a whole the Blackdown Hills start to the north in Somerset at Blagdon Hill, to the south of the M5 motorway, down to their southern extent at Honiton in Devon (the modern A35(T) road). Due to the demarcation of the CLP, only the Devon half of the Blackdown Hills was available for study. This area extends westwards to the parishes of Kentisbeare and eastwards to Chardstock (Fig. 3.1). The Blackdown Hills is the modern name for this area, and is recorded in use by 1806, with a reference to it by Tristram Risdon a century earlier (Vancouver 1808, map 1 335; (Polwhele 1793–1806, 335). In a report dating to 1690 of a 'bewitching' in the area there is a reference to the road from 'Hidon Clist [Clyst Hidon], and so for Black Down'. This may be a reference to the area of common with that name situated in Culmstock, rather than the hills themselves. This is further supported by the presence of a trackway link to the main roads to Taunton.

The nature of the landscape is one of secluded combes, and this is key to the character of the Blackdown Hills as a whole. For example, by driving along the modern day main roads that bypass the hills it is very difficult to gain a true picture of the intricacy of the winding valley systems, a seemingly impenetrable and enclosed area of high land (Fig. 3.2). It is this idea of seclusion, and the idea of the Blackdown Hills' marginality, which are crucial factors to the use, management and perception of the landscape within this area.

It can be seen, therefore, that landscape here raises a number of questions; how does this landscape develop in the medieval period, and did the segregation continue into the heart of the Blackdown Hills, between the sheltered valleys, or even between parish and manorial centres? The Blackdown Hills are clearly an example of a regional cultural unit: did the idea of *pays* work here at a smaller community level, and is it visible in field morphology and/or landholding

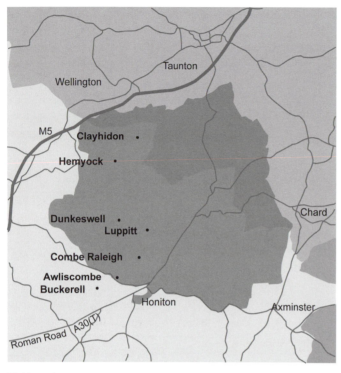

Not to scale

FIGURE 3.1. Location
of the Blackdown Hills
region

patterns? In order to elucidate how the landscape(s) within the Blackdown Hills was structured and evolved, a smaller section, in effect a microcosm of the Blackdown Hills, has been designated for study containing all the elements which make up the area as a whole.

Introduction to the Blackdown Hills study area

In order to understand the landscape of the Blackdown Hills, it is fitting to concentrate on a sample area. In order to sample a true reflection of the region, a study area consisting of a 170km² block of the Devon side of the Blackdown Hills has been highlighted to create a transect north-south across them. Within this study area, six parishes have been focused on (south to north): Buckerell, Awliscombe, Combe Raleigh, Luppitt, Clayhidon, and Hemyock. Reference is also made to a seventh parish, Dunkeswell (Fig. 3.3). As mentioned in Chapter One, much of the parish of Dunkeswell was non-titheable (only 240 fields are mapped) and has not been included as a primary parish as it would be difficult to make an authoritative examination of the parish due to the small number of fields available for study. However, it is important that the parish is included both so that comparisons can be made and because of its manorial and ecclesiastical influence (see below).

Introduction to the parishes

FIGURE 3.2. Looking
northwards towards the
Blackdown hills – note
their image as a solid
physical barrier

The discussion of the parishes will start with those in the south of the study area on the periphery of the Blackdown Hills, work northwards towards the Devon/Somerset border and the heart of the region, and will discuss not only the parish itself but also consider the case study area without the restrictions of parish boundaries, so as not to limit the interpretation of the landscape as a whole.

The first parish to be discussed is that of Buckerell which lies on the southerly edge of the study area, and on the southern perimeter of the Blackdown Hills, representing the lowest lying parish within the transect. Buckerell lies on the slopes between the Clyst Valley to the west and the Blackdown Hills proper to the east (outside of the AoNB and ESA designated area). This is an important part of the Blackdown Hills as it is through this area that the major routes pass including the Roman road (now the A35(T)). The name Buckerell occurs relatively late in relation to the other parishes (see below), recorded as *Bucherell* in 1165 (PND 1932, 610), indicating an enclosed parish. As will be discussed, the name Buckerell was not recorded until the twelfth century and was thought to have been part of the Awliscombe estate prior to this date (Reichel 1928, 35).

Buckerell is divided from the neighbouring parish of Feniton to the east by the Vine Water River, on the west from Awliscombe by Wolf River and the high ridge known as Buckerell and Bushy Knap. The parish abuts the Iron Age Hillfort of Hembury to the north, and is bordered by the river Otter to the

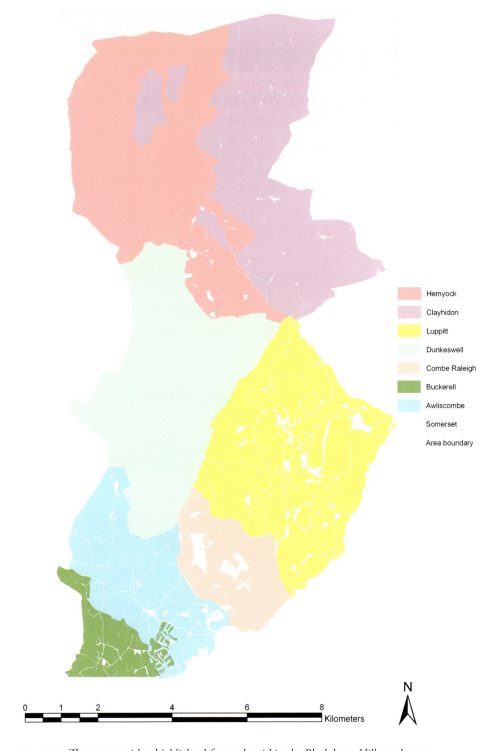

🟥	Hemyock
🟪	Clayhidon
🟨	Luppitt
🟩	Dunkeswell
🟧	Combe Raleigh
🟩	Buckerell
🟦	Awliscombe
	Somerset
	Area boundary

FIGURE 3.3. The seven parishes highlighted for study within the Blackdown Hills study area

south giving Buckerell parish a triangular shape, perhaps reflecting the nature of its formation

Neighbouring Awliscombe lies on the border of the AoNB designation and is situated in the valley of the river Wolf between the Buckerell/Bushy Knap ridge and St. Cyres Hill, a flat plateau which forms one of the upland ridges of the Blackdown Hills, and which defines the parish's shape. Awliscombe is listed in Domesday under various spellings, but the modern name is generally accepted to be topographical and derives from the Old English for the coomb (or valley) of the river-junction (Gelling 2000, 93). This suggestion is reinforced by its location. Along with Buckerell, Awliscombe forms the southern reaches of the transect across the Devon side of the Blackdown Hills, and will serve as a comparison with those parishes which lie within the heart of the region.

Combe Raleigh lies between Awliscombe and Luppitt and is shaped by two valleys which run across its length. Although it is assumed by some that Combe Raleigh acquired its name from Sir Walter Raleigh, this is merely folk belief as the name can be testified earlier. Combe Raleigh is recorded in Domesday as *Otri* (DB, 23,21), no doubt like many of the place-name derivatives in this area referring to the river Otter. The Combe prefix may arise from two sources; either as a topographical description of the valleys created by St. Cyres Hill, Carpenter's Hill and Combe Hill, or from *cumb*, a manor which was first recorded in 1242 (PND 1932, 638). Raleigh was a much later addition to the name added by Sir John Raleigh who owned the manor here in 1292 (Polwhele 1793–1806, 329). Combe Raleigh is also known as Combe Saint Nicholas, presumably named after Saint Nicholas who is dedicated in the fifteenth century church, reflecting an alternative to the Raleigh family name.

Luppitt parish is situated in the centre of the study area and is positioned over both valley and upland. Its diamond shape means that its northern tip is the point of convergence for four other parishes (Dunkeswell, Upottery, Clayhidon, and Hemyock). The centre of Luppitt is divided by Hartridge (which mirrors St. Cyres Hill to the west) which runs north–south across the parish. The name Luppitt is suggested to mean *Lufa's* pit or hollow and this may refer to a hermitage or monastic cell, but this cannot be verified (PND 1932, 641–2).

To the north of the study area, lying on the border between Devon and Somerset are the parishes of Clayhidon and Hemyock. Clayhidon, named after the Hidon family who held much of the parish (see below), is the longest parish in Devon and is bounded on two sides by Somerset (Wellington to the north and Churchstanton, previously part of Devon, to the east). In turn, Hemyock is a large parish which straddles both the upland moors and the valley of the river Culm. Both Clayhidon and Hemyock incorporate some of the highest prominences within the Devon side of the Blackdown Hills, but are also divided by a river valley, providing distinct variations in topography (see below). The -ock suffix is interesting as it is thought to derive from the celtic word *cẹd*, *coid*, or *coed* meaning forest or wood, and that the ock is an adjective of *cẹdiōg* 'wooded' (Gelling 2000, 190). This is one of the few instances of celtic spelling in this area of Devon.

The seventh parish, which will be discussed in less detail as previously explained, is Dunkeswell in the centre of the study area and to the east of Luppitt. It is important to acknowledge Dunkeswell not only for its position within the heart of the Blackdown Hills but also because of the presence of the thirteenth-century Cistercian Abbey: Dunkeswell Abbey of the Blessed Saint Mary. The name Dunkeswell derives from the Old English for *Duduc's Spring* (Gelling 2000, 31), which may suggest a holy site within the landscape and the reason why the abbey was sited here. The establishment of this monastery and its subsequent estate has a definite and notable affect on the surrounding communities insofar as documentary sources are concerned, and thus it is important to consider the impact that such a formalised community would have on the landscape.

Perception of landscape in the recent past

From the description of the steep sided valleys and the external perception of the area being marginal and secluded, it is not surprising that the Blackdown Hills are party to a number of folk stories and myths. For example, stories suggest that the narrow wooded combs had a sylvan charm, and that smugglers and thieves used them in order to evade capture aided by the difficult terrain (Coxhead 1954, 92–3). As mentioned above, tales of 'bewitchings' by the ghosts of the Monmouth Rebellion were even reported in papers and in one case, in court. More fanciful are the tales of fairies and pixies, spirits and devils, and even dragons dwelling within the rough heath land and wooded valleys that cut deeply into the hills. These ideas will be discussed in more detail in Chapter Six, but they play a significant part in how the Blackdown Hills are viewed, and also added cultural factors to the individual *pays*.

Physical elements of the Blackdown Hills

It is important to discuss the physical components that create a landscape. This is particularly relevant within the Blackdown Hills as the combination of topography, geology, and soils create a distinct backdrop for their inhabitants.

The geology of the Blackdown Hills as a whole is very distinctive as the underlying bedrock of the study area is Upper (Keuper) Marls; this is capped by a layer of valley gravels in the river valleys and hill slopes, and hilltops with Upper Greensand (GS, 326 and 340; 311). Todd (1987, 4) suggests that because of this geological formation, the Blackdown Hills are seen by many as being separate from the rest of Devon and Somerset. Thus, the Greensand which underlies the hills creates a very different landscape to the other upland regions of the South-west such as Exmoor, Bodmin Moor, or Dartmoor which may have afforded a different management routine in the past. The occurrence of this locally available chert is noticeable in the vernacular buildings, which used the toffee coloured stone in construction.

In terms of topography, the Blackdown Hills as a whole contain some of the highest peaks outside of Dartmoor and Exmoor, with the Greensand plateau on the Devon side ranging from between 250 and 270 metres above sea level. Because of the high quantities of rivers and streams within the study area, the land is cut by a series of river valleys that vary between 80 and 140 metres. This formation creates a number of sheltered basins in the Greensand hills surrounding the valley's steep sided ridges; a characteristic of the Blackdown Hills.

As a result of the rock's impermeability, Greensand is considered suitable bedrock for stream catchments. The river valleys consist of alluvium on top of valley gravels, and above the Greensand plateau lies clay with inclusions of flint and cherts (GS, 326 and 340; 311). The study area itself is fed by six major rivers, 73 tributaries, and numerous man-made leats and drains diverting springs and ground water. To the south of the study area, the main river is the river Otter which runs north-east to south-west and forms the southern border for Luppitt, Combe Raleigh, Awliscombe and Buckerell. Into this feeds Vine Water (the border of Buckerell and the parish of Feniton) and the river Wolf which flows north–south through the centre of Awliscombe parish. Figure 3.4 shows the river valley between Buckerell and Awliscombe and illustrates the typical landscape of the southern half of the study area. In the northern half of the study area, the river Culm runs east–west through the parishes of Hemyock and Clayhidon. Springs are also common in the Blackdown Hills, many of which were utilised within Clayhidon for spring-fed mills. Running off the Culm is Bolham river which flows through Bolham Water in Clayhidon (Fig. 3.5), which in turn feeds into the Madford river. This river flows north–south through Hemyock and forms the parish border with Dunkeswell to the south-west. Comparison should be made between figure 3.5, taken in the heart of the Blackdown Hills region, and the southern area of the Blackdown Hills shown in figure 3.4. The area illustrated in figure 3.5 is Bolham Water in the parish of Clayhidon, and shows the steep hillsides and the secluded valley below.

The pattern of soils reflects the topography and geology of the Blackdown Hills. The hillslopes along the valley of the Culm River consist of typical humic gley soils, which occur because of a combination of fluctuating groundwater and low permeability (Clayden 1971, 44). In the valleys, in particular around Awliscombe and Buckerell, the soil type is stagnogleyic argillic brown earths. Brown earths are acidic and generally well drained but palaeo-argillic brown earths are associated with less well drained soils. In the Blackdown Hills their distribution corresponds with the hilltops. The occurrence of these brown earth soils with the Greensand bedrock causes poor drainage of surface water, leading to 'poorer' conditions agriculturally (*ibid*. 1971, 40). Vancouver (1808, 51) suggested that the land within the Blackdown Hills would perform well once properly drained and cultivated, and the number of drainage channels which cross the study area seem to verify this fact.

FIGURE 3.4. The southern part of the Blackdown Hills, the low lying parishes of Awliscombe and Buckerell

FIGURE 3.5. In the heart of the Blackdowns – the northern half of the study area, Bolham Water in Clayhidon

The occurrence of marl pits on the Blackdown Hills is prolific and provides an insight into the nature of the soil and its use. Because of its alkaline properties, marl was generally extracted from the subsoil and mixed with the more acidic topsoil in order to improve existing arable land, particularly in heathland areas, and Williamson (2002, 69) suggests they correspond with enclosed land in the eighteenth century. As will be seen below, enclosure occurred in a piecemeal fashion in the Blackdown Hills, and by the time of the Tithe Survey many marl pits were redundant with several former quarries utilised as orchards or copses.

In terms of climate, the Blackdown Hills experiences varying extremes of weather because of the topography, like the other upland areas in the South-west. Vancouver (1808, 10) suggests that 'the southerly winds are by far the most violent and common; but those from the opposite quarter are found to be the most destructive to fruit, and injurious to vegetables in the spring of the year'. However, despite this he argues that the area does not seem to be as prone to 'local disadvantages' as other parts of Devon (*ibid.* 1808, 10).

Previous archaeological research

In light of the lack of archaeological research outside of the region of Dartmoor (something which is beginning to be reversed), gaining an image of the archaeological heritage for the Blackdown Hills is not without its problems. Evidence within the archaeological record for prehistoric and Romano-British activity is difficult to identify, although there are a number of flint scatters found within the parishes of Awliscombe and Luppitt. The Neolithic activity on the Iron Age Hembury Hillfort provides much of the tangible evidence for the prehistoric period here. The Roman Road and the encampment on Hembury give snapshots that there were some 'external' influences entering the Blackdown Hills, but this evidence alone is of little consequence.

However, there is one source of evidence which can help gain more of a picture of previous activity within the Blackdown Hills. Perhaps the most visible feature, and thus the most researched, is the production of iron in the area. The remnants of an ironworking tradition are widespread within the Blackdown Hills as a whole, and the study area is no exception. One of the largest smelting sites was in Hemyock (although levelled and cleared sometime within the last fifty years). Approximately 500 tonnes of tap slag was thought to have been piled up in the area, along with furnace lining and possible smithing slags (Griffith and Waddell 1996, 31). Hackpen Hill, to the north of the study area, has also been identified as a site of iron extraction, through aerial photographs that show numerous pits in pastoral fields (*ibid.* 1996, 32).

There is evidence of an iron processing site dating to AD 55/75 at Sweetlands Farm in Upottery, which lies to the east of the study area. Further radiocarbon dates have been taken from Hemyock and Dunkeswell providing two phases of activity, in the Romano-British and early medieval periods (Griffith and Waddell 1996, 34).

Work undertaken by CLP at Bywood Farm in Dunkeswell also indicates a significant iron production site in the Romano-British period (Wiecken 2004). Taken with the other known sites which occur in neighbouring Hemyock it can be suggested that there was large scale iron production in the Blackdown Hills during this time. Griffith and Waddell (1995, 14) suggest that these earlier dates infer that the area was exploited or controlled by the Roman army during the early part of the conquest, and it is known from Todd's excavations in the 1980s that an organised military settlement was located on Hembury Hillfort. This activity was dated by small samian ware assemblages to between AD 50 and AD 70 (Todd 1984, 264). It is therefore not inconceivable to suggest some kind of central organisation of iron manufacturing in this area. This however ignores the possibility that the local population could have been responsible. Furthermore, evidence that iron production continued into the early medieval period suggests this was small scale 'indigenous' exploitation of natural resources.

Development and evolution of the Blackdown Hills landscape

The following section outlines the transition occurring in estate structure from the earliest available record (Domesday Survey of 1086), followed by discussion of the field systems, field-names, settlements, roads and droveways, and evidence of industry for each parish, to draw together ideas regarding the development of the medieval landscape and the relationship between the landholding patterns, and field and settlement morphology.

Estate structure

The creation of estates provides the framework in which the elements of the historic landscape were developed and managed. It is crucial, therefore, to discuss the possible manorial and ecclesiastical divisions which occur in the present parishes. As discussed in Chapter Two it is noted that the Tithe Survey represents the landownership structures for the nineteenth century, but it is clear that the patterns characterised by this data give valuable information to help elucidate medieval estate structures.

In reference to ecclesiastical structures, the primary influence within the Blackdown Hills study area is the thirteenth century Cistercian abbey at Dunkeswell. The Monastic cells of Taunton Priory and Newnham Abbey also have ties with the area. However, unlike the study area of Hartland Moors (see Chapter Four) there are no clear large scale manorial influences within the Blackdown Hills rather, a number of smaller manorial holdings. This can be seen in tables 3.1 and 3.2 which list thirteenth- and fourteenth-century landholders. As a result of this lack of one dominating estate, each parish within the Blackdown Hills study area will be discussed in turn, starting with the lower lying southern parishes of Awliscombe and Buckerell, with a concluding summary of the overall patterns emerging. This is crucial as it is important to consider the study area as a holistic unit rather than a series of individual parishes.

Awliscombe and Buckerell on the southern edge of the Blackdown Hills are the most low-lying parishes. For this area the earliest documentary sources are the Domesday records. From the Domesday entry it is clear that Buckerell and

Awliscombe were treated as one unit. Therefore, when discussing estate structure Awliscombe and Buckerell should be considered together. The settlement name of Buckerell is not listed in the Domesday records, but Awliscombe is thought to have three sets of records attributed to it for Domesday: *Avlescome*, *Horescome* (or *Holescvbe*), and *Orescome*.

The primary holders of the Domesday entries in this area were Reginaldus de Ashborn, who was listed as holding half of *Ouliscombe* (FA, 1899, 367), and the brothers Ralph de Pomeroy and William Cheever (Fig. 3.6); many settlements held by them were divided between the two (Thorn and Thorn 1980, vol. 2 chapter 19). The presence of Ralph de Pomeroy and William Cheever is interesting in relation to the hamlet of Weston. Weston, formally known as Waringston(e) or Warin's Town (Reichel 1928, 42), is situated on the border between Awliscombe and Buckerell, and is thought to be represented in Domesday as *Otri* (DB, 19,27; 34,24). There are two listings for Weston, one held by Pomeroy, the other by Cheever. The later parish boundary between Awliscombe and Buckerell Weston divides the hamlet in two along the road, and this may suggest the shared nature of this settlement and the subsequent field pattern.

Figure 3.7 shows the holdings of the Abbey of Dunkeswell, and by the thirteenth century the *Testa de Nevill* lists that half of Weston (then Waringston) was held by the Abbot of Dunkeswell, and half by the Heirs of Galfrid Fitz William (Whale 1898, 45) (see Table 3.1). By the Tax Roll of *c.* 1303 (Table 3.2), the estate was held jointly by the Abbot and John Tolyro. By this date the Abbot of Dunkeswell also held Bywood in Dunkeswell, and also Buckerell (Whale 1899, 47–49). However, it seems that Weston was jointly owned throughout its history, and this is further confirmed by the patterns of field systems here.

Thus, by the thirteenth century, Weston was part of the Dunkeswell Abbey estate. However, after the dissolution, the manor of Waringstone (which in 1545 was recorded as being part of Awliscombe) along with Rapshay in the neighbouring parish of Gittisham and Bystock in Withycombe Raleigh, were sold to an Exeter merchant called John Drake. The calendar of grant of monastic lands lists free rents at Waringstone at 6s 1d; customary rents at 116s 6d; and court profits of 13s and 4d (Youing 1955, 54 m.2). 700 oaks of 60 to 80 years growth in woods at Colyton Raleigh, Eastbudleigh and Awliscombe were also sold off with Waringstone at this time (Youing 1955, 54 m.3), although there is no indication of where these woods may have been located.

By 1611 the manor was in the hands of the Henley family (Polwhele 1793–1806 vol. 2, 274). Henry Henley 'dismembered' the manor and 'granted the royalty of it, with the manorial right to Thomas Courtenay, with Robert Gidley holding the estate in the late eighteenth century' (*ibid.* 1793–1806 vol.2, 274). By the time of the Tithe Survey Lewis Gidley only held five fields to the east of Weston, all of which were in Awliscombe, but no other land in the study area.

To the north of Weston lies the holding of Ivedon, thought to be the two Domesday entries *Otri(e)* (DB, 19,42–3; 34,45). Also known as Evadon or Ivydown, Reichel (1928, 28) suggested that these two Domesday holdings

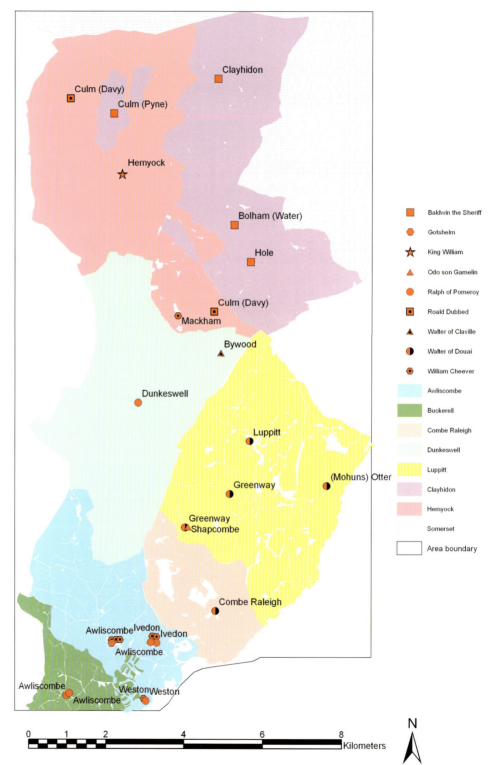

FIGURE 3.6. Distribution of eleventh century Domesday Survey Landholders within the study area

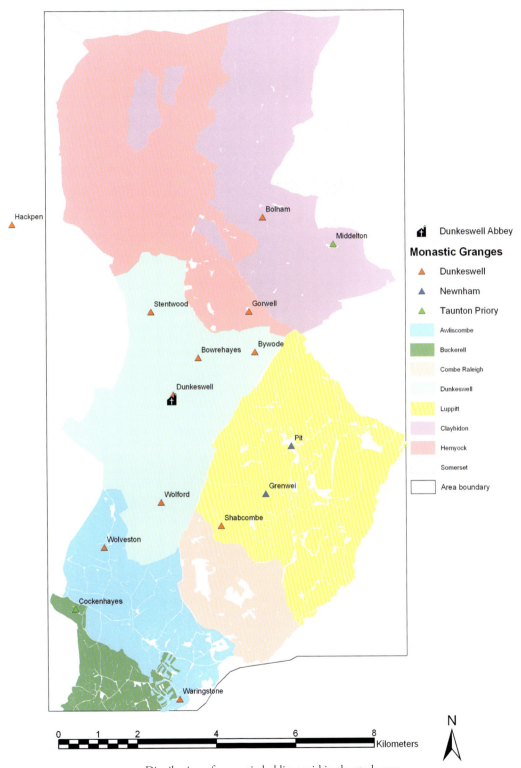

FIGURE 3.7. Distribution of monastic holdings within the study area

Index no.	fees of...	Testa de Nevill name	Testa de Nevill holder	Testa de Nevill fee		modern name
128	Toriton	Cumbe	David de Wideworth	1/2		Culm Davy
292	The Honour of Gloucester	Marlecumb	William de Colhegh	1/4	per medium	Collyhayes
527	Okemeton of John de Curtenay	Hidune	Richard de Hidune	1/6		Clayhidon
528	Okemeton of John de Curtenay	Culum	Herbet de Pynn	1		Culm Pyne
529	Okemeton of John de Curtenay	Nauicote	Jordan fitz Rogo	1/2		Newcourt and Hole
763	Honour of Beri-William Capernun, Custos of Heir of Henry de la Pomeray	Aulescumbe	Roger Giffard	1/2		Buckerell
764	Honour of Beri-William Capernun, Custos of Heir of Henry de la Pomeray	Otery	Abbot of Dunekuuill	1		Half of Waringston (Weston)
765	Honour of Beri-William Capernun, Custos of Heir of Henry de la Pomeray	Trilbehegh	William and Alexander	1/12		Hembury Fort House
809	Braneis-William de la Londre de Ballo Domini Regis	Iuedon	Robert de Stanton, Richard de Bembyry and William de Tracy	3/4		Ivedon
810	Braneis-William de la Londre de Ballo Domini Regis	Aulescumbe	Roger Giffard	1/3		Awliscombe
811	Braneis-William de la Londre de Ballo Domini Regis	Otery	Heirs of Galfrid fitz William	2		Half of Waringston
812	Braneis-William de la Londre de Ballo Domini Regis	Godeforde	Reginald de Albo Monasterio	1/8		Godford
833	Galfrid de Mandeville of the Honour of Merswode, in Sumerset	Cumbe	Matthew de Banton	1		Combe Raleigh
834	Galfrid de Mandeville of the Honour of Merswode, in Sumerset	Holediche	Reginald de Mohun	3		Holdich (listed with Mohun's Ottery)
834	Galfrid de Mandeville of the Honour of Merswode, in Sumerset	Otery	Reginald de Mohun	3		Mohun's Ottery

TABLE 3.1. Listing from the thirteenth-century *Testa de Nevill* for the Blackdown Hills

index no	Hundred	Holder	Name	Fee	Modern Parish	Modern Name
1010	Axeminstre	John de Carru	Ottery Moun	1 1/2	Luppitt	Mohun's Ottery
1010	Axeminstre	John de Carru	Loupitte	1 1/2	Luppitt	Luppitt
1026	Hemyok	Margery de Dyneham	Hemyok	1/2	Hemyock	Hemyock
1027	Hemyok	Margery de Dyneham	Hydon	1/2	Clayhidon	Clayhidon
1028	Hemyok	Abb. of Donekeswill	Bywode	1/4	Dunkeswell	Bywood
1030	Hemyok	Abb. of Donekeswill	Ouliscomb	1/4	Buckerell	Buckerell
1031	Hemyok	Regd. de Ashborn	Ouliscomb	1/2	Awliscombe	Awliscombe
1032	Hemyok	John Tolyro & Abb. of Donekeswill	Wyryngston	1/2	Buckerell	Weston
1033	Hemyok	Regd. de Clyfford	Godeford	1/8	Awliscombe	Godford
1034	Hemyok	-	Hokerigg	1/8	Dunkeswell	Hookedrise
1035	Hemyok	Heir of John Terry	Nonycote	1/2	Clayhidon	Newcott
1036	Hemyok	John Tolyro	Colm Pyn	1/2	Hemyock	Combe Pyne
1037	Hemyok	John Wogham	Comb Widiworth	1/2	Hemyock	Combe Davy

TABLE 3.2. Listing from the thirteenth-century Ed roll 1 for the Blackdown Hills

could be divided, with *Otria* thought to cover 352 acres, and *Otri* (an outlying settlement of the Tiverton Hundred) totalling 80 acres. The *Testa de Nevill* Tax Roll of 1234–42 lists the estate as Iuedon, and as being held by Robert de Stanton, Richard de Bembyry and William de Tracy. Tracy also held the neighbouring estate which bore his name. By 1779 Ivedon was held by the Pring family (Polwhele 1793–1806, 328), and it was this family who continued to hold the land around the estate into the nineteenth century.

As mentioned above, to the east of Ivedon lay the estate of the manor of Tracey, whose manor house has recently been partly demolished. Listed as Park House on the Buckerell Tithe in 1845, and Tracey House in 1846 on the Awliscombe Survey, the estate was the seat of William Tracey and was passed to the Chad family between *c*.1400 and 1800. It is thought the earliest phase of this manor is now covered by tennis courts, and that the present house, which has a construction date of 1763, overlaid and incorporated the second smaller house which had a plan dated to 1703 (SMR ST10SE/31). Polwhele (1793–1806, 328) suggests that Tracey Hayes was a Pleasant House (a house which supported grounds and servants and may be primarily for seasonal visting) and this is supported by the recording of a pleasure ground in the field names at Tracey (TA 799), which by the time of Tithe Survey was owned and held by Henry Buckland Lott. The final estate in Awliscombe is Wolverstone which lies to the north of the parish. Wolverstone is not a Domesday holding, but was a grange of Dunkeswell Abbey until the dissolution.

Apart from sharing the estate of Weston, Buckerell also contains three further estates. One of the earliest documented records of the name Buckerell occurs in 1165 in the Pipe Rolls as *Bucherell* (PND 1932, 610), suggesting that, by this time, there was some form of settlement or estate structure bearing this name. However, it has been suggested that Buckerell equated to the Domesday record of *Orescome* (Awliscombe), and Reichel (1928, 35) notes that in many cases subsequently it has been referred to as 'old Awliscombe'. As noted   to above, during the early part of the fourteenth century Buckerell was held by the Abbot of Dunkeswell, but by 1316 the *villa de Bokerell* is recorded in the Feudal Aids as part of lands belonging to Margaret Dynham, who was married to Jocei Dynham, who held the manor of Harton in Hartland (see Chapter Four). Margaret Dynham also held the manors of Hemyock and Clayhidon in this period, both of which will be discussed below.

South of the estate of Buckerell is the site of medieval Barton and the seat of the Fry Family, which is thought to be under what is now Deer Park Hotel. The present building was constructed by Nicholas Fry (Polwhele, 1793–1806, vol. 2 275; SMR ST10SW/11). The last of the Fry family (Henry Fry, Nicholas' grandson) died in 1772 leaving the estate to his widow. Polwhele (1793–1806 vol. 2, 275) records that the 'ancient name' for Deer Park was Hoke-Deers held after the Conquest by Matthew de Buckington (although it is not known how long after the Conquest he took over the lands at Deer Park, or for how long), and that the grounds were formally a chase. This name does not occur elsewhere, and therefore there are doubts over its validity.

To the north of the parish, Reichel (1928, 42) identifies another small estate at Cockenhayes, now Hembury Fort House. The *Testa de Nevill* lists that the *fees* were of the Honour of Beri-William Capernun, *Custos* of the Heir of Henry de Pomeroy, and held by William and Alexander, presumably the heirs. Again, the influence of the Pomeroy Family is evident within this small parish. The estate appears in the records again in 1346, when Cockenhayes was given to Taunton Priory. The estate later became part of the lands of Prodham owned by the Whiting family, passing then to Henry Ashford in the eighteenth century (Polwhele 1793–1806 vol. 2, 274), and by the time of the Tithe Survey, to William Porter.

Both Awliscombe and Buckerell see a number of large estate holdings and the influence of both Dunkeswell Abbey and the priory at Taunton, however, moving northwards from these parishes to the small parish of Combe Raleigh, this pattern of estate holdings changes.

Combe Raleigh, which borders Awliscombe to the north-east, and Luppitt to the south-west, may provide an interesting comparison to the neighbouring parishes in terms of estate structure. There is only one listing for the parish of Combe Raleigh within Domesday, recorded as *Otri* in the lands of Walter of Douai, and as mentioned above the volumes of *Devon Place-Names* suggests a manor called *Cumb*, although there is no tangible evidence to support this name. As mentioned in the introduction, the Raleigh suffix, it is suggested, was added by Sir John Raleigh during the Elizabethan era (Polwhele 1793–1806, 329).

There are also few documentary sources which point to there being a number of manorial centres in Combe Raleigh, and this may be because of the parish's small size, or perhaps the result of a complete domination by one lord. During the thirteenth century the estate of Cumbe was held by Matthew de Banton, and Polwhele (1793–1806, 329) supports this by stating that 'Cumbe' comprised the whole parish. This is supported by the evidence derived from the Tithe Apportionment relating to landownership. The arrangement of landownership within this parish has an interesting distribution as it is dominated by one person, Mary Bernard, and this may reflect the lack of numerous estates (see Fig. 3.16). Although the nineteenth-century historic landscape cannot be used to suggest distributions earlier than the late medieval period, it can be suggested that the pattern of landownership at Combe Raleigh has an earlier origin.

Ellishayes was a freehold of the manor of Combe Raleigh, held by the Jervis family (who constructed the Exe Bridge in Exeter) and subsequently by James Nott. The Tithe Survey indicates that the fields around this farm make up part of the small area which was not owned by Mary Bernard, but was instead held by Mary Graves (identified as purple on Fig. 3.16), indicating its autonomous status.

By comparison with Combe Raleigh, the parish of Luppitt appears to be an amalgamation of a number of estates. Within Domesday there were four listings which are now attributed to named sites in Luppitt, namely: [Mohun's] Ottery, Greenway, Shapcombe, and Luppitt itself.

In Domesday, Mohun's Ottery was also listed as *Otri* and held by Walter of Douai, with land covering five hides (DB, 23,18). The estate was also known as Ottery Fleming held by the Stoke-Flemings of Dartmouth Castle, and then became the seat of the Mohun family by 1242 at the latest, when Reginald de Mohun is listed in the Tax Roles. It was the Mohun family who established Newnham Abbey in Axminster, and the land given over by William de Mohun to the order was the Pit estate, which was Luppitt itself (Polwhele 1793–1806 vol. 2, 330). As mentioned in the previous section, it was said that Pit refers to the Lufa's pit identified in the PND for Luppitt, and that it was a former religious cell, the monks of which went on to form Newnham Abbey (*ibid.* 1793–1806 vol. 2, 330).

In 1219 *Otri* was recorded as a township (FamF, 70), and by 1303 Johannes de Carru [Carew] is listed as holding *Otery Moun* and Luppitt, see below (FA,1899, 366). In the sixteenth century Nicholas Carew married Margery Dynham, the eldest sister of John Dynham of Hartland (who will be discussed in more detail in Chapter Four) who, along with her son Nicholas, inherited a share of the great Dynham estate when it was divided into four on the death of John in 1501 (Fox and Padel 2000, xxvii). The Carew family continued in residence at Mohun's Ottery through the fourteenth–sixteenth centuries until Nicholas' son George Carew died on the *Mary Rose* in 1545, after which the estate passed to his brother. Peter Carew also died without issue, allowing for the estate to become part of the Kirkham Manor through the marriage of their sister Cecil into the Southcote family, and then to Thomas Southcote (Polwhele 1793–1806 vol. 2, 330). Polwhele (*ibid.* 1793–1806 vol. 2, 331) states that from 1685 the property was divided by the Southcotes, with much given to Sir Walter Yonge (who later bought the remaining lands making the estate one complete unit again), with seven large tenements given to Edmund Walrond of Bovey.

In 1542 as part of his inspection of England's monastic libraries, John Leland visited this area of the Blackdown Hills. On route to Dunkeswell Abbey he was invited by George Carew to stay at Mohun's Ottery (Chandler 1996, 34, 43). In part three of Leland's itinerary he states that 'George Carew hath a goodly meaner parke at Mohun's Oterey' (Leland 1535–1543, 240–1). However, the area around Mohun's Ottery is classed on the Tithe Survey as non-titheable in the nineteenth century, therefore there is no record in the historic landscape to confirm or refute this. It was recorded as recently as the late eighteenth century that the estate was a 'manor and park', but by the nineteenth century it had 'long been converted to tillage' (Shirley 1867, 89). However, there is evidence of fishponds associated with Mohun's Ottery, marked as Rookery on the 1:10,560 OS map. It is also clear from the aerial photographs that there is evidence of a ring-fenced enclosure around the settlement, and this will be returned to in later sections.

A second non-titheable area corresponds with the fields and farm of Shapcombe to the south-west of Luppitt. In Domesday Shapcombe was listed as added to the estate of Greenway, also in Luppitt (DB, 23,20), and before 1066 was listed as possessing land within Broadhembury, a parish to the west of Dunkeswell (DB, 42,16). By the medieval period at least one part of this manor became a component of the estate of Dunkeswell Abbey; perhaps the area located within Luppitt parish. After the dissolution in 1554, the manor was bestowed to Elizabeth Gravener, a widow living in London (Youing 1955, 124), and it is clear that by 1674 the estate of Shapcombe was still significant enough to be listed as a separate unit from Luppitt parish in the Hearth Tax. The manor of Greenway was also listed in Domesday records as held by Walter of Douai (DB, 23,20), and was later listed as a park and included as part of the land given over by William de Mohun to Newnham Abbey (Polwhele 1793–1806 vol. 2, 331). It was thought that at Greenway there was an associated chapel that became a Mill-house (Polwhele 1793–1806 vol. 2, 331), and earthworks in this area suggest a number of buildings and associated small field patterns, perhaps remnants of a small settlement.

The first three parishes discussed so far lie on the southern fringes of the region, with Luppitt closer to the heart of the study area and the Blackdown Hills region. The final two parishes are located to the north of the study area on the border with Somerset and fall in the centre of the Blackdown Hills.

The parish of Clayhidon (and also Hemyock, see below) acts as a transitional point within the Blackdown Hills, lying on the boundary between Devon and Somerset (which is defined by its northern boundary). Clayhidon is situated in the heart of the range and provides the division between the river valleys and hills of the southern Blackdown Hills and the true upland reaches on the northerly Hills. In Domesday there are four recorded names that are now recognisable within Clayhidon, namely Culm Pyne, Bolham, Hole, and Clayhidon itself.

Held by Baldwin the Sheriff in the Domesday listing as *Colvn* (DB, 16,122), Culm Pyne estate was, as stated by Polwhele (1793–1806 vol. 2, 335), held by the 'very anciently inheritance' of the Pine family and then passed to Sir Piers Courtenay, the younger son of William Courtenay of Powderham. Culm Pyne was held for a Knight's Fee, and this evidence of parochial parish operation can be seen as late as the Tithe Survey, with the small parcel of land around Culm Pyne being tithed to Clayhidon but located in Hemyock (Fig. 3.22).

The second of the four Domesday references refers to Bolham. Bolham Water sits in the sheltered valley of Bolham river (see Fig. 3.5), and the extent of the estate lands can be gleamed from an entry in the Feet of Fines for 1244. The Feet of Fines discusses an agreement between the Abbot of Dunkeswell and Richard de Hidon. This records that Richard gives and grants moiety (the division of land into two equal parts) of 40 acres of 'the land of Bolham where it lies towards the east, and a moiety of the land of Bywud [Bywood in Dunkeswell, see below] wherever it lies to the south' to the Abbot in return for orisons (Catholic prayer and communion) for himself and his family (FamF, 397). Some of the Bolham estate is included with lands of the abbey at Dunkeswell listed for sale after the Dissolution between 1538 and 1558 (Youing 1955, m3–6). This is perhaps one of the most helpful sources for identification of manorial centres, listing the manors belonging to Dunkeswell Abbey before the dissolution as allocated to the Earl of Bath in 1545. The Manor of *Boleham* is listed as belonging to Clayhidon and Hemyock and its associated common at *Rydewoode* [Ridgewood] to the north of Bolham is also among the parcels of land sold off.

Within the area of the Bolham estate there is a further manor known as Denshayes. Denshayes is thought to have been an estate within the Bolham area, owned by a family of the same name, and incorporating what are now the farms of Dences, Lanes, Battens and Troakes. It is also thought that Troakes Farm was the '*capitale Message* or manor house of the farm called Denishayes otherwise Denhayes', and it is known through estate archives that there were a number of demolished houses and plots on this land (CLHG Box of Blackmore Family Deeds: indenture 1749). Bolham itself was said to have been 'alienated before 1228 to the family of Daneys' (Reichel 1928, 41), and by the early 1700s the manor of Denshayes is listed as being part of the Manor of Bolham (Hawkins 1965, 55).

Neighbouring Bolham to the south is Hole. In the Exon Domesday *Holne* is recorded as being formally waste, but after the Conquest it became part of the lands of Baldwin the Sheriff, held by Otelin, and containing two villagers and 5 acres of pasture (DB, 16,124). The reference to waste could refer to two things, either that it was demolished or destroyed, or that the land was unproductive and waste ground (Thorn and Thorn, 1980 pt2 chapter 3). The area now named Hole is moorland, suggesting that the Domesday volumes may have been referring to the latter, although this cannot be proven.

In the Domesday records, the manor of Clayhidon was also held by Otelin from Baldwin (DB, 16,111). The small hamlet which now carries this name is also the location for the parish church which lies to the north of the parish some distance away from other settlement foci. Like in Luppitt, much of the land in Clayhidon was at some point held by monastic estates. Osbern and Geoffrey de Hidon (the family from which the parish got its name) gave certain parts of Clayhidon to Taunton Priory (the order to which they became canons) in the early 1100s (SRO DD/x/COC no.5/no.1).

A final manor can be identified at Middleton to the east of the parish between Bolham and Hole. The Manor of Middleton formerly held by Taunton Priory was brought to Sir Edward Seymour (the late son of the Duke of Somerset) in 1553 after the Dissolution, breaking its ties with Taunton Priory (Youing 1955, 117 m.4).[1] The lands surrounding Middleton will be discussed in more detail below.

In the neighbouring parish of Hemyock, the estate of Hemyock was held as Land of the King in Domesday, with land for 12 plough along with 12 villagers and 12 smallholders (DB, 1,8). The Exon Domesday states that it was later purchased by Baldwin for £6 by weight. Hemyock was also the chief manor of the Hundred (Reichel 1928, 39), which Fox suggests made a difference in the Hartland area in terms of nucleation of settlement patterns (see Chapter Four), and raises the question of whether the same can be suggested for the Blackdown Hills; this is something that will be returned to later.

The Manor of Hemyock has been identified as Madford. One of the earliest recordings of the manor of Madford (or Madehayes) is in 1369 and states that it held half a furlong of land which was given by Henry I to Robert Foliot (*Testa de Nevill* ref, 423). On the 1961 1:25,000 Ordnance Survey map the site of the earlier Madford Manor is listed at the present location of Lemon's Hill Farm. The name of Madford has moved a short distance to the west where there is a new Madford House and a hamlet of the same name.

Like Clayhidon, Hemyock also contains an estate held for a Knight's Fee (FamF, 25). Combe Davy, or Cumbe, was held by David de Wideworth in the thirteenth century, and by the Tax Roll of 1302 the estate was listed as Comb Widiworth. Presumably it was also this same Wideworth who gave the Davy name to the estate. Culm Davy is interesting because of the clearly defined enclosure associated with the settlement. From the Tithe Survey, a teardrop-shaped enclosure neighbouring the hamlet of Culm Davy can be seen, and within this area the church and other buildings are located.

Summary

As a whole, the study area shows a number of estates which made up each parish, with only Combe Raleigh experiencing a single manorial centre. In terms of the origins and development of Devon's historic landscapes, this provides a number of case studies to target and discuss the relationships between the patterns of Tithe landholding and the physical attributes of the landscape.

During the medieval period the landownership in the Blackdown Hills is also dominated by the monastic estates. From the Feudal Aid dated for 1303 it can be seen that the Abbot of Dunkeswell held a quarter of Bywood and of Awliscombe (*Ouliscombe*). The Abbot of Dunkeswell and Johannes Tolyro are recorded as holding a half of Wyrngeston (Weston) on the Buckerell/Awliscombe border.

It is clear that in the medieval period Dunkeswell Abbey (with, to a lesser extent, Taunton Priory and Newnham Abbey) had an influence on the already existing landholding setup. The holdings of Dunkeswell Abbey within the Hemyock Hundred (which does not include Luppitt and Combe Raleigh) included Dunkeswell itself, Waringstone (Weston) in Awliscombe/Buckerell, Bolham in Clayhidon, Bywood, Stentwood, Wolford in Dunkeswell, and Awliscombe (FF1 nos. 283, 297, 541, Fees, P.1443; Rot Ch pp. 164–5 in Summerson 1985, 21). Bowerhayes in Dunkeswell, Gorwell in Hemyock and Hackpen in neighbouring Uffculme, were also former granges of the Abbey, as was Wolveston (Wolverstone) in Awliscombe and Shapcombe in Luppitt which was held in the Axminster Hundred (Youing 1955, 131 m.14).

The Dissolution came to Dunkeswell on the 14 February 1539, when the Abbot surrendered the monastery. After the Dissolution this large estate was divided and its pieces either sold or held by the Crown. The manor of Dunkeswell along with the site of the abbey itself, the granges of Bowerhayes and Bywood, a watermill and 'three parts of a meadow' at Shapcombe in Luppitt remained in the hands of the Crown between 1558 and 1559, being rented out to John Gennynge and John Michell (Youing 1955, 131 m14). The manor of Wolverstone, part of Bolham manor, and the lands of Awliscombe were also held by the Crown (*ibid*. 1955, 131 m14). Dunkeswell Abbey had nearly 6000 acres of land, which, three months after the Dissolution were given along with the rectories at Dunkeswell and Awliscombe to John, the first baron Russell (Finberg 1969, 268–9). Ridgewood Common, the upland moor associated with Bolham manor, was sold and rented separately from the rest of the property, and two-thirds of the manor of Shapcombe was sold to Elizabeth Gravener, a widow from London. The rest was held by military tenure in Chief of the Crown as mentioned above (Youing 1955, 119, m.124).

Elements of the historic landscape

Although there are interrelations between components of the historic landscape (such as settlement pattern and field setup), each will be discussed separately for each parish within the study area, starting with field systems. This is to enable clear comparisons between the parishes within the study area and elucidate any similarities or differences between them. Here the patterns of Tithe Survey landholdings will also be discussed in relation to the historic landscape. Key to the discussion of landscape development is the occurrence and distribution of field-names. Within the GIS database this information can be added to the nineteenth-century Tithe Apportionment and queried across the study area. This large scale investigation, which crosses parish boundaries, allows patterns of landscape development to be suggested through the distribution of particular linguistic elements.

Field systems

Within the Blackdown Hills a number of elements can be seen making up the historic landscape as visible through the Tithe Survey and Apportionment. Thus, the nineteenth-century agrarian landscape of South-west England contained elements which were the end product of many periods of enclosure. Most notable are the strip-like patterns, the irregular patchworks around many old single farmsteads, and the more rectilinear construction of the later field boundaries (Shorter *et al.* 1969, 134).

Figures 3.8 and 3.9 show the patterns of nineteenth-century fields and their patterns of Tithe Survey landownership and land use. In order to understand these patterns as a whole region, the study area will be discussed first at a parish level. Apart from Awliscombe and Buckerell, each parish in the Blackdown Hills study area will be discussed as a separate unit. Buckerell and Awliscombe are discussed together as a result of their shared field pattern. The parish discussion will start with the southern parishes and work northwards across the Blackdown Hills. After each parish has been considered individually, a summary discussion will examine similarities and differences between the parishes.

In terms of general field patterns, Buckerell parish is dominated by fairly large regular square fields (Fig. 3.10). Where the hamlet of Buckerell is now situated there is a distinct enclosure of fields, located next to the parish church and bounded on three sides by roads, with the fourth enclosed by a small wooded area (Fig. 3.11). This may indicate the area of the former manor. A second distinct enclosed area of fields can be seen associated with what is now known as Deer Park. This area is partially interesting as it is thought to be a medieval Deer Park, and is described in 1633 as a hunting chase (SMR ST10SW/52). Caution must be taken when discussing any field-name in Devon with the element park, as the term refers not only to a landscape garden or hunting chase, but also to enclosed fields (Field 1993, 25).

The presence of the hill and earthwork known as Bushy Knap near to the area thought to be Deer Park is interesting. There has been much conjecture surrounding the origins and function of both Bushy and neighbouring Buckerell Knap, from Motte and Bailey to ornamental park feature (see the work by the CLP in Hawken, 2005). However, regardless of its origins, it is possible that, in the latter part of its existence, Bushy Knap would have made a convenient viewing platform for not only the deer park below, but also out to Honiton and the landscape beyond. The site of Deer Park was a medieval Barton (Lord's residence and land that was occupied by a bailiff) and has undergone a series of rebuilds before its present arrangement. The Tithe Survey shows that both the land around Deer Park and Bushy Knap are owned by William Meade Smythe, MP for Drogheda in Ireland between 1822–1826, who died in 1866. As means of a comparison, Buckerell Knap formed part of the lands within Buckerell owned by George Barons Northcote of Feniton Court in the neighbouring parish of Feniton.

The fields at Deer Park are clearly part of later enclosure, evident through the shape of the boundaries which form a large curving enclosure. Furthermore, woodland or tree field-names provide an idea of the extent of woodland along the high ridge of land on which the features of Bushy and Buckerell Knap sit. By combining these names with the shape of the fields here, it can be seen that a tract of woodland ran along the western side of the ridge, bordering Deer Park to the south. The use of field-names and field morphology allows for the mounds, and whatever construction that may have been built upon them, to be placed in a landscape context. It is possible to suggest a landscape which contained wooded slopes, with a deer park to the south-east of the parish, associated with a series of large, fairly regular fields on the lower ground. These regular fields between Buckerell, the ridge and surrounding Deer Park suggest a sequence of later enclosure and thus, it could be suggested, represent the former deer park itself.

Awliscombe, by comparison, has a combination of both larger regular fields as seen in Buckerell and smaller more irregular fields dispersed around settlement foci (Fig. 3.12). The field arrangement around Wolverstone, the small hamlet and former manor to the north of Awliscombe, is revealing. There are three areas designated as common remaining in the northern corner of the parish, and surrounding them are a series of late enclosed fields, identified by their regular straight boundaries with the field-name 'breach', meaning to break the ground with a plough (Field 1993, 80; TA 22–4, 25). In an area that was former turbary and waste, a number of fields also have field-names showing names with the inclusion of breach. These lie on the boundary with Dunkeswell to the north of an unenclosed area defined on the Tithe Survey as common. This suggests that these areas were used for some kind of ley agriculture or convertible husbandry (as discussed in Chapter One) where the common ground was taken under plough at particular times and then later enclosed permanently. In terms of Tithe Survey land use (see Fig. 3.13) the fields here are listed as 'arable'[2] with some pasture, which also would suggest this type of land management.

Not all of the fields in these two parishes are as easily categorised into large and regular or small piecemeal enclosures. There is also evidence of a number of blocks of strip fields which have survive. There are remnants of possible strips surrounding the hamlet of Wolverstone that can be recognised from their field boundaries. To the west of the hamlet and below the areas of common it is clear that there are a number of fields with inverse 'S'-patterns, and also evidence of doglegged boundaries, which suggests removal of strips. Here the land is held by Drewe Edward Simcoe, and occupied by three tenants, Francis and William Pring, Edward Peacock, and Roger Rosier, who occupy small blocks of fields. Such evidence may indicate how the original strips were sold off and enclosed.

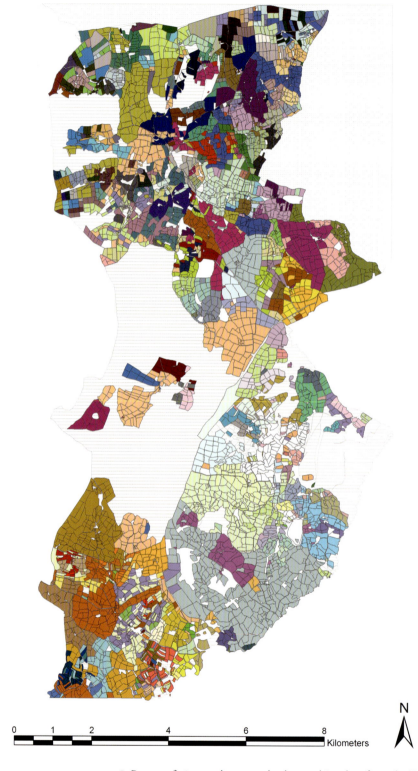

FIGURE 3.8. Pattern of nineteenth century landownership taken from the Tithe Survey

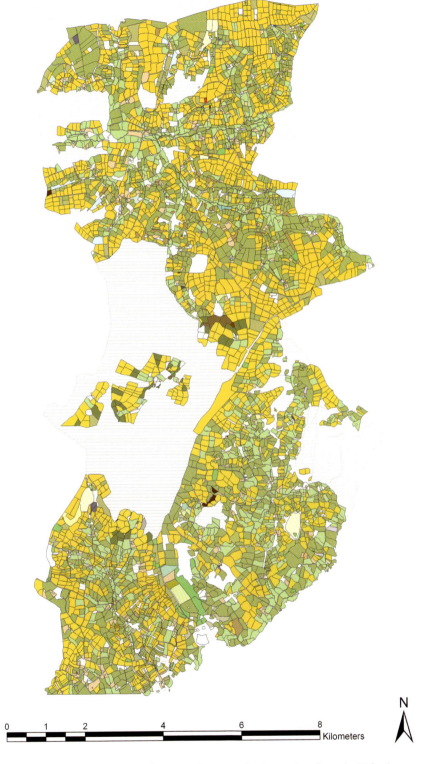

FIGURE 3.9. Pattern of nineteenth century land use taken from the Tithe Survey

However, it is clear that the fields lying on the eastern border with Awliscombe and continuing into Buckerell around the hamlet of Weston show a different setup to the rest of the parishes (Fig. 3.14 and Fig. 3.15). From the information gained from the Tithe Surveys for both parishes it can be seen that in the nineteenth century Awliscombe and Buckerell were involved in sharing-out of strip fields, alternating possession of the fields lying between themselves and those lying over the parish boundaries. This may also be evidence to support the idea that Buckerell was in fact part of Awliscombe in the early medieval period (see above). This pattern of fields illustrates the presence of a former irregular open field system; by the time of the Tithe Survey the strips that are held by Awliscombe are seemingly unevenly divided between two owners, William Pierce and Nathaniel Bishop, with Pierce holding the majority. What is worthy of note is that these two men owned no other land within the parish, but are key landowners in Buckerell. The landownership pattern within the Buckerell

FIGURE 3.10.
Landownership patterns
for the parish of
Buckerell

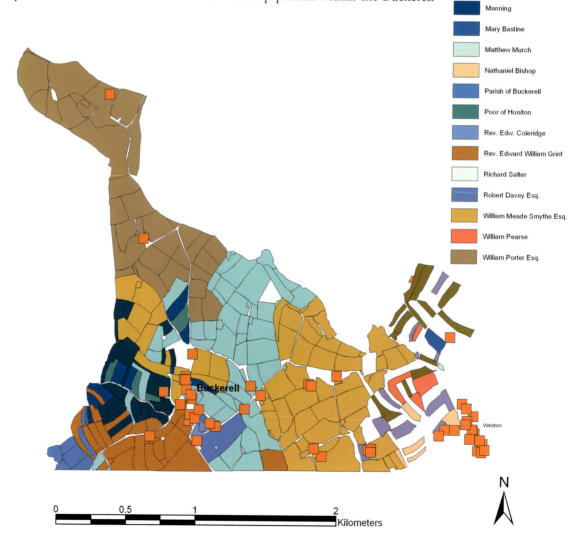

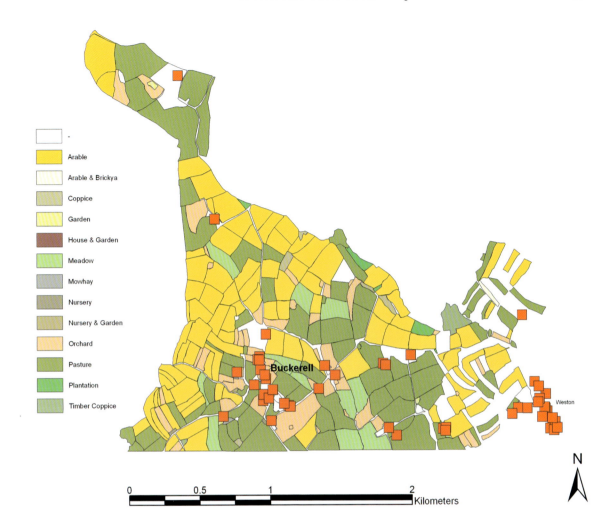

FIGURE 3.11. Land use patterns for the parish of Buckerell

strips was also defined by Pease and Bishop, as well as James Notley and John Pady. Pady is also the occupier and only owns fields within the strips; Notley, however, owns a significant amount of land in Awliscombe but no land (apart from in the open field) in Buckerell.

This landownership pattern and its relationship with Weston suggests the extent of the agricultural lands connected with the early manor. It is clear that the parish boundary (marked in red on Figs. 3.14 and 3.15) that divides Awliscombe and Buckerell lies over this field pattern, suggesting that the layout of the open field was earlier than the creation of the parishes in the twelfth century.

There are further indications of strip fields lying on the boundary between Buckerell and the parish of Feniton to the south-west. Here the strips are grouped in a gore, with a corresponding field-name meaning a triangular holding of land (Rackham 1986, 165). There are indications that the strips lying

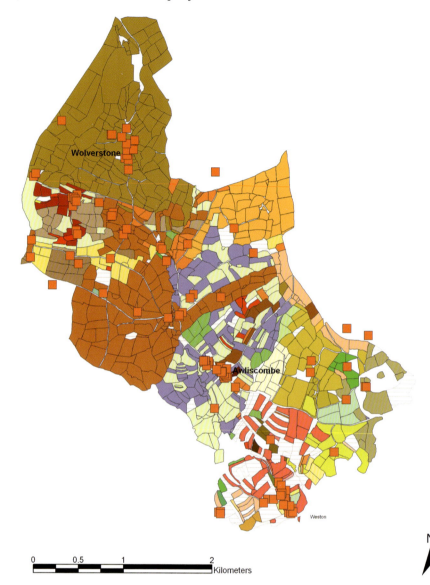

FIGURE 3.12.
Landownership patterns
for the parish of
Awliscombe

on the border of Buckerell and Feniton were larger than the surviving blocks
seen on the Tithe Survey, with a second -gore field-name occurring in fields to
the south of the strips. Interestingly the pattern of these fields continues into
Feniton, with one cut by the parish boundary, suggesting that the boundary had
previously followed the line of a strip, and signifying that the field pattern was
not constrained within what are now unitary borders. Within Feniton (which
lies outside of the study area) there is no clear evidence of strips as there is in
Buckerell within the modern landscape. However, on the Tithe Survey there
are clear indications that the strips continued over the parish boundary. The
doglegged boundaries clearly indicate where the furlong blocks formerly existed,

FIGURE 3.13. Land use
patterns for the parish of
Awliscombe

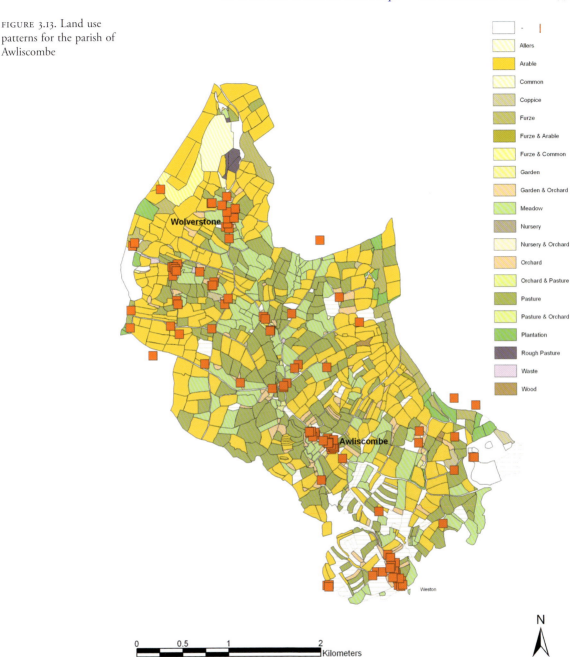

	-	
	Allers
	Arable
	Common
	Coppice
	Furze
	Furze & Arable
	Furze & Common
	Garden
	Garden & Orchard
	Meadow
	Nursery
	Nursery & Orchard
	Orchard
	Orchard & Pasture
	Pasture
	Pasture & Orchard
	Plantation
	Rough Pasture
	Waste
	Wood

Wolverstone

Awliscombe

Weston

0   0.5   1   2
Kilometers

N

creating the same pattern seen in Buckerell. Field-names provide little clue to
the antecedence of these fields, with only Starve Acre, suggesting infertility
of the soil, giving any indication to former practices here. In terms of land
use, there is a predominance of 'arable' which is to be expected, with pasture
and meadow occurring in single fields. Interestingly, the Feniton fields do not

FIGURE 3.14. The hamlet of Weston and the associated relic open field system

FIGURE 3.15. Pattern of landownership surrounding the hamlet of Weston relating to the relic open field

show the diversity in landownership seen in Buckerell, with a one-landlord collaboration (George Barons Northcott and Elizabeth Woolley) holding the strips.

The land between Buckerell and Feniton was not organised in the same manner as the open field at Weston as there is not the same arrangement of fields alternating between parishes. However, it is clear that the fields existed prior to the formation of the parish boundary. Therefore, it can be suggested that whereas the open field at Weston was under the control of one manor and retained a fossilised relic of this within its later field pattern, the strips at Feniton were controlled by more than one centre. The settlements of both Buckerell and Feniton are close enough to be associated with this open field, as is the settlement now known as Curscombe Farm (whose name was listed in Domesday) in Feniton, and Avenhayes Farm in Buckerell.

The distribution of gore elements within the Tithe Survey field-names of Awliscombe and Buckerell suggests areas of possible open field which have not survived in the field morphology. This may reflect a wider distribution of these field types than are seen in the historic landscape, and there are a number of blocks of strips elsewhere within the parish of Awliscombe generally associated with settlement of some kind. To the north of the village of Awliscombe a number of blocks of strips can be identified from the Tithe Survey. It is clear that some of these strips have been removed to create larger fields, but the zigzag line of Church Lane gives an indication of the furlong blocks. A suggestion as to how tightly packed together these fields were can be gleaned from the field-names: names such as Minnow Meads (TA 734), Minney Meads (TA 733), and perhaps most telling Buddle (TA 735) which, in the Devonshire dialect, means to suffocate (Downes 1998, 55). In terms of patterns of landholding, they are divided between James Thomas Notley and the Calwoodley Charity Trust in alternate strips, and occupied by Francis Pringle senior and Daniel Pring.

Because of the nature of Tithe Survey landholding, the parish of Combe Raleigh provides an interesting comparison to its neighbours Awliscombe and Buckerell. In general the field pattern within Combe Raleigh is large but irregular (Fig. 3.16), but there is also some evidence for inverse 'S'-fields, for example between Ellishayes Farm and Windgate Farm, to the north of the parish. This is however, by and large, the exception. By the eighteenth century, it is known that within Combe Raleigh all but St. Cyres Hill was enclosed, totalling some 300 acres in all (Polwhele 1793–1806, 328). This enclosure generally occurred long before the sweeping enclosure of the Parliamentary Acts which affected the northern parishes in the early part of the nineteenth century.

The lack of enclosure on St. Cyres Hill can be tentatively dated. Around the year of 1795, General John Graves Simcoe established an emplacement of 200 guns on the unenclosed St. Cyres Hill (manned by the men of neighbouring Luppitt) as a response to the Napoleonic threat (Toulson 1999, 58). However, by the time of the Tithe Survey, even St. Cyres Hill was divided with regular fields. Aside from the later enclosure of St. Cyres Hill, for the rest of the parish this early enclosure appears to be the result of piecemeal activity. Commentators of the late eighteenth and early nineteenth century present a confusing narrative for Combe Raleigh. Despite Polwhele's statement that the whole of Combe Raleigh was enclosed early, the same commentator thought that parish was still considerably wooded with ash, oak and elm as late as the eighteenth century (Polwhele 1793–1806, 328). What may be seen here is the different categorisation, and worth, of woodland. It can be seen from Tithe Apportionment that there are areas of coppice and woodland listed, but not in significant quantities (Fig. 3.17). On the Tithe Survey, recorded some forty years after Polwhele's survey, there are significant amounts of pastoral land and furze that may have provided the preservation of wood species recorded by him, but thought of as rough pasture.

It can be suggested that there is evidence of assarting into woodland taking place around Aller Farm situated on the eastern slope of St. Cyres Hill. Firstly, the name of the farm itself is revealing, with Aller meaning alder, but aside from this, the patterning of the fields themselves is indicative of cutting into woodland or uncultivated ground. The field-names themselves, such as Hungerlands, suggest the poor quality of the land here, and if the formation of the enclosed landscape was piecemeal as suggested, then this type of small scale prospecting into more marginal land may have been common.

Another example of small scale land intake occurs at Ellishays Farm (which, as previously stated, was a free holding of the manor), that lies to the north of Combe Raleigh settlement. Here a kidney shaped ring-fenced enclosure (which respects the contours of the river valley) can be seen as being associated with the settlement. This field pattern is very similar to model suggested in figure 1.4 discussed in Chapter One which show such ring-fenced enclosures associated with individual settlement, usually held by one owner. The enclosure is divided into four fields which show blocks of meadow, pasture, and 'arable' and may suggest some form of ley or convertible husbandry. At neighbouring Windgate Farm, there is a clear evolution of land enclosure occurring in the organisation of the field structure. Here the Tithe Survey land use lists alternate fields of 'arable', meadow, coppice, orchard, and pasture neighbouring the farm, with the named 'First', 'Second', and 'Third' Meadows lying adjacent.

In relation to Tithe landownership, this parish is dominated by one landowner; Mary Bernard. This is unusual in comparison with the surrounding parishes, and indicates that a different structure occurs here. In order to define individual holdings where field patterns give little clue, the Tithe Survey land occupier records provide a starting point. There is also a predominance of one occupier within Combe Raleigh, Henry Godfree Ridler, which adds little information to the picture already gained from the field systems. However, the smaller holders can give an idea of former tenure, highlighting blocks of fields, for example around the holdings of Stonehayes, Tower View Farm, Crook Dairy and Windgate Farm to the east of the parish. This is by no means exact or wholly satisfactory as a method, but may add another dimension to the organisation and management of the landscape here.

The diamond shaped parish of Luppitt lies to the north of Combe Raleigh in the centre of the Blackdown Hills study area, and acts as a transitional point between the lower outer edges of the Hills and the inner more upland areas. The field patterns within Luppitt show a different formation to what has been seen within Awliscombe, Buckerell and Combe Raleigh, but there are also some common elements between them. Figure 3.18 shows the pattern of landownership in Luppitt, and this is immediately different from the more southerly parishes. Land use too is also more fragmented than seen in Awliscombe, Buckerell and Combe Raleigh (Fig. 3.19).

An area within Luppitt parish whose field patterns can immediately be recognised as distinctively occurs to the west of Dumpdon Hillfort (Fig. 3.20

FIGURE 3.16.
Landownership patterns
for the parish of Combe
Raleigh

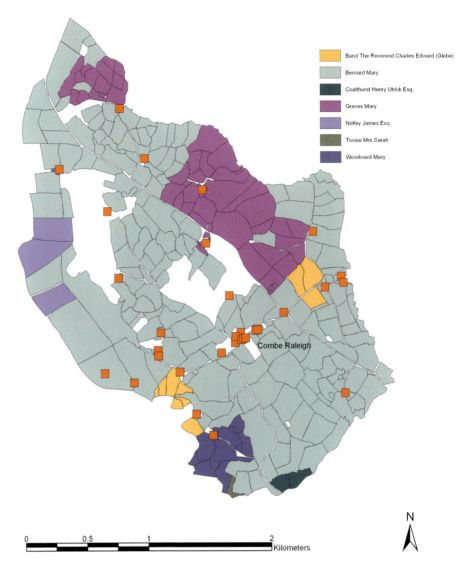

Combe Raleigh

	Band The Reverend Charles Edward (Glebe)
	Bernard Mary
	Coalthurst Henry Utrick Esq.
	Graves Mary
	Notley James Esq.
	Twose Mrs Sarah
	Woodward Mary

0   0.5   1   2
Kilometers

N

and Fig. 3.21). An irregular patchwork of small fields, some of which show evidence of former strips and S-shaped boundaries are visible, and a number of elements can be identified amongst this assortment of field types. There are a number of droveways leading from the top of Dumpdon Hill, an area encompassed by the earthworks of Dumpdon Hillfort, which provides the only common directly accessible to the hamlet, funnelling down into Higher Wick (and also towards the hamlet of Beacon to the north).

The fields in this area show no visible pattern which could suggest intakes of land deriving from the farms within the hamlet of Wick. A suggestion could be made for fields attached to the farm at Wick Cross illustrating a number of small 'infields' radiating from the farm and eight further fields, which, according to the Tithe Survey, show alternation between meadow, 'arable', and pastoral fields.

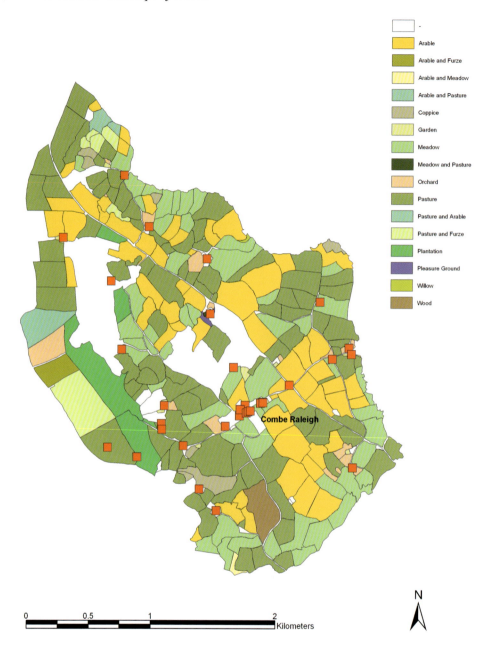

Arable
Arable and Furze
Arable and Meadow
Arable and Pasture
Coppice
Garden
Meadow
Meadow and Pasture
Orchard
Pasture
Pasture and Arable
Pasture and Furze
Plantation
Pleasure Ground
Willow
Wood

Combe Raleigh

0   0.5   1   2
Kilometers

N

A second much smaller intake of fields (recorded in the Tithe as consisting of orchard, pasture and 'arable') can be seen occurring around Rollshayes Farm, and the 'hayes' suffix is interesting as this is considered to be a name indicating woodland clearance. The 'hayes' element does not frequently occur within the field-names of the Blackdown Hills study area, and this stands out as an unusual instance. The lack of constancy between farm and fields suggests an earlier pattern on which the medieval fields were based. This is speculative, as

FIGURE 3.17. Land use patterns for the parish of Combe Raleigh

there is no clear evidence in the historic landscape to suggest an earlier origin, but the fields' proximity and relation to the Iron Age Dumpdon Hillfort make this more plausible.

Evidence of strip fields can also be identified on the border with Combe Raleigh, just below the settlement of Wick. Within the Tithe Survey all but one of these fields are recorded as being set aside for pasture with the remaining field recorded as 'arable', which may suggest some form of crop rotation. The landownership was divided between Mary Bernard, Edward Forward Roberts, the Feoffee of Honiton, Edward Guppy and John Coffin, and Richard Burroughs. These strips possess a number of 'water' names such as Watery Lane Plot (TA 1522, 1518, 1519), and Lower Waterham Plot (TA 1523) that may be reference to poor drainage of the soils rather than their proximity to the river Wolf. Curiously, there are no holdings or settlements associated with these strips, which implies that these fields may be an indicator for an abandoned settlement, or that more strips were present associated with Wick or Tower View Farm in neighbouring Combe Raleigh.

It is possible that these irregular fields occurred on all sides of Dumpdon Hill and that what we are seeing at Wick may simply be the last remnants of a system which was cleared elsewhere. It can be seen from looking at the soils of this area, mainly stagnogleyic palaeo-argillic brown earths, that the soils here are 'poorer' agriculturally than those on the south-eastern side of the hill where the fields have been improved and are larger. This idea can be advanced by the identification of similar irregular field patterns on the eastern side between Dumpdon Hill and Whitehall Farm, and between the hill and Smithenhayes Farm. It is possible that these vestiges of a former field structure survived because it was not economically viable to improve them for the returns that they reaped. Local farmers believe that the fields on the western side were given to the poor, and this would seem sensible if the land was deemed to be of a poorer agricultural quality.

Intakes of land by individual farms are also visible in the patterns of fields within Luppitt and this can be seen at Ford Farm. The earliest date for the name of this farm is recorded in 1394, and it is possible that this intake corresponds to around this time. There are a number of discrete blocks of fields present in the parish, forming lozenge shaped ring-fenced enclosures within the field patterns. A second identifiable enclosure of fields can be seen between Hartridge to the east and the possible lands of the Luppitt estate to the west. This enclosure is bounded by a circuit of roads, which the fields inside and outside respect. This field system corresponds with Shelves Farm and Barnfield Farm, and the Tithe Survey shows a fragmented distribution of ownership. Discounting the field associated with Littletown (a dwelling clearly later than the others) there are two blocks of ownership, Russell Thomas and Mary Jane Worth. What this indicates can be one of two things, either this later tithe ownership bears little relation to the formation of this block of land, or what we are seeing is in fact a true reflection of earlier landholdings and that the area was developed through

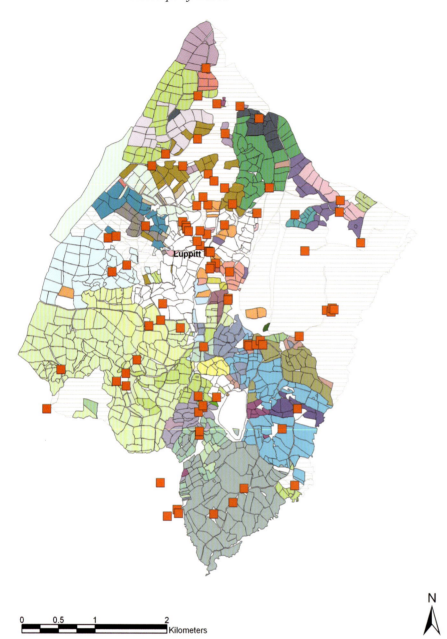

FIGURE 3.18.
Landownership patterns
for the parish of Luppitt

a number of co-operations. A number of these small enclosures (representing the setting up of land by farmsteads and settlements) occur near the hamlet of Beacon. At Beacon there are three clearly identifiable enclosures, with associated farms at their edges, suggesting that this form of piecemeal enclosure was common within the period.

To the east of Shelves and Barnfield is an individual farmstead that shows distinctively different field morphology to that seen at the other two settlements.

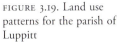

FIGURE 3.19. Land use patterns for the parish of Luppitt

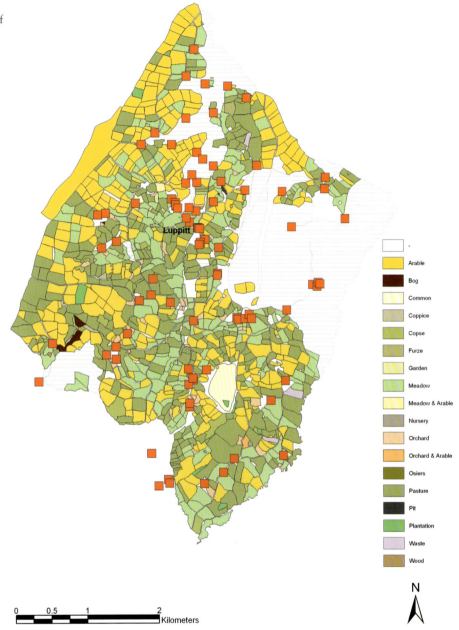

The fields around the farm of Greenway are particularly indicative of Ley cultivation and convertible husbandry. Although there is evidence of later truncation of strip fields, the typology of these strips are indicative of such agricultural practices. Further to this, the Tithe Appointment field names provide an insight into the possible use of these fields; Starve Acre, Sheepwash, Oat Moor, Raven Moor and Turf Moor. These names can indicate a number

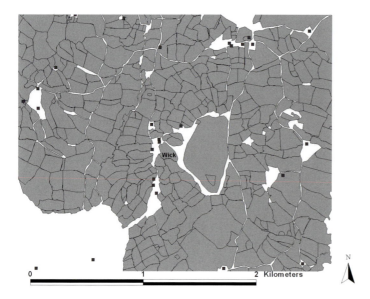

FIGURE 3.20. The irregular field system surrounding the settlement of Wick in the parish of Luppitt

of things. Firstly, the occurrence of Starve Acre suggests that this land is agriculturally poorer and therefore less productive (Field 1993, 107), while Oat Moor also indicates poor soils as oats as a crop are indicative of meagre production. Raven Moor is also indicative of this, as the raven was seen as a representation of death and starvation and is often used in field-names to

FIGURE 3.21. Looking westwards from Dumpdon Hillfort over the settlement and fields at Wick

indicate poorer conditions. The use of moor in all these cases also suggests intake from former waste or common land. The reference to Sheepwash also provides a link with how the land was managed. The name implies the field was used for the watering and dipping of animals (Field 1993, 52) and it is noticeable that a small stream flows along the northern edge of the field. Further indicators of poor soils are the three fields-names that include the 'cat' (cats/cat's brain field names refer to the rough and bumpy texture of the soil, likened to the ridges of a brain) (TA 726, 711, 715), and of particular relevance is the reference to Cats Brain, suggesting a soil consisting of rough clay mixed with stones (Field 1993, 30) which is common in this area.

Polwhele (1793–1806 vol. 2, 331) suggests that the area around Greenway was listed as a park when given over to Newenham in Axminster. Again the term park may simply refer to enclosed land; to the north of Greenway farm there is a Tithe Survey field-name listed as Hill Park, and the term is used in other areas of Luppitt. However, if the reference to park means something like an estate garden then this could explain the unusual and irregular fields here.

Moving away from these relatively early enclosed areas, within Luppitt there are a number of areas of common and moorland dispersed through the parish particularly in the northern area. Although some of the higher moorland, such as Hartridge, has been enclosed by the time of the Tithe Survey, much of the common land like Hense Moor to the north of the parish managed to avoid the early nineteenth-century Enclosure Act. Thus, much of the areas of common retained at least some of their earlier character.

There are a number of areas in Luppitt which are classed on the nineteenth-century Tithe Survey as non-tithable, in particular, the areas around the settlements of Mohun's Ottery and Shapcombe. There are a number of fields that are 'non-tithable' surrounding Shapcombe, perhaps demarcating their status as common. Polwhele (1793–1806, 331) states that there is '...a whole tything of that name, which is not charged to the land and windows in general parish levies, but separately assessed'. The field boundaries around Shapcombe suggest former droveways, funnelling out over the river into Combe Raleigh. On the 1842 Tithe Survey a non-tithable area is also associated with Mohun's Ottery. Aerial photography allows the form of the fields around Mohun's Ottery to be considered. It can be seen that there is good evidence for a ring-fenced enclosure surrounding the site of the early manor house. Further to this, sixteenth century documentary evidence relating to land management allows a glimpse of how the land was used. Leland's *Itinerary* (1535–1543, 241) describes the route from Mohun's Ottery to Colyton and discusses a landscape 'of good corn pasture and some wood'. Despite this 'missing' information, it can be seen that Luppitt seems to comprise of a number of elements which have created the historic landscape here; the numerous manors and the mix of poorer soils and higher topography have made a more patchwork arrangement of fields within the parish.

To the north of Luppitt is the parish of Clayhidon. The position of Clayhidon in the centre of the Blackdown Hills as a region acts as a further comparison to the southern four parishes, as figure 3.22, which shows the pattern of Tithe landownership, illustrates. In terms of its field structure, the parish can be divided into two sections; the southern lower area defined by the river valley of the river Culm, and the northern, more upland zone; this is also echoed in the nature of the Tithe Apportionment land use categorisation (Fig. 3.23).

It is possible to elucidate evidence of earlier farming regimes within the southern parts of Clayhidon. A good example is May's Farm, a farmstead that is associated with an area indicative of ley or convertible husbandry, as land use patterns also show alternation between strips of 'arable' and pasture. The lozenge shaped field pattern contains seven fields (similar to the model of convertible husbandry suggested by Fox and Padel in Chapter One), five of which show evidence of ploughing through 'S'-strips. The pattern of Tithe Survey landholding here is interesting. The landownership is alternated between Robert Troake and John Pring, with the Tithe Survey listing the occupiers as James Troake and John Pring (Fig. 3.24). What is interesting is that the field system associated with May's Farm takes in Hole Moor to the north, which was an area of resource under Middleton Barton's ownership throughout the medieval period (FamF, pt2, 23), and is aligned along the 700 m contour. It is possible that the same agricultural regime occurs at nearby Crosses Farm, which nestles between the moors of Newcott and Hole, and again near Middleton Barton, where a now demolished holding was associated with a small strip of three fields perched at the edge of Middleton Wood. There are suggestions of further possible medieval settlement in this area, which will be discussed in greater detail below. An interesting pattern of fields can also be seen near Hole farm which may indicate former dwellings which have been removed. In the surviving fields landownership is divided between Christopher Flood and John Hurwood, and from the field boundaries it is possible to suggest that these small plots continued southwards towards the farm. The remaining part of Hole Moor to the west of Mays Farm also shows shared landownership and tenants. Being a product of late enclosure, the moor was divided into four, and ownership was shared by John Quick, John Troakes, William Valentine and John Pring.

The manor of Middleton provides an interesting comparison to Mays Farm. Middleton is situated near Hole Moor, which was part of the medieval estate. The Tithe Survey indicates that there is a prevalence of pasture and meadow land use for this area, with many of the fields suggesting either some form of assarting from woodland, or creation of enclosures from moorland or common. 'Arable' is recorded for the higher aspects of the hills (generally in this area above 200 m), and these fields can be classed as examples of later enclosure because of their regular pattern. This may suggest something about the nature of use of moors in the earlier landscape, and echo the descriptions of upland management discussed in Chapter One. It can be suggested that the uplands were left as pasture, and ploughed sporadically, hence the Tithe listing of 'arable' or 'ploughable'.

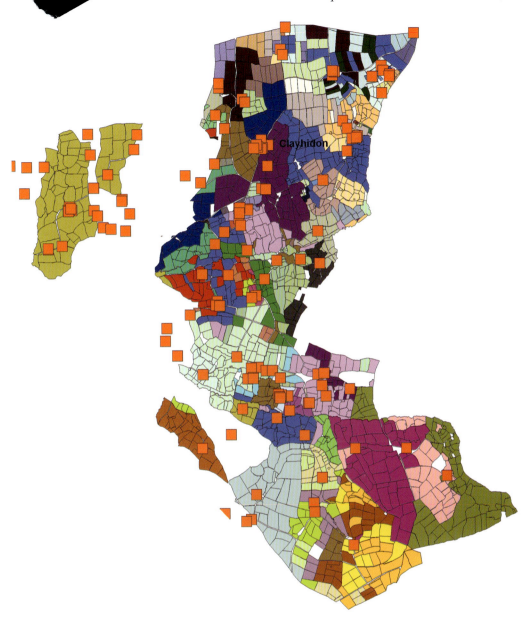

FIGURE 3.22.
Landownership patterns
for the parish of
Clayhidon

Sometime around the twelfth or thirteenth century, animals from Middleton manor along with 40 cattle of Taunton Priory were brought onto land at neighbouring Bolham for grazing (SRO DD/X/COR no 5; FamF pt 1, 22). This indicates two things; firstly the implication of cross region links with Taunton

ᴳᴜᴿᴱ 3.23. Land use
atterns for the parish of
Clayhidon

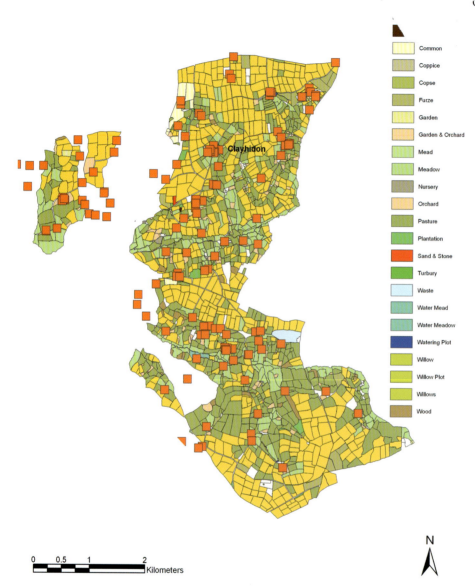

Clayhidon

	Common
	Coppice
	Copse
	Furze
	Garden
	Garden & Orchard
	Mead
	Meadow
	Nursery
	Orchard
	Pasture
	Plantation
	Sand & Stone
	Turbury
	Waste
	Water Mead
	Water Meadow
	Watering Plot
	Willow
	Willow Plot
	Willows
	Wood

0   0.5   1   2
Kilometers

N

Priory, and secondly the movement of the animals across the parish in order to
utilise dispersed grazing resources. The Tithe Survey indicates a high proportion
of pasture and meadow lands, and as part of Dunkeswell Abbey the Manor
of Bolham held the grazing land at Ridgewood above Bolham river (Youing
1955, m.4). This may indicate where such grazing took place, and field patterns
indicating droveways associated with Ridgewood. In 1545, Ridgewood Common
is recorded as being '40 acres growing "by parcelles"' (strips or blocks of land),
and was enclosed during the wave of Parliamentary Enclosure (Youing 1955,

FIGURE 3.24. Evidence of earlier patterns of landholding at May's Farm in Clayhidon

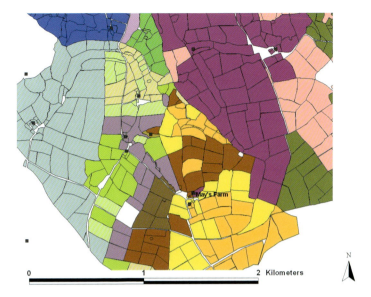

63 m.8–9). On the Tithe Survey the waste to the east of the late enclosure at Ridgewood is described as 'Undivided Lands' (TA 1078), implying that a small area of common still remained after the Act.

The river valley associated with the river Culm is characterised by fields recorded in the Tithe Survey as being pasture or meadow, with orchards found surrounding the settlement holdings and 'arable' upon the higher ground. These fields appear to follow the contours, with regular late enclosed uplands and slopes, interspersed with more irregular plots along the valleys. By querying the Tithe Apportionment through the GIS, it can be seen that field-names containing the element 'mead' occur predominantly along river valleys, on the land below 170 m (Fig. 3.33). This is what would be expected for meadow land, and this may indicate the organisation of earlier fields which have since been reused or divided.

The northern half of the parish of Clayhidon shows another pattern emerging from the Tithe Survey. Like Luppitt to the south, there was a significant amount of moorland and common within Clayhidon. Common land was found on the higher ground towards the Somerset border, and in total, the parish held significant acres of waste and moor. There is also evidence here of squatter settlements upon the common land which will be discussed below. Much of the land in this central area of the Blackdown Hills, both in Devon and Somerset, was not enclosed until a private Act of Parliament in February 1812. Between this date and 1821, the 600 acres of waste and common were put under enclosure, resulting in a group of 144 fenced and ditched fields (CLHG). Much of the northern hills of Clayhidon were included in this, which caused the loss of 600 acres of the manor's common land in both Devon and Somerset that was replaced by an allocation of a mere 40 acres of turbary that could be accessed

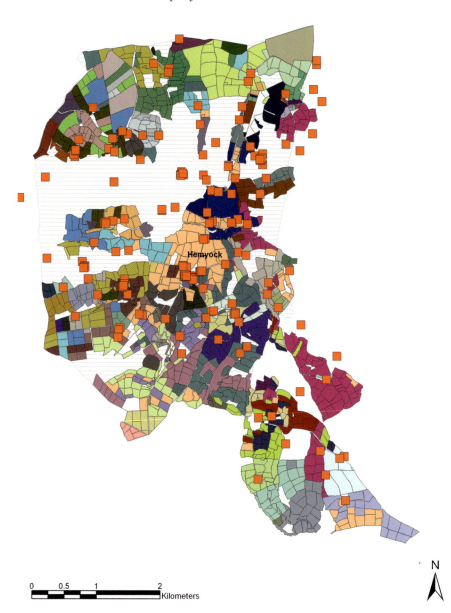

FIGURE 3.25.
Landownership patterns
for the parish of
Hemyock

Hemyock

N

| 0 | 0.5 | 1 | | 2 |

Kilometers

by general rights. Thus, when considering this act of enclosure (which led to agricultural land within parishes such as Clayhidon selling for approximately £20 per acre) the loss of common rights must be considered. This is discussed more in Chapter Six.

Hemyock, like Clayhidon, lies on the northern boundary of Devon, and is characterised by the river valleys of the Culm and the river Madford (flowing north–south). However, Hemyock does not seem to have followed the same patterns of land management that Clayhidon experienced, and may reflect

FIGURE 3.26. Land use patterns for the parish of Hemyock

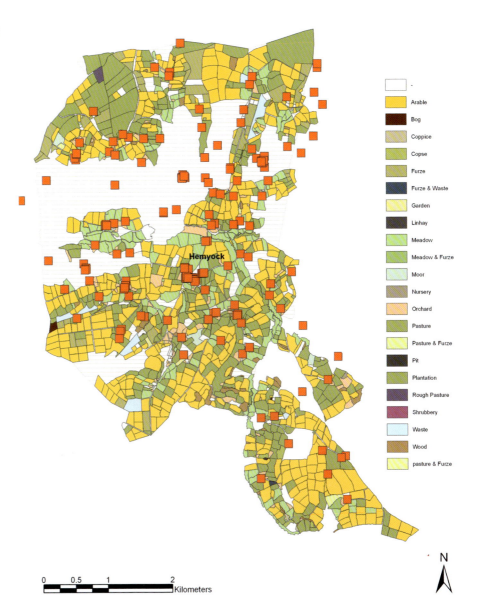

not only subtle differences in topography but also in different management strategies and landownership patterns (Fig. 3.25). As a whole, Hemyock parish shows a number of individual field systems made up from a mixture of irregular small fields, and some later enclosure found mainly on areas that were previously moor or common (Fig. 3.26).

Madford (identified at Hemyock's Hundred manor) had two commons; Blackdown Common which now lies in Culmstock, and the southern part of Hackpen Down. It is known that this area of common ground was designated for the grazing of animals from the feast of St. Michael [29 September] to the Purification of the Blessed Virgin Mary [2 February] (Reichel 1928, 33). In 1249 at Hackpen in Uffculme, the Abbot of Dunkeswell agreed with the neighbouring landowner to have common pasture in lands, woods and meadows but to leave Hackpen Hill for the neighbour to assart and the abbot to use as pasture after the harvest (Hallam 1981, 167). Blackdown Common remains unenclosed, but Hackpen Hill was part of the nineteenth-century Parliamentary Enclosure and is divided by regular field systems, and a small part of Hackpen Common remains. Before this enclosure however, tenants of manors in Hemyock, and also Clayhidon, were given the perhaps unusual opportunity to legitimately 'breake upp or eare any parte of the lordes waste to sowe any grayne in, payenge for every acre iiii*d*. [5 pence] as longe as they shall sowe hit' (Reichel 1928, 33; Finberg 1967, 106).

In the northern area of the parish, the patterns of fields near to the hamlet of Culm Davy are perhaps the most interesting as they show a number of different systems in operation. To the east of Culm Davy hill is a circular enclosure of fields, cutting across the contours and bounded by roads or tracks. Within this enclosure a number of smaller field systems can be identified along with their associated farmsteads. Around this area are two telling farm names, Whitehams and Whitemoor Farm (which on the Tithe Survey is held within Clayhidon parish and was thought to be part of a Knight's Fee). The inclusion of white in such names can suggest a number of things. Firstly it is thought to indicate poor fertility of land (Field 1993, 32), and this area in Culm Davy is situated in land which is today rough grassland and on the Tithe surrounded by a significant area of common, furze and pasture. Further, white can also suggest clearance, which corresponds with the field pattern that we can see here. The field pattern is one of small irregular fields, indicating a piecemeal arrangement cutting into the moorlands, and the system associated with Whitehams shows a setup similar to that found at Greenway in Luppitt; a mix of pasture, furze and arable land recorded on the Tithe.

Summary

What we can see from looking at each of the six parishes in turn is that as we move northwards through the Blackdown Hills there are significant changes occurring. The parishes in the southern reaches of the hills, in the areas with lower altitude, show a different structure to those in the north. In Awliscombe, Buckerell and Combe Raleigh the fields are large and fairly regular, with evidence of open field cultivation. Both Hemyock and Clayhidon have smaller more irregular fields and in Clayhidon large areas were left unenclosed until the nineteenth-century Act of Enclosure. This is in contrast to the centrally lying Luppitt whose uplands remained largely unaffected.

At this point, the parish of Dunkeswell, which lies to the west of Luppitt and to the north of Awliscombe, should be mentioned. As highlighted earlier in this chapter, the Cistercian Abbey founded at Dunkeswell at the beginning of the thirteenth century had an impact on the estate structure of the study area, and interestingly, only 280 fields are listed within the Tithe Survey for the parish. Therefore, only a small amount of land within the parish can be mapped, and figures 3.27 and 3.28 show the patterns of Tithe Survey landownership and land use for the available fields in Dunkeswell.

The untitheable land within Dunkeswell can be divided into two categories: land that was former common, and land which forms the remnants of the Abbey. Much of this untitheable land was held by Elizabeth Posthuma Simcoe, either as part of a farm estate, or, as the Tithe Survey indicates, large areas of former common. However, the non-titheable area around Percy Farm lying to the east of Dunkeswell settlement is recorded on the Tithe Survey as being owned by Mrs Graves, which may indicate an earlier independent manorial setup which can only be accessed through the patterns of landholding.

The areas of titheable land which are included in the Survey lie to the south of the parish around Dunkeswell Grange, towards the centre of the parish around the main settlement, and to the north of the parish around the former grange of Bywood Farm (Fig. 3.29). Interestingly land belonging to the estate of Bywood is recorded within Dunkeswell village around 2 km away from the farm. It is known that within living memory people still used oxen for ploughing at Bywood and at other farms in the Hills (Ken Farmer, *pers comm* 2003) which could influence our interpretation of medieval field patterns. The ownership and land use patterns here show mixed cultivation, and were owned by Elizabeth Simcoe.

Dunkeswell Grange is situated to the south of the parish, and was also owned in the Tithe by Elizabeth Simcoe, who made this house one of the Simcoes main residences. From this it would appear that the land in Dunkeswell belonging to the former Abbey was bought by the Simcoe family, who also owned Hemyock Castle.

Even from the small amount of information we have for the historic landscape of Dunkeswell it can be seen that the picture of the development of the medieval landscape is as complex as the neighbouring parishes of the Blackdown Hills study area.

A further layer of information can be added to the field morphology in order to gain greater insight into this historic landscape. This layer is the occurrence and distribution of nineteenth-century field-names accessed through the Tithe Apportionment.

Field-names

The use of a GIS database allows for large quantities of information to be stored, manipulated and queried. This querying mechanism is particularly useful when discussing the distribution of field-names as such a study would be nearly impossible to carry out without such a tool. A number of different

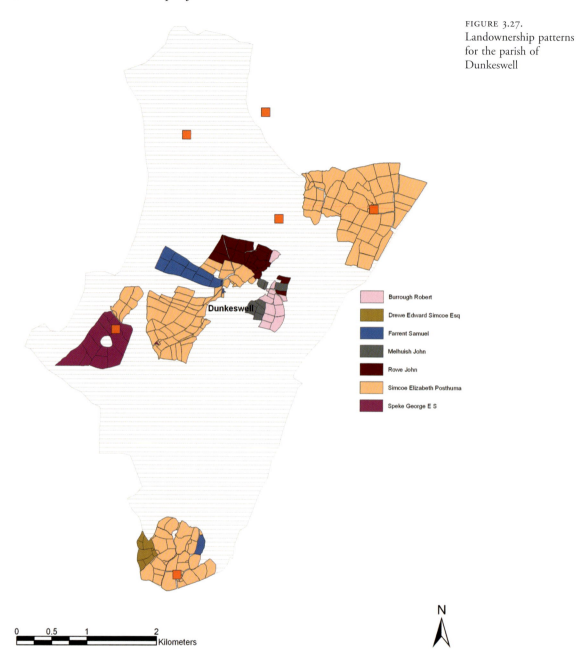

FIGURE 3.27.
Landownership patterns
for the parish of
Dunkeswell

field-names have been studied (see Appendix 1, Tables 1–11) but key names
have been highlighted for discussion; those containing acre, park, gore, and
moor elements.

Within the Blackdown Hills study area just under 10 per cent of the Tithe
Survey fields digitised contained the element 'acre', with the highest percentage
occurring in the parishes of Dunkeswell, Luppitt and Clayhidon (Fig. 3.30). As

FIGURE 3.28. Land use patterns for the parish of Dunkeswell

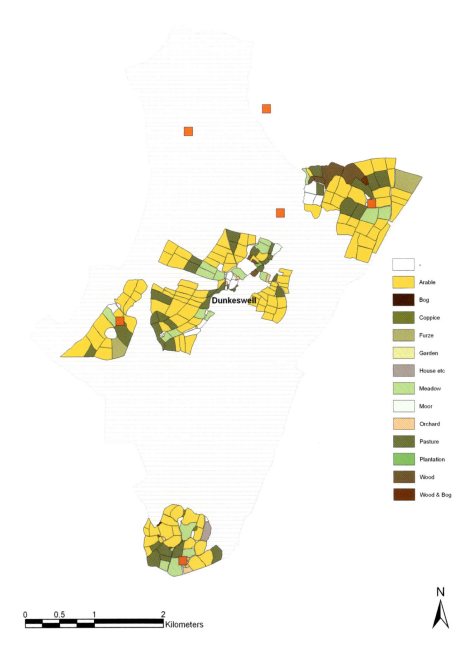

a whole the distribution of 'acre' field-names within the Blackdown Hills study area occurs predominantly in the more elevated parishes (Hemyock, Clayhidon, and the northern parts of Dunkeswell and Luppitt) and is concentrated on the upland plateaus above 240 m in the north of the region, or on the steep-sided slopes of the ridges in the south. The field morphology corresponds with

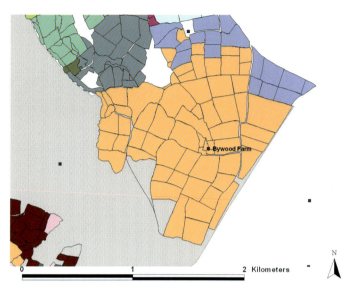

FIGURE 3.29. Pattern of Tithe Survey landownership at Bywood Farm in Dunkeswell showing the distribution of land held by Elizabeth Simcoe

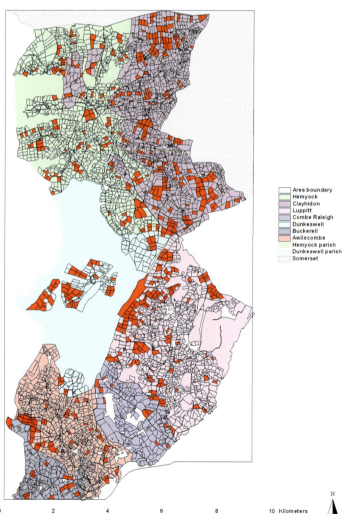

FIGURE 3.30. Distribution of field-names which contain acre elements

the rectangular parallel boundaries associated with later enclosure, and forms distinct blocks suggesting the pattern of enclosure.

Further, it is worth noting that the occurrence of 'park' elements within the Tithe Survey fields corresponds with those containing 'acre'. This category does not contain fields which are known to correspond with pleasure parks (such as the fields adjacent to the manor of Tracey in the parish of Awliscombe) or other such 'artificial' landscape. The 'park' element, from the Old English *pearroc*, is particularly common in Devonian and Cornish field-names and relates to an enclosed piece of land (Field 1993, 25). Although the spread of -park names in the Blackdown Hills is not as widespread as the 'acre' field-names (Fig. 3.31), they are most prominent in the lower lying parishes of Awliscombe and Buckerell to the south of the study area. For example, as table 6.2 shows, 10 per cent of the Tithe Survey fields in Buckerell contained the element park within their name. In Luppitt the occurrence of 'park' elements is particularly indicative of later enclosure, and names such as Great and Little Rye Park can be found throughout the parish. 'Park' elements occur in large fields on the southern slopes of Dumpdon Hill and in relation to the rectangular enclosures on Harts Ridge. The 'park' field-names occurring in large irregularly shape fields to the south of Dumpdon Hill have led to the area being identified as park land. This may be incorrect, but it is clear that the occurrence of this name around Dumpdon Hill suggests a change in the field pattern, leaving small irregular fields to the west of the Hillfort, and creating large fields to the east.

Other earlier field patterns may be suggested from the occurrence of gore elements in field-names. Using the field-name element 'gore' and querying the Tithe Apportionment data within the GIS for both Awliscombe and Buckerell it is possible to suggest by the limited distribution that this inclusion could be an indicator for areas of former open field. The field-name element occurs not only in the strips on the Buckerell/Feniton border but also within the open field pattern by Weston. A further name can be identified lying between Combehayes Farm to the north and the settlement of Buckerell to the south corresponding with a block of fields which, on the Tithe Survey, show landownership alternating between George Barons Northcote, 'Manning', and the Poor of Honiton (see Fig. 3.97b).

Luppitt, Dunkeswell, Hemyock and Clayhidon contain a higher percentage of fields containing moor elements within their field-names than the lower-lying southern parishes of Buckerell, Awliscombe and Combe Raleigh (Fig. 3.32). This occurrence must be because of the development of the landscape in the Blackdown Hills, mirroring other physical manifestations of the historic landscape such as the presence of open fields and nucleated settlements. The distribution of 'mead' field-names is also as would be expected, following the lines of the river valleys (Fig. 3.33).

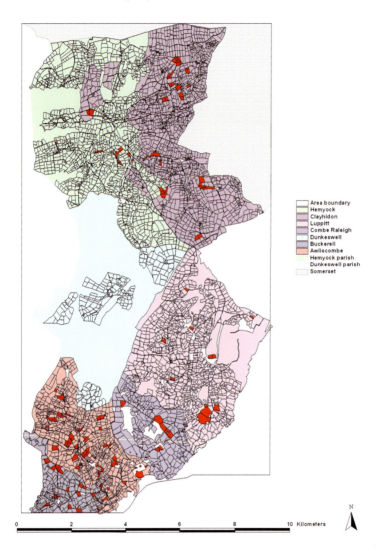

FIGURE 3.31. Distribution
of field-names which
contain park elements

Area boundary
Hemyock
Clayhidon
Luppitt
Combe Raleigh
Dunkeswell
Buckerell
Awliscombe
Hemyock parish
Dunkeswell parish
Somerset

N

0   2   4   6   8   10 Kilometers

Settlement

The discussion of field systems and field-names raises a number of questions about the nature of settlement in the Blackdown Hills. It can be seen that settlement patterns in the Blackdown Hills, like field structures, vary depending on where within the study area they occur (Fig. 3.34). No uniform pattern occurs, and as discussed in Chapter One, the trend in the literature is that Devon is essentially a landscape of dispersed settlements. Indeed, Rippon (2007, 7) states that the Blackdown Hills are in themselves the boundary between dispersed landscape and the more village dominant area to the east. Therefore in order to identify the different components in the nineteenth-century landscape (and thus elucidate the medieval structure) each parish will be considered in turn, moving from south to north.

Starting with the two southern parishes, Awliscombe combines both

FIGURE 3.32. Distribution of field-names which contain moor elements

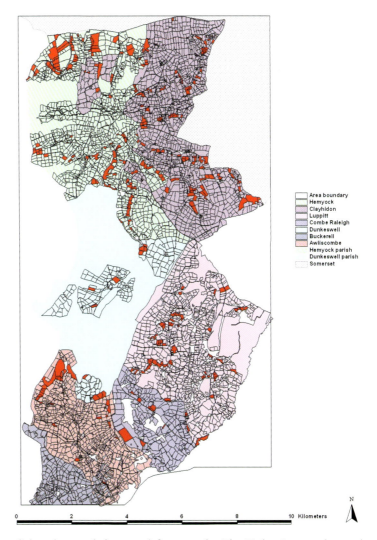

'nucleated' hamlets and dispersed farmsteads. The Tithe Survey shows that the Awliscombe settlement itself was arranged as a tight cluster of houses located around a central crossroads with the fifteenth-century parish church of St. Michael located a short distance away from the centre. A secondary settlement is located to the south of Awliscombe. The hamlet of Weston, which lies on the border with Honiton and is situated half in Awliscombe parish and half in Buckerell, is associated with the irregular open field system discussed above. As we have seen, field patterns of this kind are generally associated with nucleated settlement. This is because of the centralised organisation from manorial lords and cooperative nature of farming practices that are associated with open field systems. A second hamlet, Wolverstone, can be found to the north of the parish, and through aerial photographs it is possible to suggest that this is a contracted settlement. At Wolverstone (or Woolston on the Tithe Survey) there is evidence

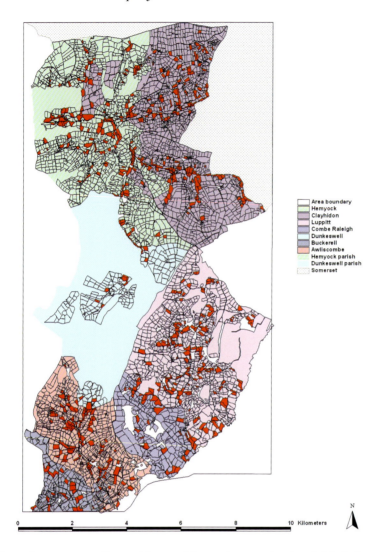

FIGURE 3.33. Distribution
of field-names which
contain mead elements

Legend:
Area boundary
Hemyock
Clayhidon
Luppitt
Combe Raleigh
Dunkeswell
Buckerell
Awliscombe
Hemyock parish
Dunkeswell parish
Somerset

0   2   4   6   8   10 Kilometers

N

of soil marks corresponding with possible settlement in the fields below the
farmstead of Culverhayes (SMR: ST10SE-078). A smaller, more disaggregated
hamlet occurs at Godford situated between Awliscombe and Wolverstone, and
all of these settlements are located on the lower ground of the valley of the
river Wolf.

Besides these nucleated settlements, there are some individual farmsteads
which tend to occur above the 140 metre contour on the slopes of Hembury and
St. Cyres Hill. Individual dwellings and associated plots can also be found along
Ridgeway Lane, in particular, Salt Box, Rushlands, and Ridgeway Farm itself.
Eight of these individual farmsteads are not present on the modern Ordnance
Survey map, four of which occur on Hembury Hill, and another on St. Cyres
Hill. The position of these suggests 'squatter' settlements, small dwellings with
associated plots of land which are found on the commons or moorland seen

FIGURE 3.34. Distribution of settlement as recorded on the nineteenth-century Tithe Survey

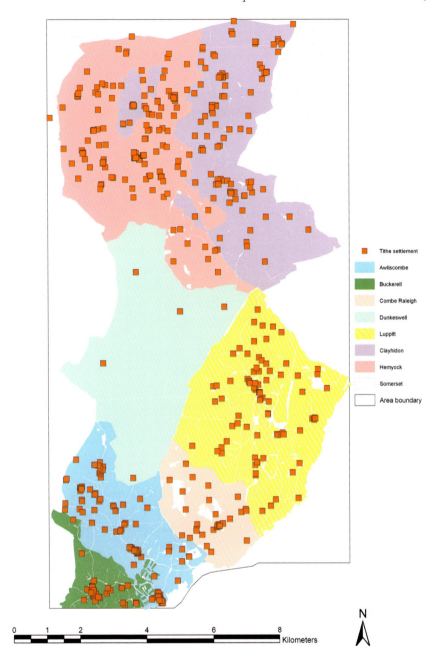

Tithe settlement
Awliscombe
Buckerell
Combe Raleigh
Dunkeswell
Luppitt
Clayhidon
Hemyock
Somerset
Area boundary

0 1 2 4 6 8 Kilometers

N

elsewhere within the study area. Squatter settlements, as introduced in Chapter One, are the reaction to lack of land, where people set up holdings on the moor (generally areas which are common ground), and take in land for cultivation.

The settlement pattern in neighbouring Buckerell could also be classed as 'nucleated' settlement as far as the Blackdown Hills are concerned, insofar as there is a cluster of dwellings around the centre of the parish. From the taxation returns of 1334 (L'Estrange Ewen 1939, 11), it can be seen that Buckerell and Waringstone (Weston) at this point were listed together as Decennary or tithing, and this is interesting in relation to the field patterns at Weston and its position on the Buckerell/Awliscombe border.

Like neighbouring Awliscombe and Buckerell, the houses and tenements that make up the Combe Raleigh settlement are fairly 'nucleated' with a few dispersed farmsteads dotted on the north-eastern side of the parish on the upland slopes. There is evidence of two squatter settlements on St. Cyres Hill, each associated with small plots of land, as seen in other parishes. Nevertheless, the majority of settlements within the parish lie within the central concentration at Combe Raleigh itself.

Thus, it can be seen that in the Southern parishes of the Blackdown Hills the general trend of settlement distribution is that of more nucleated settlement, and in comparison the settlement pattern of Luppitt is distinctly dispersed. Webber (1976, 105) suggests that the primary settlement of Luppitt is more of a hamlet, and even as late as the Tithe Survey there was little cohesion in where settlements were located in terms of identifying nucleated centres. The hamlet of Luppitt is the nearest settlement we have to this. The arching of the road creates a small focal point around the church, although this maybe because of topography enforcing nucleation rather than deliberate organisation. The settlement at Mohun's Ottery shows evidence of some form of structuring, with the dwellings located in the centre of the fields and a number of roads which spoke out from this core. Although smaller than the Luppitt settlement seen on the Tithe Survey it forms a more defined settlement pattern, with all the houses located at the centre around a central space or green. As mentioned above, Mohun's Ottery was thought of as a township in the thirteenth century, and this may suggest a reason for its cohesion.

What are clear are the small individual farms on the areas of common ground, consisting of one house and a small intake of land. This is a pattern that can be seen elsewhere within the northern half of the study area, but interestingly also in the lower reaches of the Blackdown Hills. This particularly occurs on Hense Moor, to the north of the hamlet of Luppitt, where there were at least eight individual dwellings at the time of the Tithe Survey (Fig. 3.35). These were possibly 'squatter' camps, one family building a small autonomous farm intaking a small manageable amount of land, or may refer to an agreement like that between the tenants and the manor of Hemyock Hundred (see below).

Some of these farms remained small holdings, such as Snook's Farm[3] located on the western slopes of Hartridge and first recorded in 1685, while others grew in size incorporating more land. White's Plot on Hense Moor is a good example of this, with the occurrence of white within the place-name also suggesting intake from moorland or waste, with a ring-fenced field pattern as seen elsewhere in the Blackdown Hills and illustrated in Model 4 in figure 1.4 in Chapter One.

Lying below the end of Hartridge a number of tenements can be identified grouped around a central space or green (situated on deposits of typical

FIGURE 3.35. Distribution of 'squatter' settlements on Hense Moor Luppitt. Note clearance names such as turf, fern and white.

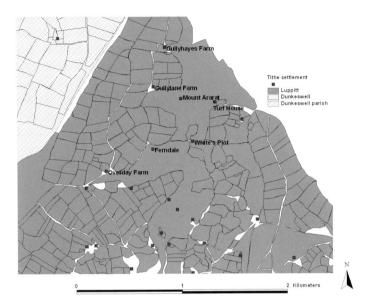

stagnogley soils and typical argillic pelosols) which are thought to produce a more agriculturally productive soil. The name *Bekyn* (generally attributed to the hamlet) is known from 1469 (PND 1932, 643), and it is thought that the cairn which lies at the tip of Hartridge was used as a fire beacon in the medieval and Napoleonic periods (NMR citing OS in SMR ST10SE/16/1), attributing the name Beacon to the settlement below. However, some would suggest that the lighting of signals and the settlement here had an even longer history, with fires being used in prehistory to communicate with other communities living on Dartmoor, although this cannot be substantiated (Cope 1998, 183). From the Tithe Survey it can be seen that there are five dwellings recorded, four around the outside of the enclosure, and one, Wrens, inside the central green, suggesting some nucleation of this small hamlet. Further, the occurrence of the green may be the result of the droveways which cut across Hartridge, and indicate grazing points along a droving route.

Looking at the northern edge of the study area, Clayhidon (alongside Churchstanton and Churchinford, now both in Somerset) is described as possessing characteristics of true Blackdown Hills villages by Webber (1976, 105). What he means by this is debatable. As discussed in Chapter One, the term village is a catchall statement that can mean different things in different parts of the country. In many models, villages are classed by their degree of nucleation and the cooperation of its community under manorial control, through open field farming. The 'traditional' view of what a village is would not include the settlements of Clayhidon. Nevertheless, Webber's description of Clayhidon as a village implies nucleation, so how this settlement pattern compares with the others within the study area is key. Comparing Clayhidon with the nucleated settlements of Awliscombe, Buckerell, and Combe Raleigh I would disagree with Webber.

FIGURE 3.36. Pattern
of Tithe Survey
landownership at Jacob's
City in Clayhidon, built
on an area of former
turbary

FIGURE 3.37. Remains
of house plot walls at
Jacob's City Clayhidon

Although Clayhidon does show a degree of cohesion in terms of settlement it is comparable with Luppitt and does not show the same characteristics as the southern parishes which are more clearly nucleated settlements. In the case of Clayhidon there is no coherent nucleation of dwellings, and as a whole the parish contains few houses or farms, such as that which occurs at Rosemary Lane to the west of the parish. At the time of the Tithe, Clayhidon settlement itself consisted of the church and three farms with a couple of smaller dwellings.

The occurrence of 'squatter' settlements is also a factor in Clayhidon, and there is evidence for a number throughout the northern half of the parish. 'Jacob's City' is a characteristic example of the type of settlements that occur in areas where available land is in short supply (Fig. 3.36). Jacob's City was a small nineteenth-century settlement in what is now known as Wiltown Valley on the

Devon/Somerset border. The squatter settlement, set up by Jacob Hutching for his family on the former turbary, only consisted of about five houses and was abandoned by the time of the Tithe (Fig. 3.37). It is known from the enclosure award for this area that there were more structures here (CLHG) and that the remnants of these have been recorded by the Community Landscapes Project. On Clayhidon Turbary, to the west of the parish, a number of small plots can be identified. Most obvious is that of Sandpit Cottage, its location associated with a spring on the turbary next to a small rectangular plot of land. Two other houses can be seen on the Tithe near to Heazle Farm, both again located in neighbouring rectangular plots opposite a spring. A further two can be found at what is now Jennings Farm. It is possible based on the Tithe Survey Apportionment that many of the plots surrounding the holdings were still held by the Hutchings family, with Jacob junior, James, John, Robert and Samuel Hutchings holding discrete blocks.

Neighbouring Hemyock shows a different pattern of settlement to Clayhidon, and Polwhele (1793–1806, vol. 2 334) suggests that by the end of the eighteenth century there are eight 'villages' recorded within the parish, namely Hemyock-town, Mountain, Borough-hill, Madford, Shuttletons, Tedborough, Millhayes, Comb-Hill, and Columb-David.

The settlement at Hemyock however, can more easily be called a village (in the Blackdown Hills sense of the word). The modern town bears little resemblance to the Tithe Holding having almost doubled in size, but the heart of the settlement remains the same. The reason for the concentration of settlements in this upland parish can be easily established; the presence of Hemyock Castle created a focal point for activity, with a number of tenements located near the dual central of the church and castle.

As identified previously, Madford is thought to be the manor of Hemyock. The distribution of Tithe Survey dwellings suggests that Madford should be classed as a hamlet, as there are a number of properties concentrated together but not associated with a church. There is also a small hamlet at Culm Davy, and Domesday records the estate in the twelfth century. However, these two settlements are the exception. By the time of the Tithe Survey, Borough Hill, Combe Hill and Tedborough were single dwellings, and Shuttleton, although listed as an estate, owned fragmented fields. The farmstead of Combe Pyne, which lies in Hemyock, was associated with the parish of Church Stanton, and in the early eighteenth century was owned by the Baker family of Somerset (Polwhele 1793–1806, volume 2 337).

Summary

The settlement pattern for the Blackdown Hills study area as a whole can be described as one that changes the further into the region one gets. It is clear that on the southern edges of the Hills the settlement pattern is more nucleated, and there are fewer isolated farmsteads. Clayhidon and Hemyock experience a significantly greater proportion of settlement dispersal. The town of Hemyock only occurs because of the presence of Hemyock Castle. Taking into consideration the apparent lack of a distinct centre and of any evidence suggesting concentration of holdings around the church area of Clayhidon, the term village which Polwhele employs is extremely misleading especially in comparison with the settlements in the lowlands fringes of the Blackdown Hills. This is the case even if contraction of settlement is taken into account. Luppitt lies truly in the middle ground, marking the transition, as it contains a higher proportion of individual farmsteads but also contains a number of hamlets, Awliscombe and Buckerell show the greatest evidence for nucleation, with dispersed farmsteads only occurring on the hill slopes surrounding Hembury. The parish of Dunkeswell cannot be included in the discussion of settlement as there is not enough information present in the nineteenth-century Tithe Survey to comment on the distribution. Those that are present (Bywood Farm, Grange Farm and Hookedrise Farm) are all individual dispersed holdings.

Roads and droveways

The final element of the historic landscape to be discussed is that of routeways, which are important as they link components such as the settlements, field systems and estate holdings together across the landscape. Webber (1976, 21) suggests that the narrow and poor condition of the numerous winding sunken lanes, droveways and packhorse tracks allowed the Blackdown Hills to stay in relative isolation well into the post-war years. Many of the roads in the historic landscape seem to have developed from tracks, and as mentioned above consist of winding sunken roads, deviating to avoid fields and follow contours and rivers. Droveways are visible within the landscape as a relic of the links between the farms and the higher ground; they were used to drive animals to and from the areas of former common land.

The Enclosure Act of the nineteenth century affected the nature of the roadway infrastructure, through the creation of linear roads bordering the regimented fields. In the areas which were enclosed by piecemeal arrangements, the roads respect the local topography, mirroring rivers, and bordering blocks of fields.

As with the other parishes, the road network in Buckerell is nearly identical to the modern layout. There are three main roads which branch off from the main settlement of Buckerell, but perhaps most interesting is Tape Lane which runs east–west into Awliscombe. This road (along with Wineford Lane and Weston Lane in Awliscombe) surrounds the area of open fields, providing the framework for the blocks of strip fields. The same occurs to the west of the parish at the second, smaller set of strip fields, where the road forks into two around the strips.

Because of the shape and topography of Awliscombe, the roads branch out from a central axis that runs along the river valley. The river runs north to south through the parish, intersecting the settlements of Wolverstone and Awliscombe. As a result the roads follow the contours of the valley, and therefore they are more linear than those within other parishes. At Laurel Bank this main road forks into two, and Weston Lane branches off cutting through the area of irregular open field. Around this area of open field the roads become more irregular and criss-cross each other, thus creating small enclosed areas. This can be seen most clearly at Tracey, where the roads completely encompass the former manor, creating the enclosure in which the settlement lies. This also occurs around Egham and Pulshays Farms, and shows a different infrastructure to the roads in the rest of the parish. Within Buckcrell droveways can be seen in the area to the west of Bushy Knap, which suggests some movement from either the Deer Park estate or Buckerell itself. There is less evidence for droveways within these two parishes. However, near Combehayes Farm there are two areas of roadside waste which form a funnel shape. This road leads to the higher ground around Hembury Hillfort, and it is at this point too that the parish boundaries converge together and open out again.

Luppitt's present roads are almost identical to those recorded in the tithe documents. Perhaps the most notable section of the former droveway lies to the west of Luppitt (which pushes out the line of the parish boundary in order to respect it). This is a large droveway lying on one edge of the parish and forms what is now Luppitt Common (Fig. 3.38). This funnels in two directions, firstly into Dunkeswell around the area of Bywood Farm (a settlement that now spans both Dunkeswell and Hemyock, and was once a grange of Dunkeswell Abbey), and secondly onto Hense Moor to the north of Luppitt parish. It is also possible that it funnelled in a third direction, dividing off to the east towards Dunkeswell and the area of common known as Rough Gray Bottom. Such use of common lands for grazing was universally practiced in Devon, and will be discussed in Chapter Seven.

A number of smaller droveways are visible within the parish, particularly around Hartridge, a former common. Here there are a number of small droves leading from the ridge; one on the western side was connected to two tracks creating routes from the settlement at Luppitt and from Hense Moor. On the eastern side of the ridge there are three visible droveways, a small track leading to the fields surrounding Mohun's Ottery, the other, a larger drove joining to a track and another droveway at the parish border leading to Braddicksknap Hill in Upottery.

The droveway at Shapcombe which appears to funnel over the river crossing into Combe Raleigh is interesting as it suggests movement of animals over large distances. Another visible droveway can be seen funnelling from the border with Combe Raleigh towards Wick (the small hamlet below the eastern banks of Dumpdon Hill) through the patchwork of fields discussed above. This droveway also appears to branch from the hamlet of Beacon to the north and suggests that animals were moved to this southerly hill rather than onto Hartridge. There is an area of roadside waste present on the road which lies between the

Luppitt Common

Luppitt
Dunkeswell
Dunkeswell parish

0   1   2 Kilometers

N

FIGURE 3.38. Evidence within the nineteenth-century historic landscape of the droveway at Luppitt

settlements of Wick and Luppitt, suggesting that there was movement of cattle between these settlements also.

Within Clayhidon the road structure has undoubtedly been affected by the Parliamentary Enclosure of the early nineteenth century. Where this occurred there are straight roads running north–south into Somerset and adjoining onto earlier routes. More recently, the roads to the south of the parish have been altered by the construction of the airbase at Upottery by Canadian and American forces during World War Two.

Those which have not been altered by these two acts have not diverted since the Tithe. There is a network of criss-crossing roads which follow the rivers Culm and Bolham, following the topography feeding down into the combes. A number of small droveways can be identified in relation to areas of former common (for example at Bolham Hill) and corresponds with the grazing patterns already discussed.

The main roads which cross through Hemyock parish converge at the central settlement at the church and castle complex, and spoke out from this point in the same way as the roads in Mohun's Ottery. There are also a number of droveways that have now been incorporated into the modern road network, notably visible in the historic landscape as strips of roadside waste, on the road surrounding the circular enclosure at Culm Davy leading to Clemant's Common on Culm Davy Hill. At Boham's Farm in Hemyock there is clear evidence of a droveway which feeds from the valley of Madford river up onto Burrow Hill. This large droveway was reused in nineteenth century for a small settlement.

Evidence of industry

There is also significant evidence of whetstone extraction in the Blackdown Hills. This occurs primarily on the Uffculme hills and in the parish of Blackborough to the west of the study area, but there is also aerial photographic evidence of extraction from the Greensand spur of Whitness Moor, just above Hembury Hillfort. This practice is relatively modern, with much of the extraction occurring in the post-medieval period.

Vancouver (1808, 421–422) recorded the population densities for each parish in Devon, also recording their occupations. This source is contemporary with the Tithe Survey and provides an insight into how the landscape was managed in the nineteenth century.

Table 3.3 and chart 3.1 show diversity between the parishes within the study area, and it is clear that the types of occupation are not defined by the location within the Blackdown Hills.[4] One pattern that can be noted is that where there was a high percentage in manufacturing there was a low in the 'other' category and vice versa. For example, Combe Raleigh had 79 per cent of the population employed in other forms of work, while only 5 per cent were in manufacturing. This appears to be a regional trend and not something seen within the other study areas (see Chapters Four and Five). However the 'all other persons' category provides little information as to other professions, and may be misleading. It is clear that this category contains children and the old, but may also incorporate positions such as domestic servants, and 'services' such as school teachers and religious leaders.

Through archaeological and documentary evidence it can be suggested that the origin of some of the manufacturing industries within the Blackdown Hills relates to the number of mills recorded in the area. Watts (2002, 73) notes that watercourses formed natural boundaries within Anglo-Saxon charters, and that mills were incorporated into these clauses, with place-names which incorporate 'mill' as secondary settlements to the estate centre. The identification of mills may be owing to the growing wool trade during the medieval and post-medieval periods. During this period the mills were used for fulling (a process for cleaning and thickening cloth), as well as production of flour and other materials such as gunpowder. In terms of the historic landscape, the evidence of 'hydraulic pumps' on the 1:10,560 ordnance survey maps indicates increased drainage of the land, and/or mills. These hydraulic systems require a height difference to allow a fall in water and a relatively constant flow (Watts 2002, 127), and the combination of these pumps with springs is interesting due to the quantity of spring fed mills in this area which would provide a constant flow of water during the winter months.

It is known that Buckerell has a water mill as early as 1238, as it is recorded in the crown pleas that 'A boy called William was drowned under Buckerell Mill wheel…' (Summerson, 1985, m24:76). However, there is little archaeological evidence for the location of this, and in the post-medieval period no mills were

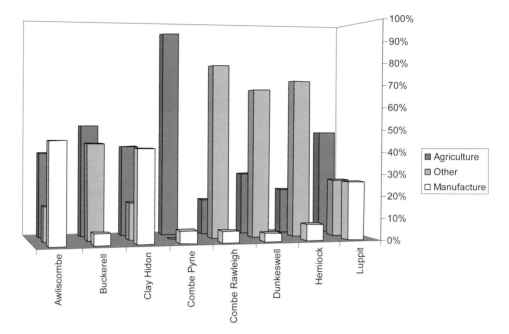

CHART 3.1. Comparative chart of the percentage of population in agriculture, manufacturing and all other forms of employment in 1801, as listed by Vancouver (1808, 421).

listed within the 1845 Tithe Apportionment. There is reference in Domesday to half a mill within *Orescombe*, which is the portion of Awliscombe that is now attributed to the lands of Buckerell, but this can only be speculation.

Within neighbouring Awliscombe there is evidence for two mills during the medieval period, one called Lower or Strickland Mill which was situated on the river Wolf, and the other at the hamlet at Godford. The mill at Godford is thought to have been operating around 1730 (SMR ST10SW/029) and was supplied with water that was fed into a dammed pond from a millrace leading from the river Wolf. However, Strickland Mill, also supplied with water via a pond from the river Wolf, was a grist mill thought to belong to the manor of Awliscombe in the thirteenth and fourteenth century, and may also date back as early as the eleventh century (SMR ST10SW/028).

It can be seen from the Tithe Apportionment that there was a mill in Combe Raleigh. The Tithe Apportionment lists a mill house and mills, suggesting that there was more than one. This was common in the South-west in the later medieval period where multiple mills were common; that is where two or more wheels were placed overlapping each other (Watts 2002, 120–121). It is known that there was a water powered mill known as Tower Mill at the site of what is now Mill house Nursery, which was destroyed by fire in 1890 (SMR ST10SE/50). A leat from this mill ran from Stublands weir to the north.

In Domesday, Mohun's Ottery in Luppitt is recorded as having a mill (DB, 23,18) These early mills were horizontal water-powered mills spanned across a watercourse (Watts 2002, 83). Thus, the settlement's present proximity to the river Otter would not rule out that the Domesday mill was a watermill. The

TABLE 3.3. Table of the percentage of population in agriculture, manufacturing and other forms of employment in 1801, as listed by Vancouver (1808, 421).

Parishes	Agriculture		Manufacture		All other people		Total	
Awliscombe	165	39%	194	46%	67	16%	426	100%
Buckerell	143	51%	15	5%	122	44%	280	100%
Combe Rawleigh	38	16%	12	5%	187	79%	237	100%
Combe Pyne	133	94%	8	6%	0	0%	141	100%
Clay Hidon	286	41%	289	42%	115	17%	690	100%
Dunkeswell	111	28%	15	4%	267	68%	393	100%
Hemiock	209	20%	75	7%	736	72%	1020	100%
Luppit	322	48%	178	26%	175	26%	675	100%

manor of Tracey also has an associated mill. Also known as Higher Griggs it lies within what is now Honiton. The first phase of the mill dates to the seventeenth century (although it is thought it could have an earlier origin) and was a flour and grist mill (SMR ST10SE -139); although between 1813 and 1836 it operated as a paper mill (Shorter n.d cited in SMR ST10SE -139).

There are a number of mills within Clayhidon, for instance, Middleton Mill situated on the Bolham river and part of the Middleton estate. Domesday also lists mills at the Clayhidon Culm Davy and Culm Pyne estates (DB, 16,111; 16,124; 16,122). In addition, it is known that in 1603/4 a watermill was recorded at the manor of Denshayes alongside four houses and 11 cottages (Hawkins 1965, 55). An account by the farmer at Palmers Farm suggests that 'long before his time' there was a spring fed mill at his farm but also, more significantly, at Battens (FamF 1998, pt4: 9). From the work undertaken by the volunteers of the Community Landscapes Project, the location of this mill has been recovered.

Concluding remarks

The occurrence of the roads and droveways avoiding field patterns and following topographical features within the study area is what Muir (2001, 20) describes as the outlines of ancient fields being 'embedded within the fieldscape'. Muir's choice of word here is particularly important in describing a landscape such as the Blackdown Hills. It implies landscapes which have evolved, knotted together and becoming ingrained over the generations, a landscape providing a truth depth of time, exactly what we are seeing within the whole of the Blackdown Hills.

At a general level the Blackdown Hills as a whole is characterised by a pattern of dispersed hamlets, individual farmsteads and semi-irregular fields systems; this is too simplistic however; what can actually be viewed is small scale autonomy that can be seen not only between north and south, but also within the parishes themselves.

The occurrence of the irregular open field patterns in Buckerell and Awliscombe, and also neighbouring Feniton, corresponds with the general idea of such systems occurring within the more nucleated settlements. Within these southern parishes it is clear that they are the product of amalgamation between a number of medieval estates, and this can be seen from the Tithe Survey landownership patterns. However, in Combe Raleigh, the landownership pattern shows a parish comprised of one estate and its corresponding nucleated settlement, but there is also evidence of small individual farmsteads occurring on the upland slopes of St. Cyres Hill.

Luppitt comprises both hamlets and dispersed individual farmsteads and squatter settlements, and also shows a diversity of field patterns. Here there were small irregular fields around the settlement of Wick, evidence of convertible husbandry around Greenway, and the upland areas of centrally placed Luppitt remained unenclosed. Furthermore the use and ultimate fate of the commons differed, when Clayhidon experienced considerable enclosure in the early nineteenth century. Clayhidon shows a distinctly dispersed pattern, with a number of small hamlets (Bolham Water area and Rosemary Lane) in the southern and central section with a few small hamlets in the northern part of the parish. Hemyock shows nucleation at its main settlement which, as mentioned previously, is undoubtedly due to the castle, but generally the parish consists of dispersed hamlets. Hemyock also shows a different field pattern to neighbouring Clayhidon. Despite the differences in field systems, the Tithe Survey patterns of land use show a mix between 'arable', pasture and meadow, interspersed with orchards in Clayhidon and Hemyock. In these parishes 'arable' occurs on the upland slopes of the Culm valley along the Somerset border, and this may be considered as arable in the sense of 'ploughable'. In other words, poorer agricultural land was taken in and out of cultivation. The number of droveways here also indicates the movement of cattle onto these hills, suggesting seasonal grazing as at Bolham and Middleton.

It is clear that topography has affected the way in which the field divisions are laid out, with the higher hills clearly enclosed later than those in the river valleys of the Otter, Culm, and their tributaries. However, the patterns of Tithe landownership show that the varied organisation of the area also play a part in the management of the landscape.

Landownership patterns for the whole of the Blackdown Hills study area show an interesting distribution. In Buckerell and Awliscombe, where there is no evidence of open field systems which make the ownership highly fragmented, owners own large blocks of land in one area of the Parish. Combe Raleigh's complete dominance by Mary Bernard epitomises this, and the southern half of Luppitt also follows this trend. In northern Luppitt however, landownership begins to be more dispersed, with owners holding smaller areas of land, and this trend is continued in Clayhidon. Neighbouring Hemyock however, shows a pattern of landownership which is more fragmented; there are no coherent blocks of owners. As the hundred centre[5] this is interesting as even though there is nucleation of settlement around the centre of Hemyock town, there is no coherence in landownership. This is interesting in comparison to Hartland and the work of Harold Fox on the impact of hundred settlements within the landscape (see Chapter Four).

At this point the issues of *pays* within the Blackdown Hills need to be raised again. It would be unwise to consider the dispersed parishes as not having a strong sense of community. This is imperative when discussing the idea that the designation of the whole of the Blackdown Hills as a *pays* region is too broad. What we are seeing here is something akin to the French meaning of the word; ie individual communities, perhaps consisting only of a few dispersed hamlets, which are shaping their environments according to their own personal needs. The perceived seclusion from the rest of Devon and Somerset poses an interesting hypothesis as to the way the landscape of the hills was manipulated and used by the communities which worked and lived within it, and will be discussed in greater detail in Chapter Six.

Notes

1   As an aside, Youing (1955, 117) states that although he was the Duke's oldest surviving son, he was in disfavour at this time owing to his mother's indiscretions.

2   When the Tithe Survey lists the land use as arable, this will be referred to as "arable" as the listing may mean "ploughable". See the Chapter Six.

3   Snook meaning odd shaped corner in the local dialect (Downes 1998, 86).

4   Dunkeswell has been included within this list for the purposes of comparison, and all spellings used in the table are written as in Vancouver (1808).

5   A hundred is the division of large areas into smaller administration, military and judicial units. This occurred before 1894 and the introduction of districts. A hundred centre is therefore the central meeting point within the defined area, and the location of so-called hundred courts.

CHAPTER FOUR

'Furthest from Railways'
– Hartland Moors

The Blackdown Hills region of east Devon represents a landscape which saw a number of different trajectories in terms of its development during the medieval and post-medieval period. These differences were partly topographic but also relate to estate and landholding structure. The Hartland Moors study area presents a comparison to the Blackdown Hills as the historic landscape is made up of a number of different zones; from the sheltered combe of Clovelly to the high cliffs at Hartland Point and the moors of Tosbury, Hendon, and Bursdon.

It must be considered then if similar patterns of land management will be seen in the Hartland Moors region as were seen in the area of the Blackdown Hills discussed in Chapter Three. Is there the same idea of small community *pays* within the area, or are there other factors at play within this region?

Introduction to Hartland Moors

The area of Hartland Moors in north-west Devon can be defined as the upland moor lands. This coastal region spans from Bideford Bay in the east, to the Atlantic coast in the west and stretches down to the Devon/Cornwall border to the south (Fig. 4.1). Like the Blackdown Hills, the name Hartland Moors

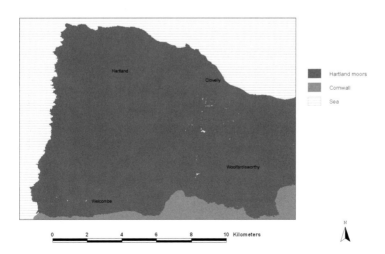

FIGURE 4.1. Area of Hartland Moors region of north-west Devon

is a modern term for this coastal region, and like much of Devon, this area of the northern coast stretching from Bideford in the north to Devil's Hole at Marsland Cliff in the parish of Welcombe in the south is designated an Area of Outstanding Natural Beauty. Much of the coastline is also owned or managed by the National Trust (Fig. 4.2).

As the name indicates, the Hartland Moors area is defined by its upland moor, that is land of 160 m or above. The region is framed on two sides by sheer cliffs; the northern coast facing onto the Bristol Channel, and the western side providing the last land mass before America. In terms of modern agriculture, it is generally considered that the area as a whole operated a mixed agricultural economy, despite its coastal position. Furthermore, Burton (1953, 9) states that on the Atlantic coast region to the west, the high price of corn pushed wheat production to the edges of the cliffs, but that the crop yields were relatively poor.

As described in the last chapter, a defining part of the Blackdown Hills was, and still is, the area's isolation and separation from the rest of Devon. In light of this, it can be argued that this is a factor that should also be considered when discussing this region on the north-western edge of Devon. Pearse Chope (1940, 1) notes that the parish of Hartland was isolated from the rest of the county, especially through the lack of rail access until the First World War; the idea that

FIGURE 4.2. The rugged coastline of the Hartland Moors study area looking south

it was 'furthest from railways'. With the rise in popularity of cars access became easier to the Hartland Moors area, and visitors from outside the immediate area came to the region more readily.

Introduction to the Hartland Moors study area

As with the Blackdown Hill, in order to gain a representative sample of the landscape of the Hartland Moors region, a 176km² area (bottom left 22021170 top right 23601281) has been designated for study. Within this defined area, four parishes will be discussed in depth; Hartland, Clovelly, Welcombe and Woolfardisworthy (Woolsery) (Fig. 4.3), but Parkham parish will also be considered as it shares the manorial holding of the manor of Bucks with Woolfardisworthy (see below). These four parishes have been singled out for enquiry for a number of reasons; primarily because they are parishes which provide good documentary material, but also because of their physical location, and the contrasting conditions not only between themselves but also in comparison to the other study areas under investigation.

Introduction to the parishes

Hartland is considered to be one of the largest parishes within Devon with the exception of Dartmoor. Therefore, this means that much of the research undertaken within the study area relates to this parish. Hartland parish has an internal boundary of some 30 miles and consists of 17,000 acres (Gregory 1950, v). Two sides of its roughly rectangular shape are bounded by the Atlantic Ocean and the Bristol Channel, and on its eastern and southern sides it is separated from its surrounding parishes by the topography which creates natural boundaries (Pearse Chope 1916, 5). The name Hartland is thought to derive from *heort*, OE for Hart (PND 1930, 72), and perhaps acknowledges the presence of stags, or the presence of deer parks (see below). However, Pease Chope (1902a, 7) suggests that this is not the case, and that the name actually refers to 'the Saxon settlement of *Heortings*, or the men of the clan of Heort'. Pease Chope is keen on the idea of clan references, and although the name may be referenced to the early medieval period, it is perhaps unwise to focus too much upon the idea of incomers. The final say must go to modern linguistics, and Gelling (2000, 245–6) proposes that the name Hartland comes from the OE with the *land* referring to an estate or new arable area, and suggests the name to mean *hart-island estate*. The parish registers of 1620 show that the population of the parish was greater than that of the nearby town of Bideford (Pearse Chope 1940, 2; 1916, 13).

By comparison in terms of size, the parish of Welcombe is a small parish lying between the river Torridge and Marsland Water, the watercourse that forms the boundary of Cornwall and the Cornish parish of Morwenstow. It forms the southern boundary of Hartland and is divided from its neighbours by a deep

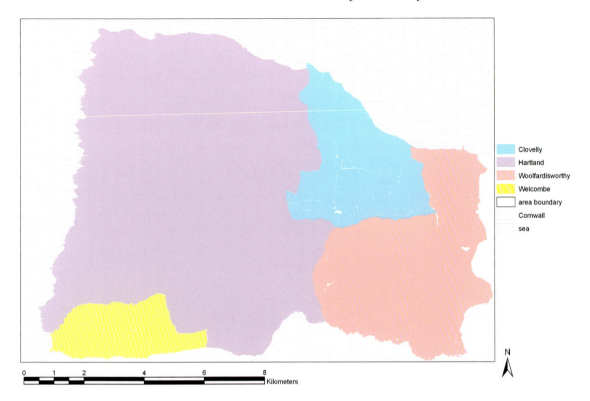

0   1   2   4   6   8
Kilometers

Clovelly
Hartland
Woolfardisworthy
Welcombe
area boundary
Cornwall
sea

N

FIGURE 4.3. The four parishes highlighted for study within the Hartland Moors study area and parishes

valley. It has been suggested that the name derives from *Wel* meaning Welsh or foreign, therefore Welcombe is the combe which divides Devon from Cornwall (or *Cornwelsh*) (Pearse Chope 1902a, 7). However, another and perhaps more likely explanation for the name is the Old English origin, meaning *spring*-valley (Gelling 2000, 30). This explanation of the name Welcombe is also descriptive of the parish's position as one of the two St. Nectan's Wells in the study area (dedicated to local patron saint, see below) is located in the centre of the settlement.

The third parish under consideration forms the eastern boundary of Hartland and Welcombe. The shape of the parish of Woolfardisworthy is like an inverted 'L' with a long extension of land stretching up to the north coast and Bideford Bay. This in itself is an interesting occurrence, as it would suggest that the community wanted to gain access to this resource, which its inland position would not allow. The positioning of this parish could be described as more 'inland' than the other three under consideration, and as such provides an interesting comparison. Only one suggestion has been made for the origin of the name Woolfardisworthy; 'Wulfheard's farm' in Old English (PND 1930,80), implying that the parish was named after one of the many farms which must have been located within the landscape. As highlighted in Chapter One, the occurrence of the -worthy suffix is important as the presence of -worthy and also -ton place-names is distinctive to the Hartland study area, providing a different linguistic trait to that occurring in the Blackdown Hills. Padel (1999, map 13.4) notes that this area shows a concentration of worthy names, as figure 1.7 demonstrates.

The final parish for study is Clovelly, which lies to the east of the Hartland Moors study area. The settlement of Clovelly lies on the north coast of Devon in Bideford Bay, and the land making up the parish is situated in the valley between Hartland and the steep cliffs. The place-name Clovelly is thought by some to be of 'celtic' origin from the prefix of the name in the Domesday spelling *Clovelie*, which Burrow (1980, 64) indicates as evidence of a retention of pre-English culture. Significantly in the late nineteenth century, this was thought to have still been noteworthy, with Warden Page (1895, 7) suggesting that the 'clans' of the northern coasts were 'a different race' to those in the south. However, PND (1931, 70) suggest that the later spellings of the name include a first element that could be the Welsh *Clawdd* meaning ditch, in reference to topography or Clovelly Dykes. There is no land between the Hartland Moors region and Carmarthen Bay 50 miles to the north (Pearse Chope 1916, 5) and therefore it is not inconceivable for the name to travel across the Bristol Channel, but this is perhaps unlikely. It is however more credible to suggest that the Old English prefix, a compound of *cloh* meaning ravine (PND 1931, 70), is the more plausible source. Gelling (2000, 83) concurs with this and suggests that the name derives from the OE *clof* or *clofa* meaning 'something cut' and that *clof* had a topographical meaning similar to that of the related Old Norse word *klofi* meaning 'crevice'.

Perception of landscape in the recent past

During his visit to the region in the late nineteenth century, Warden Page (1895, 162) suggests that the area of Hartland Moors was 'just the place where you would expect to find old-world manners and customs, old-world fashions and old-world furniture', and Vancouver (1808, 407) makes the statement that the longevity and health of the population within the Hartland Moors area was attributed to the 'regularity of exercise necessarily connected with rural life'.

Perhaps unfairly Polwhele (1793–1806, 419), who was travelling through the area in the nineteenth century, remarks that the parishes of Welcombe and Woolfardisworthy 'will furnish little, on which to remark'. Hartland also does badly, with Warden Page (1895, 157) stating that: 'Hartland – I speak of the district, not the village, though that is dull enough – has in the country inland little to recommend it'.

Harsh criticism indeed, but Warden Page did not stop there, as he also describes the area between the village of Clovelly and Hartland (around the sheer cliff of Gallantry Bower) as a 'wild country' (*ibid.* 1895, 161).

Nevertheless, Clovelly itself fared better, becoming popular with the 'gentlemen' travellers of the nineteenth century, and consequently their writings provide us with an image of the landscape in this period. Around Clovelly, the fields on the lower slopes are described as 'rough with brakes, and woodland along the coastal cliffs, and the river valleys with dense foliage of ferns, mosses and wild flowers' (Warden Page 1895, 150). Charles Dickens and Wilkie Collins (1860, in Simmons 1971, 70) described Clovelly in 1860 in their short story *A Message from the Sea*, describing the cliffs as 'red-brown… richly wooded to their extreme verge', and emphasised the quaintness of the village with its steep row of houses.

The area is also rich with stories, such as the tale of 'Cruel Coppingar'[1], and other folklore and myths. For example, the scale of construction at Clovelly Dykes in the centre of Clovelly parish has even meant that modern folklore names the site as the Arthurian city of Camelot and this will be discussed in more detail in later chapters. The Arthurian associations are undoubtedly later, but perhaps build upon earlier myths used to explain the presence of large scale earthworks seen at Clovelly. As is discussed elsewhere (Franklin 2006, 156) Hartland Point to the west of Clovelly Dykes might provide a link to these earlier myths. *Hercvlis* or Hercules Promontory, one of only three named Roman sites within Devon (as listed by the Ordnance Survey Historical map of Roman Britain) led the antiquarian Camden in 1789 to state that the name arises from Hercules, who came to Britain to fight giants, and suggests evidence of Phoenician sailors trading with Devon (cited in Pearse Chope 1940, 6); also a fact suggested by Polwhele (1797, vol. 1, 136). There is no evidence of occupation in the Romano-British period for this area. However, most of west Devon is aceramic at this time and the Romano-British activity on Exmoor to the east cannot rule out some contact this far west.

The ideas highlighted above regarding cultural regions or *pays* and folklore are discussed at greater length in Chapter Six, but, it can be seen that just as a number of folktales and legends have developed on the Blackdowns, it seems that this coastal moorland also attracted myths.

Physical elements of the Hartland Moors Region

As in Chapter Four, it is important to discuss the physical components of any landscape under consideration in order to determine whether they have an effect on the organisation of the landscape.

The geology of the study area is particularly regular, consisting of sandstone and shale, with alluvium along the rivers courses. As a result of this geological formation, the topography (away from the sheer coastal cliffs) shows a number of combes following the lines of rivers, forming a series of isolated valleys. These isolated valleys are key to the discussion about distinct cultural units or *pays*, as it is this type of environment which facilitates strong community-based societies which differ from those surrounding them.

In terms of soils, the Hartland study area has a very similar construction to that of the South Hams area, consisting of mainly brown earth with shale and slate. The Bideford coast region around Clovelly is characterised by soils from the Manod Association; free draining loamy soils over the palaeozoic siltstone and slate. These are suited to grassland, either permanent and rough grazing, or leys, especially when limed and fertilised, with some arable cropping on the gentle slopes (Findlay *et al.* 1984, 227–230). On the upland areas, the soils are part of the Onecote Association and the Hallsworth 2 Association. The soils of the Onecote Association which are predominately in the Hartland area are clayey and loamy cambric stagnohumic gley soils that can sustain the production of large yields of grass, but are susceptible to rapid deterioration and waterlogging if not carefully managed. Revision to rough pasture can be caused through plough smearing during reclamation (Findlay *et al.* 1984, 255–6). These areas are therefore suited to rough grazing, but only after draining of surface water and sporadic springs. The Hallsworth 2 soils form a band across from the Atlantic Coast to Wellington in Somerset. These are severely waterlogged soils when undrained, thanks to their slowly permeable dense and coarsely structured subsoil (*ibid.* 1984, 193–5). This means that agriculturally the land is under ley; permanent, often rough, pasture, with the remaining areas covered in coniferous forest, scrubby deciduous woodland, or *Molina* Moor.

It must be remembered that these classifications of land use are based on modern technology and economic variables. However, when used as a guide it can be suggested that the Hartland Moors study area soil make-up creates an environment that is generally suitable for mixed farming and dairying but is too heavy for intensive arable production. This is a factor that is comparable with the Blackdown Hills as the soil structure in that area reflects the same agricultural variables. Therefore, if the physical variables are taken alone, we should see an agricultural landscape with similar features in both study areas.

In terms of drainage, there are ten major rivers in the Hartland study area, feeding into the sea and usually creating a waterfall. Abbey river, river Torridge, and Clifford Water make up the main water courses which are fed by a number of tributaries. Clifford Water forms the boundary between the parishes of Clovelly and Woolfardisworthy and Marsland Water forms the southern boundary of Welcombe, and, as mentioned above, divides Devon from Cornwall.

Climatically, the Hartland Moors study area is in an area with an annual rainfall of over 1000 mm a year, and a growing season of 275 days (Caseldine 1999, 33). This, combined with the strong Atlantic wind (emphasised by the occurrence of Windways, Windy moor and Windbury field-names within the Tithe Apportionment), makes for a distinctive climate.

Previous archaeological and historical research

Much of the known archaeology within the Hartland Moors study area is prehistoric. There are a significant number of flint scatters dating to both the Mesolithic and the Neolithic periods, and a number of Bronze Age barrows recorded on the moors of the region. The occurrence of Clovelly Dykes, a large four-banked earthwork typologically dated to the Iron Age, suggests a large motivated prehistoric community occupying the lands here (or at least significantly sized to support the act of constructing of such an earthwork).

There are three possible Cliff Castles within the study area suggested by typology to be Iron Age in date. The structure about which the most information is known occurs in Hartland at Embury Beacon on the western coast. This was later used for an Elizabethan beacon giving the site its name. This feature was excavated in 1973 as a result of the threat of rapid coastal erosion, and pottery from this excavation places the site in the mid- to late Iron Age, along with evidence of a crucible and stone whorl also recovered from the site (SMR SS21NW/501). The second is situated on the northern coast at Windbury Head, also in Hartland (Pearse Chope 1940, 8), but there has been no excavation of this site. As mentioned above, there is a suggested site on Hartland Point itself. This third location is more uncertain, as there are few archaeological remains here to confirm its existence. As discussed above, this part of Devon is generally considered to be aceramic for the period between the end of the Iron Age and the early medieval period, leading to a void in our understanding. For the early medieval period there is evidence of a possible early Christian graveyard, thought to be associated with an early Chapel in South Hole in Hartland (SMR SS21NW-506; Pearce 1985, 267–9). The identification of such early medieval settlements could provide clues to the origins and development of the late and post-medieval landscape, and aid the identification of past land use through the nineteenth-century historic landscape.

Development and evolution of the Hartland Moors landscape

Estate structure

In Chapter Three it was seen that in the Blackdown Hills there was a series of small manorial groups which made up the parishes within the study area. Both the Blackdown Hills and the Hartland Moors area were influenced by monastic houses during the Middle Ages, but the way in which Hartland's manorial structure was made up differs noticeably from the Blackdowns. There has been significant historical research, in particular relating to the early manorial organisation of the Hartland region, undertaken by Robert Pearse Chope who lived in the Fattacott area of Hartland, H.S.A Finberg, and in the 1980s by Harold Fox (cf. Pearse Chope 1902b; Fox 1986). Pearse Chope (1902b, 420) suggests that what is now Hartland parish was essentially an ecclesiastical unit and much of the land holdings are not recognised within Domesday accounts. A significant influence on the area and particularly on the parish of Hartland was the church. Before the arrival of the Regular Canons of the Order of St. Augustine of Hippo, there was a college of 12 secular canons at Hartland founded by Gytha, wife of Earl Godwin and mother of King Harold, at the site of the early medieval chapel (Fig. 4.4) (Gregory 1950, vii). Gytha maintained the canons on the land which she dedicated to them. Around 1169–70, the

FIGURE 4.4. Stained glass window in St. Nectan's Hartland depicting Gytha, founder of the secular college which became Hartland Abbey. Also crest of the Dynham family and the Abbey

FIGURE 4.5. St. Nectan's Church at Stoke Nectan in Hartland which dominates the small settlement in which it is located

FIGURE 4.6. St. Nectan's Well in Stoke Nectan in the Parish of Hartland. The spring marks the spot where St. Nectan placed his severed head

Augustan canons, possibly from Notley in Buckinghamshire, arrived at the college to serve in the abbey founded by Geoffrey (Summerson 1985, 62), and it is likely that the land which Gytha gave over to the college became part of the larger monastic holdings of the abbey.

It is known that in the period before the Reformation there was, besides the abbey, a large parish church, St. Nectan, at Stoke, and in excess of 11 small chapels dotted through the countryside (Hoskins 1959, 77; see Table 4.3). The hamlet of Stoke St. Nectan is thought to be the manorial centre which is associated with Hartland manor (see below). However, the extent of the church here has caused much discussion as the size of the building does not represent the density of population in this settlement (see for example Pearse Chope 1902b), and is undoubtedly a symbol of the manorial power here (Fig. 4.5). Again there is reference to the Welsh Saint Nectan,[2] with a well dedicated to him located nearby to the church (Fig. 4.6), mirroring the same configuration of holy well and church that occurs at Welcombe.

The Dissolution of Hartland Abbey came on the 22 February 1539, and afterwards Stoke St. Nectan was passed to the Abbott family. It is known that on the 25 January 1777 a grant of the priory of Hartland and other lands at Stoke were awarded to a William Abbott, reducing the size of the monastic estate (Hartland Town Trust Archives). It was William Abbott who was ultimately responsible for the construction of Hartland Quay in the late sixteenth century (Fox 2001, 16).

It is possible to identify two influences occurring within the Hartland Moors study area. Finberg (1956) notes that the manor of Harton was a royal estate in the ninth century as in Domesday it is listed as an entity held before 1066 by Gytha, wife of Earl Godwin and mother of King Harold. Post-Conquest it belonged to King William, Harold's victor (DB, 1,30). It is also thought that in this period Lundy Island, which lies to the west of Hartland, was surveyed as part of the manor of Harton (RH. i. 73b, 89b). It can be seen through later documents that during the thirteenth century Lundy was used for supplying the estate of Sir John Dynham (Woolgar 1999, 502), suggesting that the island's resources were being exploited to their fullest extent.

It is also suggested that prior to the death of William I, the manor of Harton was held *in capite* directly by the king with no under tenants. It was only after William's death that Harton was granted to the Dynham family (see Table 4.1, listing the *Testa de Nevill* records), where it remained until the reign of Henry VII (Pearse Chope 1940, 26). Pearse Chope (1940, 26) continues by suggesting that this Dynham manor was the head of a barony as well as of the hundred, and also of the rural deanery. In 1235 the Feudal Aids record that Oliver Dynham also held the manor *in capite* (FA,341-2), and between 1284 and 1286 the Borough of Harton was created through a seignorial grant. By 1299 there were 13 burgesses recorded for the borough, each paying the sum of one shilling (Finberg and Beresford 1973, 91–92; Pearse Chope 1902b, 425–8). Oliver Dynham received a charter from Edward I giving him and his heirs the right to hold weekly markets within Harton, a yearly fair on the eve of the feast of St. Nectan, and the right to preserve game on his demesne lands (Gregory 1950, v).

Furthermore, the IPM collated for Oliver Dynham recorded in 1298 that he held *Hertilonde* as a *capital message* with a courtyard, a herbage and garden, but also significantly list the acreage of land under an agricultural regime; namely 112 acres of arable, 6 acres of meadow, 60 acres of pasture, a wood, and two parks. By 1301 the manor of Hartland included two parks with deer, a preserve or fishpond in Boterbiri [Butterbury] and Hyndeherton, watermills at Herton and Egereston [Eddistone], and woods at Eapham and Boterbiri (IPM, 29 Edw. I File 129 (2) m.1). This increased by 1428, when the manor had 34 messuages, two parks with deer lands, three corn mills, and one fulling mill (IPM, 7 Henry VI file 40 (56) m.9).

The location of the two deer darks may be suggested by the place-names North and South Deerpark located to the west of the settlement of Hartland

Index no	fees of…	Testa de Nevill name	Testa de Nevill holder	Testa de Nevill fee		modern name
295	The Honour of Gloucester	Clovely (1)	Roger de Giffard	1/4	per medium	Clovelly
129	Toriton	Molleford	Reginald Beupel, Roger Giffard & Prior of Frithelarestok	2		Milford
130	Toriton	Hole and	Reginald Beupel, Roger Giffard & Prior of Frithelarestok	2		Southhole
131	Toriton	Herdcywyk	Reginald Beupel, Roger Giffard & Prior of Frithelarestok	2		Hardisworthy
359	Particular Fees of the King in Chief	Hertilande	Galfrid Dynanth	2/3		Hartland
357	Particular Fees of the King in Chief	Wollecumb	Robert de Merland	2/9		Welcombe
132	Toriton	Almereston cum membris	Reginald Beupel, Roger Giffard & Prior of Frithelarestok	1	per medium	Almiston
132	Toriton	Almereston cum membris	Reginald Beupel, Roger Giffard & Prior of Frithelarestok	1	per medium	Bucks
132	Toriton	Almereston cum membris	Reginald Beupel, Roger Giffard & Prior of Frithelarestok	1	per medium	Walland
296	The Honour of Gloucester	Wolfaresworth	William de Hamptenesford	1/2		Woolfardisworthy
541	Okemeton of John de Curtenay	Asmundesuurth	Reginald Bernehus and William de Strokeswurth	1/2		Ashmansworthy
541	Okemeton of John de Curtenay	Asmundesuurth	Reginald Bernehus and William de Strokeswurth	1/2		Stroxworthy

TABLE 4.1. Listing from the thirteenth-century *Testa de Nevill* for Hartland Moors

on Pearse Chope's (1902b, map 2) map of the Hartland manorial holdings. The first recorded use of the place-name Deerpark is thought to be *Deareparke* in 1566 (PND 1931, 78), suggesting that the name may have survived as indicator of the use of the area long after its original foundation.

Comparing this to the suggested location of the manor of Harton itself, the extent of the thirteenth-century manorial lands is thought to have been delimited with marker stones at Hartland Mill, Cutcliff (Cutliffe) Lane, Rosedown Farm, Ballhill, Ford Lane, Larkaborough Gate, and Thorn Cross, with a further stone possible at Harton Cross (Hobbs 1995) (Fig. 4.7). Much

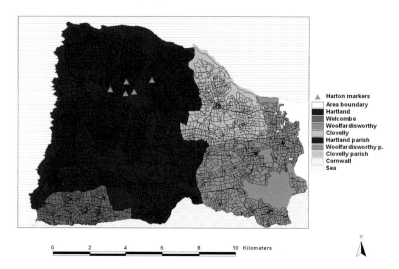

FIGURE 4.7. The position of markers which delimit the boundary of the manor of Harton

land and property was held outside this, and the deer parks are situated on the edge of this defined area. It is known that the manor house of Harton was in the middle of demesne within the South Deer Park near to what is now the town of Hartland (Pearse Chope 1916, 14).

It cannot be underestimated how much of an impact the Dynham family had in the Hartland Moors area, during the medieval and post-medieval periods (like in the Blackdown Hills, where the Carew family, who became part of the Dynham's line through marriage, owned Mohun's Ottery). The Dynham family ran large estates, and the manor of Harton held a considerable part of what is now the parish of Woolfardisworthy (Pearse Chope 1916, 13), and also land in the 'modern' parish of Welcombe (see below).

The 1566 Dynham Survey covered large areas of the parish, and listed 92 free holdings within the Dynham manor plus 60 customary holdings and 46 Barton tenancies as a lease of demesne land (DRO Z17/3/19; Wickes 1979/80, 4). It is interesting that the Hartland manor had more than 87 free tenants in 1301, compared with only eight free tenants out of a population of 129 in Ottery St Mary in east Devon (Hatcher 1988, 676). This may be because of the sheer size of Hartland, as Ottery is smaller in area than Hartland, but it is still a considerable number. It is also worth noting that Hallam (1981, 21) argues that Devon was one of the least free counties in England. Thus what we are perhaps seeing within the Hartland study area is different organisation occurring within Hartland manor.

The Harton estate and its predecessors undoubtedly turned the, at times unfavourable, environment to their advantage. In the eleventh century it is considered that cattle were dominant in the economy of the west of the county, because of suitable grazing land. This dominance of cattle rearing occurred in a rough band which stretched from the Hartland Coast and the Somerset border, down the Cornish coast and across eastwards to Okehampton (Hoskins 1959, 50). In particular, Hartland and also Clovelly had high numbers of cattle and sheep; 137

and 700, and 45 and 100 respectively (DB, 1,30; 1,59). In the fourteenth century the same can be seen in the proportions of cattle, pigs and sheep consumed within the household of Sir John Dynham, as in the years between 1372–3, 72.5 percent of the meat consumed was bovine (Woolgar 1999, 134).

The manor of *Walcome* was owned by the Bishop of Coutances, Geoffrey of Mowbray, who was awarded large tracts of land after the Conquest, particularly in Somerset and Devon that formed his personal fief (DB, chap 3 part II). At some point the manor of Welcombe became part of Hartland manor where it remained until 1508 when St. Nectan's Chapel and graveyard was dedicated, and became a parish in its own right (Pearse Chope 1902a, 21; Pearce 1985, 265). It is thought that the dedication of the church at Welcombe to St. Nectan shows the significance of the saint through the scattered communities within the area (Burton 1953, 164). The fact that Welcombe was part of Hartland manor means that it is perhaps more likely that the same saint dedications were made. Furthermore, the inhabitants of Welcombe were required to keep in repair part of St. Nectan's churchyard wall in Stoke, showing the dependence of their chapel to the Hartland parish church (Pearse Chope 1902a, 21).

The first part of this section has mainly focused on the role of two major forces, the Dynham family and the church. It is clear from documentary sources that there was a great deal of ill feeling between the Abbey and the Dynham family, particularly after Oliver Dynham seized the abbey in 1261 during a vacancy in the position of abbot, and 'consumed its goods against the will of the canons and extorted large sums of money from them' (Pearse Chope 1902a, 19). Eleven years after this event (with the Abbey restored back to the monks), it is also recorded that there was a fight between the lord's men and the abbot's men in the parish church. This resulted in the Bishop being brought to Hartland to reconsecrate the church and reconcile the two groups, absolving many of the lord's household for the earlier trespass (*ibid*. 1902a, 19). Hostilities between the Dynhams and the Abbey continued right through the fifteenth century until the Dissolution.

It is clear that the dual power of the Hartland Abbey and the Manor of Harton had a considerable impact on the estate structure of the Hartland Moors study area. However there were also other smaller manorial setups (Fig. 4.8). Milford in Hartland was thought to have been a discrete manorial estate and the layout of its fields and common indicates this. The same can be applied to Hartisworthy to the south of Milford, South Hole, and also Meddon. Milford was recorded in Domesday as *Meleforde*, and there is evidence that this holding, which was recorded as serving five villagers, has a pre-conquest origin (DB, 36, 4).

In comparison to Hartland, what is now the parish of Clovelly has a more simple manorial history, but is perhaps the area that has the least written about its manorial set-up. Before the Conquest, some of the area that is now Clovelly parish was held by Bertric, son of Algar, and then by his successor Queen Matilda, with the estate passing on to King William on her death in 1083 (DB, 1,59;

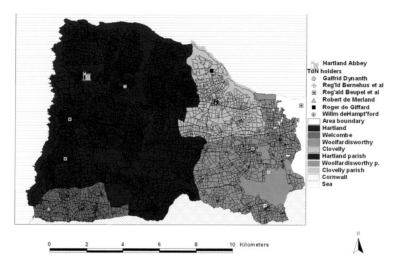

FIGURE 4.8. Estates listed in the *Testa de Nevill* in the Hartland Moors study area in relation to Hartland Abbey

24,21 part two). In terms of later estate structure, the Tithe Survey gives a good indication of the later holdings. From the listings of landowners within the tithe apportionment it is clear that almost 90 per cent of the land within Clovelly is held by Sir James Hamlyn Williams, Bart of Clovelly. This mirrors the estate structure and pattern of landholding seen in the parish of Combe Raleigh in the Blackdown Hills (see Chapter Three), and may illustrate a similar development in the two parishes.

Hoskins (1952a, 306) suggests that, having once been part of the manor of Hartland, Clovelly may have been 'carved out of Woolfardisworthy at some date', perhaps created as a separate ecclesiastical entity in the twelfth century.

Within the neighbouring areas, the manor of *Olvereword*, which later become Wolsworthy (now known as Woolfardisworthy) was owned by the King's Thane in 1068, in this case probably Colwin the reeve, a thane formally of Queen Edith but who transferred his services to William (DB, C2 part II). There is a link with Hartland Abbey as the manorial church of *Olvereword* was given over to the abbey after its formation (*Oliver Mon* 1946, 204; DB, 52m4 part II).

Domesday also lists a number of other holdings corresponding with the modern hamlets of Almiston, Ashmansworthy, and Bucks or Bokish. Later part of Woolfardisworthy, Almerscote (later changed to Almiston) meaning *Aelfmær's cote* (PND 1931, 80) was thought to be part of a hundredal grouping with Dilly in the parish of Yarnscombe, and later became part of the Honour of Torrington (DB, ch. 42 part II). Also part of Woolfardisworthy parish, Ashmansworthy was part of the land held as Land of Baldwin the Sheriff in Domesday, and seems to have been a sizable holding. The entry lists six villagers and four smallholders dwelling within the estate, with 60 acres of meadow, and plot of pasture one league long and half a league wide with 100 sheep and 25 cows (DB, 16,31). The name Ashmansworthy is thought to derive from the OE *Æscmund's worþig* (PND 1931, 81), and the field formation, discussed below, suggests the possible outline of such a farm holding. Again, here we see the occurrence of -worthy and -ton place-names, emphasizing this convention.

Bucks is listed in Domesday as *Bochewis* and the first element is thought to translate to the OE *bōc* meaning 'book' which is suggested to denote that the area was held by charter (PND 1931, 81). Bucks later became a key fishing centre in the area when a harbour was constructed in the seventeenth century (Fox 2001, 16). A statement which is worthy of note is that made by Warden Page (1895). He states that the people of Bucks Mill had a reputation for keeping themselves apart from their neighbours, and that it was rumoured that their speech and appearance was different to the adjacent settlements, and that this was because of 'a strong strain of Spanish blood in their veins...for it is said that their forebears were shipwrecked Spaniards' (*ibid.* 1895, 149). Aside from the Spanish ancestry, the occurrence of these different cultural identities is interesting particularly in terms of the idea of distinct *pays* regions. It can be suggested that this small settlement situated at the bottom of a steep valley by the sea was deemed to be completely separate in terms of ways of living from those who surrounded it, further adding to the notion that *pays* should be discussed not only at regional or parish level, but also for small units such as settlements.

Buck's Mill is also interesting, and unusual. The area lies on the boundary of two parishes, the western side within Woolfardisworthy, the eastern within Parkham. This mirrors the argument seen in the Blackdown Hills relating to the hamlet of Weston which was divided between Buckerell and Awliscombe. In the case in the Hartland Moors study area, the administrative duties were divided at Bucks Mills between the two parishes, with the land in Parkham falling under the manorial control of the Coffin family, which later became the Pine Coffin estate (Hoskins 1954, 236).

Summary

Besides the few small individual manors, the Hartland Moors study area is dominated by two large manorial centres, the Abbey of Hartland, and Harton Manor held by the Dynham family. The lands of the Hartland estate also extended through what are now the parishes of Welcombe and Woolfardisworthy. Because the Harton estate controlled much of the land within the study area it is crucial to look at the area as a whole rather than as discreet parishes and to understand the wider implications of such an influence within the landscape which continued beyond the self-contained borders of the parish.

The predominance of the lands held by Lewis William Buck in Hartland and Welcombe is interesting in comparison to the distribution of lands held by Sir James Williams in Clovelly and Woolfardisworthy. This suggests two predominant land owners in the nineteenth century, which mirrors the holdings of the Dynhams, the Abbey of Hartland, and the dominance of one estate in Clovelly.

Elements of the historic landscape

The discussion of estates in the Hartland Moors study area has illustrated that the pattern of landholding is complex, and ownership oversteps parish boundaries. How this relates to the historic landscape needs to be discussed, in particular with reference to the relationship between these patterns of landholding and the resulting field and settlement morphology.

Field systems

It can be seen from figures 4.9 and 4.10 that between the four parishes there are notable differences in the patterns of Tithe Survey landownership and land use. To discuss these patterns further, as with the Blackdown Hills, each parish will be examined in turn, starting with the largest parish Hartland.

The Tithe Survey for the parish of Hartland has become significantly damaged, leading to missing data. Despite this, it can be seen from figure 4.11 and figure 4.12 that even with the damage there are distinct patterns of landownership and land use occurring within the Parish. Within the Hartland parish, the first focal point must be the land associated with the manor of Harton. As mentioned previously, the manor house of Harton was located in South Deer Park and that place-name evidence has provided an insight into the extent of the deer park associated with the manor. The marker stones that are positioned around the present town of Hartland indicate the extent of the manor of Harton, and correspond to a defined field pattern. The occurrence of the name Rosedown (one of the farms used as a

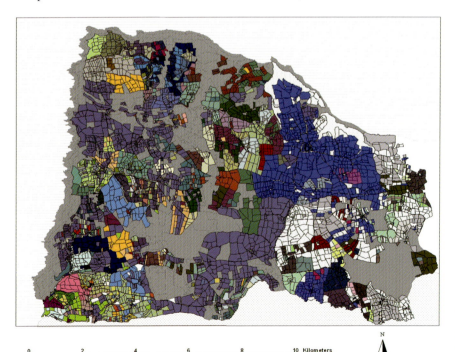

0   2   4   6   8   10   Kilometers

N

FIGURE 4.9. Nineteenth-century Tithe Survey landownership patterns for all four parishes

FIGURE 4.10. Nineteenth-century Tithe Survey land use patterns for all four parishes

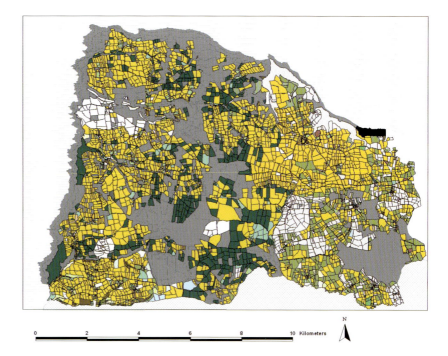

FIGURE 4.11. Landownership pattern for Hartland Parish

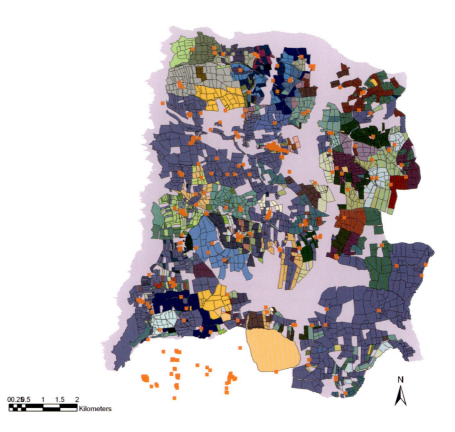

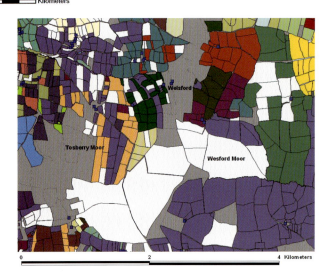

FIGURE 4.12. Land use
pattern for Hartland
Parish

FIGURE 4.13. Field
systems around the
settlement of Welsford in
the parish of Hartland

marker for the Harton estate) is also a possible indicator of the land use in this part of the landscape. The Assize Roll of 1299 lists the name as *Rosdone* which PND suggest is a hybrid name with a first element that is Cornish, meaning moor or wasteland (1931, 75) and many of the field-names also allude to this with reference to moors or rough ground.

TABLE 4.2. Division of land holding in Harton, as listed in the IPM for Oliver Dynham dated to 1298.

	free tenant	burgesses	villeins	farmers	Total
1 acre	1	-	-	-	1
3 furlongs	20	-	-	-	20
2 furlongs	22	-	-	-	22
1 furlong	17	-	-	-	17
1 1/4 furlong	1	-	-	-	1
1/2 furlong	-	-	100	-	100
1/3 furlong	-	-	22	-	22
1/4 furlong	-	-	17	-	17
a burgage	-	13	-	-	13
farmers	-	-	-	20	20
Total	61	13	139	20	233

The IPM for Oliver Dynham, dated to 1298, also lists the number of free tenants, burgesses, villains and farmers holding lands within the Harton Manor, as shown in table 4.2. It can be seen that 233 people within the manor of Hartland are recorded in the IPM as paying rent to Oliver Dynham at this time. As mentioned in Chapter One, the term 'furlong' in this period referred to a group of furrows running parallel to each other, rather than a length, so the division of the distribution of land through each of the four categories provides an interesting suggestion of how the estate was divided during the thirteenth century. Free Tenants hold the largest portions of land (between 1 acre and 1¼ furlongs), with the Villains holding between half and a quarter of a furlong. The separate category of farmer is interesting as it suggests a distinction between free tenants, villains and farmers.

Moving away from the Hartland estate, there is evidence for a possible open field system around Welsford in Hartland parish (SMR SS225SE/69). Welsford is a small hamlet situated between Tosberry and Welsford Moors. The area of possible former open field is situated to the east of the settlement, indicated in the historic landscape as a series of dog-legged boundaries representing the extent of former furlongs (Fig. 4.13). These fields have encroached upon Welsford Moor which remains unenclosed. The tithe landownership for the area is interesting because the area around the manor is owned by Lewis William Buck esq. (who also owned the majority of the land within Hartland on the Tithe Survey) and Sir James Hamlyn William, the lord of the estate of Clovelly. From the proximity of Welsford to Clovelly it can be seen that the ownership of land crosses over the parish boundary (see Fig. 4.11).

Tosberry Moor experienced a different fate, and it is clear that there are a number of straight surveyed fields running against the contours up the side of the slope. This is mirrored on the Tithe Map of 1842 which shows the land divided into a number of smaller fields within these strips. The ownership here seems to be divided between two owners; Lewis William Buck and John Pillman (as can be seen in Fig. 4.13). Again the fields associated with the settlement of Tosberry encroach into the moor, showing an earlier phase of enclosure activity, and show an irregular pattern that could be associated with an open field strip system. The topography for both Welsford and Tosberry is undulating, creating a number of hilltops and valleys ranging from between 170 and 210 m. The soil here is also relatively poor draining and susceptible to waterlogging after ploughing, indicating why enclosure occurred at such a late date on the moors.

To the south of Tosberry is the unenclosed Bursdon Moor. Pearse Chope's (1902b, map 5) map of the Hartland manorial lands lists Bursdon as holding two free tenants' holdings. Gelling indicates that there are a number of place-names in the parish of Hartland with the suffix -don, which she suggests derives from the OE *dūn*, meaning Hill (2000, 141, 148). The Tithe shows that many of the field-names indicate some sort of reclamation from the moor, and marsh; Newfoundland (TA 3147) for example is typical of this (Field 1993, 81).

As the examples suggest, Parliamentary Enclosure is not as visible in the Hartland Moors study area as in the Blackdown Hills. The nearest known example is Parkham Ash in Parkham parish, lying on the border of Woolfardisworthy. It is known that the Parkham Ash area was subject to Parliamentary Enclosure in 1850 (SMR SS32SE/40). This hamlet lies on an upland scarp of 175 m, and thus is typical of the late enclosure of moorland and upland areas which occurred in the nineteenth century.

A notable fate on the uplands in the Hartland Moors study area is the combining of land. Fox (1989, 50) notes that there is evidence of attachment of land to other hamlets causing a decline in a settlement. In particular this was thought to have occurred at Hendon, which was taken by a farmer in the settlement of Netherton further to the north of the parish so that the moorland could be used for pasturing cattle, maximising the resources which the area had to offer.

It needs to be established whether the extension of already existing holdings have an archaeological effect on the landscape, as visible in the associated fields, settlements and roads. The formation of field systems around the former Domesday holding of Ashmanworthy and farmstead of Dipple [first listed as a personal name in the lay subsidies of 1330s] again shows evidence of strips and the amalgamation of a number of convertible husbandry or Lay field strips. In addition to this, Hoskins (1943, 80) considers the enclosure of the waste in the 276 years between 1566 and the Tithe Map survey of 1842, and discusses that the lay manor added land to existing farms rather than creating new properties. Table 5.2 shows the amount of land attached to farms within Hartland in 1566 and 1842, and the increase in acreage added from enclosure of waste.

Three farms had a significant increase of 100 acres or more in the period between 1566 and the nineteenth-century Tithe Survey. Noticeable amongst these is Hendon (which experienced the greatest increase), which could be explained by the incorporation with Netherton which Fox identified. Seckington is noteworthy as it is situated in the centre of large enclosed fields bounded on two sides by rivers; Clifford Water to the east, and Seckington Water on the south-western side, and on its northern side by the modern A29(T). Interestingly there are a number of dog-legged fields to the west of Stitworthy Farm (now in Woolfardisworthy), suggesting a former strip system in operation here, also confirmed by aerial photographs. The air photograph shows evidence of a number of removed field boundaries, all of which were recorded on the Tithe Survey. This shows that this strip system continued until modern farming processes make the field formation redundant. The formation of the field boundaries form a number of discrete blocks and could imply the amalgamation of a number of other properties. As mentioned above, within this parish, landownership is not helpful thanks to the dominance of Sir James William Bart, but the land occupier may be of more use. Here four names are listed (Thomas Hamlyn, John Downing, William Claverdon and Thomas Chang) distributed in a more irregular pattern, mirroring a former strip system which has seen the amalgamation of strips.

As mentioned above, probable medieval open field (or possible lynchets) are also recorded at South Hole in Hartland on the western coast (SMR SS21NW/507), having been retained in the modern field boundaries. Here a number of strips are present within the Tithe Survey, with the ownership alternating predominately between John Colwell, Henry Adams, and Lewis William Buck (Fig. 4.14). Interestingly (and perhaps evidence of separate structures occurring) different patterns of ownership can be seen at Hardisworthy and Milford to the north, although they show similar field patterns. South Hole was a Domesday holding, and from this entry it can be identified that Saewin held this farmstead before 1066. Thus, the occupation of the site itself had a long antiquity, which provides an interesting backdrop to the field systems recorded here. Four defined lynchets are evident along the eastern slope overlooking the settlement. This is a steep slope which rises to the cliffs at Gull Rock and Broadbench Cove, and through analysis of the topography along it, it can be seen why the preservation of such regimes can be found here. The Tithe Survey Apportionment indicates a predominance of arable within the strips, with arable and coarse pasture recorded on the commons at the cliff edge. It has already been established that cereal was grown on the cliff edges when there was the need or demand, but its occurrence on such a large scale suggests that what is occurring, at least in some cases, is the instance of convertible or ley husbandry.

Furthermore, the former manor of Milford, situated on the western coast of Hartland, also provides a good example of a distinct estate setup. The boundaries of this hamlet are delimited by watercourses, and a well and a spring are located at the edge of the settlement. By overlaying the patterns of fields as seen on the tithe map onto the historic landscape a number of blocks divided into strips can be seen (see Fig. 4.14). These fields have sinuous inverse S-shaped boundaries divided into furlong blocks. The headlands formed through ploughing these strips create what is now the boundary between

Milford Common (which is situated on the cliff edge) and the fields. The landownership here is listed as John Haynes esq., Richard Dennis, William Caller Senor, and again Lewis William Buck. The common associated with the settlement is held separately by Anne Morrison and others, who hold most of the land around the farm of Ackworthy, across the river to the east. This may reveal that even though the common is attached to the estate of Milford, others held the rights to it.

Hoskins (1952a, 314 n2) suggests open fields occurred at Brownsham, Exmansworthy, Long Furlong, Pitt, Blegberry, and around the settlement of Hartland. Within Hartland it is clear from the Tithe Survey that there are a number of areas which may have experienced an open field type structure which later became enclosed. This is particularly clear from the Apportionment lists of landowners, which show the dispersal of ownership through the strips, mirroring the pattern seen in Awliscombe and Buckerell. This is particularly evident within the Milford, Elmcott and Hartisworthy area on the western coast of Hartland, and Hennaford in Welcombe and Bucks Mill in Woolfardisworthy (see below).

As discussed previously, the Tithe Survey landownership patterns in Clovelly parish are vastly different to its neighbours, as it is dominated by one owner: Sir James Hamlyn Williams (Fig. 4.15). This is similar to the pattern seen in Combe Raleigh in the Blackdown Hills, where it reflected the dominance of one manor. This could also be argued for Clovelly. In terms of field patterns, Clovelly is more similar to its neighbour Hartland. Like those seen at Milford in Hartland, in Clovelly the fields positioned on the northern coast are large and generally rectilinear in shape, cutting across the contours and edge of the steep cliffs (and in later years the Hobby Drive[3]). The same configuration can be seen around Embury Beacon and Welcombe Mouth on the western coast, but within Hartland they are generally smaller, and at times (such as at Brownsham on the northern coast) nearly strip like. The remnants of former organisation of these fields occur through the land ownership seen in the Tithe Survey, with a number of individually owned fields forming the former strips. In terms of land use, Clovelly as a whole is recorded as being predominantly arable within the tithe, with woodland and timber plantation and some pasture found towards the coast and with rushy pasture along the Clovelly/Woolfardisworthy border where Clifford Water runs through (Fig. 4.16).

Welcombe lies to the south of Hartland and displays a pattern of landownership similar to its neighbour. As mentioned above, it is thought that Welcombe was once part of Harton estate, and this may explain the similarities between the two parishes. Land use patterns are also similar. In Welcombe, 352 fields are listed as arable (not counting those fields which are listed with a joint land use such as arable and pasture), some 54 per cent of the total land use for the parish (Fig. 4.17). Pasture only takes up 12 per cent, which includes fields listed as meadows (no separate distinction is made). From the field-name evidence derived from the Welcombe tithe apportionment for the strips around the fifteenth-century hamlet Upcott there are frequent references to higher or lower lands, and to their contemporary land use of waste and marsh.

Hollacombe is situated in Welcombe on the boundary between that parish and Hartland. This farmstead is on the boundary of Hendon that Pearse Chope (1902, map 2) suggests was part of the Demesne and Barton land of the manor of Hartland, and could indicate the farm's possible use within the estate. There is a reference to Walter de Holecomb in the 1332 lay subsidy, but it is possible that the name of the person came from the settlement rather than the other way round as the PND suggests (1931, 80). The name is probably derived from the OE *holh cumb* or Hollow valley. This corresponds with the farmstead's positioning as it lies on the slopes of a valley.

As a parish, Woolfardisworthy shows discontinuity with the other three parishes, and this is because of the nature of its field patterns. Nevertheless, there is some similarity between Woolfardisworthy's distribution of Tithe Survey landowners and Hartland and Welcombe (Fig. 4.18). This is significant; here fields are in small, fairly regular strip-like formation, only differing towards the coast near Bucks Mill, reflecting that the arable was held in sub-divided fields (Fig. 4.19) (Astill 1988b, 81). The small blocks represent the relative poor quality of the soil, allowing for crops to be divided over a number of fields in order to maximise yield. The change of field patterns at the cliffs continues the same coastal trends in field patterns at Clovelly.

The arrangement at Bucks Mill is interesting, as it suggests an open field type of field pattern associated with a nucleated settlement (see below), and mirrors the trend for nucleated settlements and strip fields seen on the western coast in Hartland. This may illustrate the cohesion of people and skills occurring in these coastal hamlets.

Summary

From its field patterns it can be seen that as a whole the Hartland Moors study area is characterised by a number of distinct features. Inland, fields are generally smaller and irregular. In comparison with the coastal areas, two forms of field pattern emerge. Around Bideford Bay the fields are larger and more regular in layout and shape. Along the Atlantic and the north-western coast, and generally associated with the mouths of rivers, the fields are small and strip-like.

On the uplands it is important to recognise the dominance of moorland, much of which was enclosed late in the post-medieval period, during the late eighteenth and nineteenth centuries, with some evidence of Parliamentary Enclosure. These can be identified by their regular field pattern, which are juxtaposed to the earlier patchwork of encroachment occurring in relation to settlements. As a whole, looking at the Tithe Survey, Hartland Parish shows far greater evidence for fragmentary ownership than neighbouring Clovelly, but shares this patterning with Welcombe. The land use shows a predominance of arable and coarse pasture, with some meadow. Furthermore,

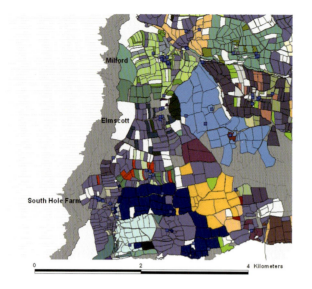

FIGURE 4.14. Strip
fields surrounding the
settlement of South
Hole, and also the
settlements of Elmscott
and Milford in the parish
of Hartland

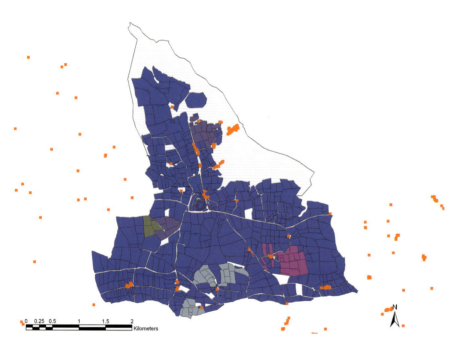

FIGURE 4.15.
Landownership pattern
for Clovelly Parish

the Tithe Apportioment indicates the practice of convertible or ley husbandry
through a number of the entries referring to 'Arable occasionally' or 'Arable
and occasionally …' It is also possible for this type of agricultural practice to
occur within the open fields, before the enclosure of the strips recorded in the
Tithe Survey.

FIGURE 4.16. Land use
pattern for Clovelly
Parish

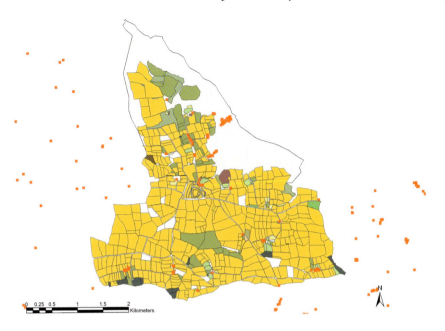

FIGURE 4.16. Land use
pattern for Clovelly
Parish

Field-names

In light of the patterns of field morphology seen in the nineteenth-century
historic landscape in Hartland Moors, it is now valid to discuss these patterns
in relation to their field-names. As figure 4.20 shows, the occurrence of acre
field-names is less common in the Hartland Moors study area, with an average
of just under 4 per cent of the total number of digitised fields containing such
an element (see Table 6.7).

In comparison, within the Hartland Moors study area, 12 per cent of the
fields digitised contained the park element within their field-names (Fig. 4.21).
These fields occur on the steep hill slopes, but not on the hill tops or on areas
of moor. This can be seen particularly in Clovelly, the parish with the highest
concentration of park field-names within the Hartland Moors study area. The
concentration of park field-names around the settlement of Brownsham to the
north of Hartland parish highlights the distinct S-shaped fields located to the
east of the dwellings. The occurrence of Oven Park within the Brownsham fields
may further confirm the process of later enclosure in this area. The inclusion
of oven in field-names is suggested to derive from the OE *ofniman* meaning
'to seize', and can signify land removed from regulated common-field systems
and let for rent, usually as pasture (Field 1993, 18).

The practice of land being removed from common or moorland is interesting,
and the distribution of moor field-names in the Hartland Moors study area
ignores parish boundaries, giving an indication of the extent of pre-enclosure
moorland in this area of north Devon (Fig. 4.22). Occurring in nearly 10 per
cent of the total digitised fields in the study area, these moor names are most

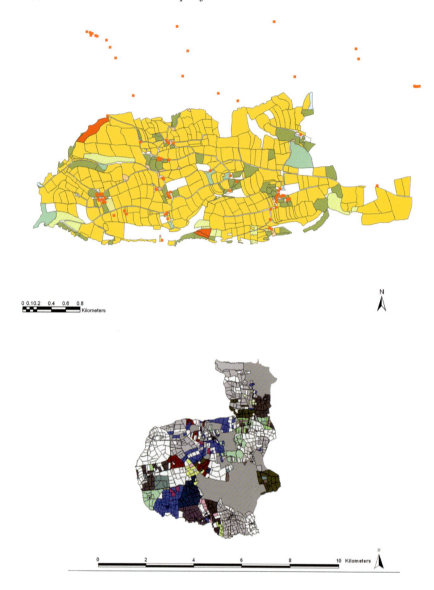

FIGURE 4.17. Land use pattern for Welcombe Parish

FIGURE 4.18. Landownership pattern for Woolfardisworthy Parish

predominant in the parishes of Woolfardisworthy and Clovelly (Table 6.3). This is distinctly apparent around Hendon Moor to the south of Hartland parish where the adjacent fields in Welcombe parish contain the moor element within their field-names, and this also disrespects roadways which cross them. The occurrence of moor field-names in the parallel bounded strip fields directly to the east of Bursdon Moor, also in Hartland parish, also confirms the encroachment onto the more 'marginal' land.

The final element is that of mead field-names, which, as in the Blackdown Hills, occur along the river valleys in the more fertile alluvium which occurs there (Fig. 4.23).

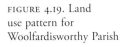

FIGURE 4.19. Land
use pattern for
Woolfardisworthy Parish

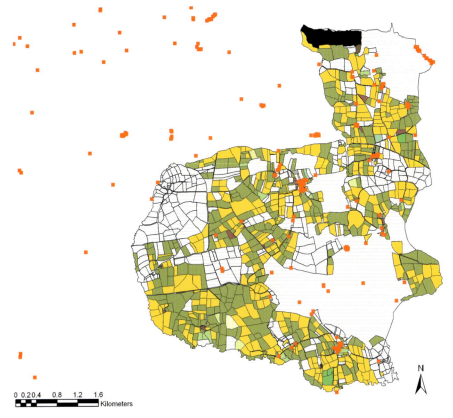

FIGURE 4.20.
Distribution of field-
names which contain
acre elements

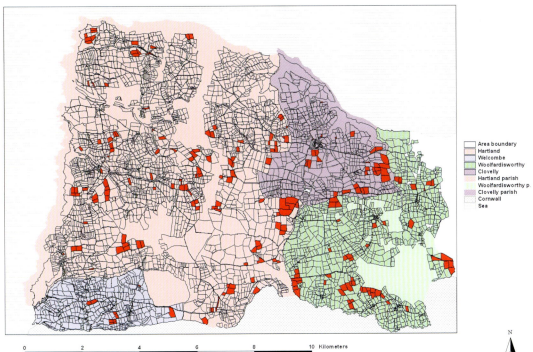

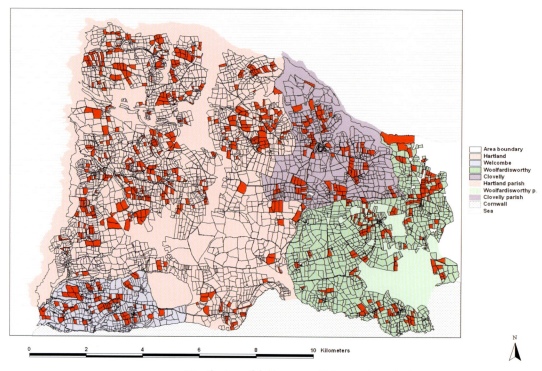

FIGURE 4.21. Distribution of field-names which contain park elements

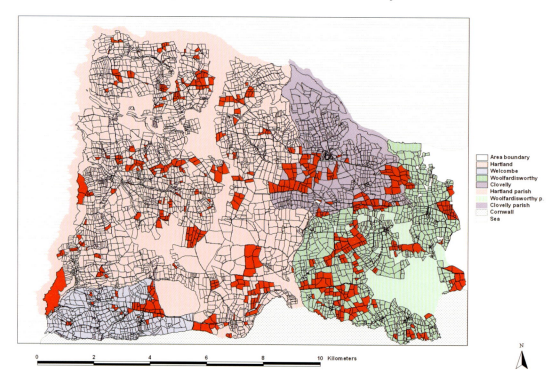

FIGURE 4.22. Distribution of field-names which contain moor elements

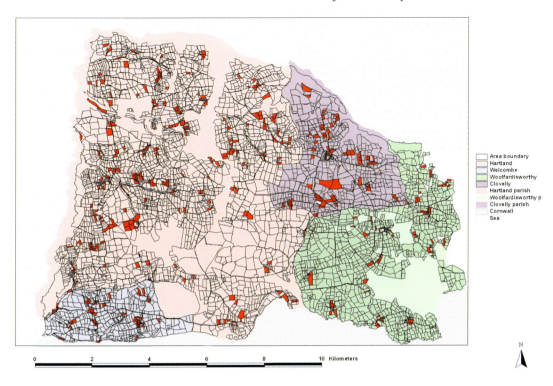

FIGURE 4.23. Distribution
of field-names which
contain mead elements

Settlement

When describing the landscape of this area, Warden Page (1895, 160) mentions
the lack of individual dwellings outside of the main settlements such as
Hartland itself (or indeed the smaller hamlets) stating that only a few occurred
along the Hartland Road which linked the villages of Clovelly and Hartland
together. Figure 4.24 shows the distribution of settlement at the time of the
Tithe Survey. Hoskins (1952a, 290) states the 'village' of Hartland is an example
of a 'Midlands' style settlement with related open field systems organised
by a central lord. This is different to what we saw in Chapter Three as the
Blackdown Hills were blanketed in individual farmsteads and small hamlets,
with 'nucleated' settlements predominately in the southern half of the study
area. However, it was also noted that even though the so-called 'big village
set-ups'[4] could be found in Hartland (along with the South Hams, especially
in Modbury, see Chapter Five) it was comparably rare in contrast with single
farmsteads and hamlets (Hoskins 1959, 30). Interestingly, in relation to the
other study areas, Fox (1983, 40) argues that any such nucleation occurs
around the former manor of the Dynham lords. It is clear to see that the
presence of the Dynhams in Hartland created cohesion of settlement, and
this is a significant factor. However, as mentioned previously there were other
factors at work within the region and there were a number of smaller manorial
holdings operating outside the Dynham estate. This pattern is mirrored in the

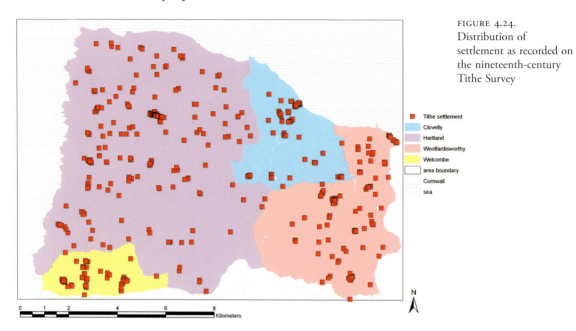

FIGURE 4.24.
Distribution of
settlement as recorded on
the nineteenth-century
Tithe Survey

■ Tithe settlement
  Clovelly
  Hartland
  Woolfardisworthy
  Welcombe
  area boundary
  Cornwall
  sea

FIGURE 4.25. The
nucleated village of
Clovelly

TABLE 4.3. Table showing the increase in farm size through enclosure in Hartland (After Hoskins 1943, 80)

Farm	Area in Acres		
	1566	1842	increase
Brownsham	69.25	171	101.75
Farford	47.5	147	99.50
Gawlish	44.75	68	23.25
Hescott	61.5	120	58.50
Mettaford	64.5	122.5	58.00
Sutterland	40	99	59.00
Moor	46	74	28.00
Beckland	37.5	67	29.50
Blegberry	97.75	166	68.25
Bremlidge	46	75	29.00
Thorne	46	83	37.00
Lower Velly	29.75	50	20.25
Butterbury	119	213	94.00
Hendon	210	366	156.00
Seckington	200	328	128.00

evidence seen through the study of the nineteenth-century historic landscape. The information gained from the Tithe Survey points to this patterning of settlement, as can be seen on the western coast of Hartland, and also at Bucks Mill and Clovelly (Fig. 4.25).

The fields around South Hole, Hartisworthy and Milford indicate a separate estate structure, and the settlements themselves could be described as nucleated, with holdings positioned around a central enclosure. However, these are merely hamlets consisting of a few dwellings dotted along the eastern coast. Thus, aside from the Dynham holding, the Hartland Moors area shows signs of a settlement arrangement that remains dispersed, with widely spaced hamlets (generally of two or three farms) (Fox 1983, 40), and isolated farmsteads only along the access road. The settlement of Seckington was formally part of the Hartland Abbey estate (Youing 1955, 17), and its role as a separate entity within a larger estate may go some way in explaining the layout of the field systems discussed previously. It was thought that this settlement could be described as a village (in the Devon sense of the word, again see Chapter One), and that it had almost completely disappeared by the second half of the eighteenth century (Hoskins 1940, 11).

The arrangement of settlements explains the increase in acreage in agriculture shown in table 4.3 and the arrangement of the fields into small discrete units corresponding with these former holdings. This contraction of settlement was a common occurrence within the Hartland Moors area. Fox (1989, 50) discusses the Accession Rolls for the Duchy of Cornwall dating to 1365 for Hartland, which suggest a 'wrecked landscape', and that folk-memory indicates the existence of a hamlet at Hendon moor from the rhyme 'Yennon [Hendon] was

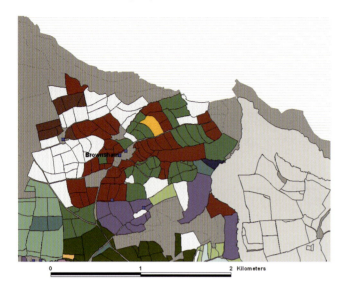

FIGURE 4.26. Settlement of Brownsham in Hartland parish and related fields showing Tithe Survey landownership

a market town when Lunnon [London] was a furzy down'. However, caution must always be taken when discussing folk stories as the rhyme, or variations of it, has been attributed to a number of former settlements throughout Devon. Nevertheless, the Accession Rolls indicate that five of the farmsteads within Hendon were deserted and by the mid- eighteenth century had reverted again to moorland again (Fox 1983, 41). Further to this, the settlement of Brownsham which once contained 14 farms contained only eight dwellings, with many holdings added together (Fig. 4.26). There was also the total abandonment of the hamlet of Youlden (Fox, 1989 50), which again explains the 101 acre increase in land between 1566 and the Tithe Survey.

Interestingly, though perhaps coincidently, this contraction and abandonment of settlement corresponds with a movement from the inland areas to the coasts in the fourteenth and fifteenth centuries. The court rolls indicate that there was a movement of villeins from Hartland to the parish of Northam, which contains the port of Appledore (Hartland account of 6–7 Hen IV in Fox 2001, 162). This movement to the coast is considerably earlier than the creation of the quays at Hartland and Clovelly which were not constructed until the late sixteenth century (*ibid.* 2001, 16) (Fig. 4.27). However, it is known that after the construction of the quay at Hartland in the sixteenth century other buildings quickly followed (Fox 2001, 17), creating a settlement (if perhaps seasonal) at the coast. It is also known that in recent history many families moved from their dwellings to one farm. For example, at Gawlish in Hartland at one point 32 families were living at the farm (*pers comm* Steve Hobbs Harton Town Trust). Thus, the number of farms recorded is reduced, but the same amount of people are still present. A similar inland to coastal shift can be suggested in the South Hams region of Devon, and will be discussed in the next chapter, but it is useful to refer to such a transition here. With this movement we do not see the creation of fishing villages and cellar settlements like those that can be

FIGURE 4.27. (opposite page) The late sixteenth-century quay at Clovelly and the remains of the late sixteenth-century quay at Hartland, destroyed in a storm

seen on the southern coast of Devon. However, the evolution of Clovelly and Bucks Mills in Woolfardisworthy to their present state must be attributed to the need for access to the sea. Bucks Mill is a nucleated settlement with related strip fields, and was divided into two authoritative units, and this division may have occurred as a result of a need for access to the sea and other manufacturing resources.

Caution needs to be taken however, when comparing the earlier work of Hoskins and that of Fox. As shown in table 4.3, there was an increase of 156 acres at Hendon between 1566 and 1822, which on its own suggests that the idea of a wrecked landscape are not as simple as first thought. The increase relates to the reduction in the number of farmsteads causing amalgamation of a number of land units into one. Thus, a simultaneous contraction in one sector of the rural landscape causes a continued growth in another, resulting in a distorted image of what is really happening in these areas. The landscapes are not wrecked in the true sense of the word, merely managed in a different formation; populations are moving to exploit other industries within the region.

Another influence in the siting of settlement in the region may be gleaned through the establishment of the religious buildings in the landscape. Records dating to 1400 list 14 chapels that were licensed for the Celebration of the Divine Service by Bishop Stafford (Table 4.4). Pearse Chope (1902a, 21) doubted the existence of some of these chapels, although archaeologically there are tangible links to individual sites. Despite surviving evidence for these medieval chapels being scarce, their approximate location is recorded, which reveals an interesting distribution. By looking at the associated field patterns, and using

TABLE 4.4: Chapels dedicated by Bishop Stafford in 1400 (after Pearse Chope 1902a)

Name	Location	Parish	Archaeological Evidence	Existence doubted by Pearse Chope
St. Mary	Fire Beacon	Hartland		No
Holy Cross	Clifford & South Hole	Hartland		No
St James	Exmansworthy	Hartland		No
St Wenna	Cheristow	Hartland		No
St James	Milford	Hartland		No
St Clare	Philham	Hartland	St Clare's well with image of saint at back	Yes
St James	Velly	Hartland	Field Names	Yes?
Holy Cross	Clifford	Woolfardisworthy		Yes
St Leonard	St Leonard's	Hartland	Remains	No
St Clare?	Galosh	Hartland		Yes
St Michael	Kerbstone	Hartland		Yes
St Martin	Mendon	Hartland		No
St John	Long Furlong	Hartland	Rumour that Piscina is in Morwenstow	Yes?
St Anthony/Andrew?	Harton	Hartland	Fields names/St. Andrew's Well	Yes?

the morphology of other surviving settlements in the parish, it is possible to conjecture that these chapels are not isolated churches but were associated with hamlets that are now, at most, one or two farms.

Milford again provides a clear example of this, and it is known that there was an early medieval chapel listed at South Hole, suggesting a link with the settlement and field systems discussed above. As can be seen, all but one of these chapels are within what is now Hartland parish, with only Holy Cross at Clifford (now in Woolfardisworthy) deviating from this. Furthermore, the occurrence of a dedication to St. Wenna at Cheristow is interesting, as St. Wenna is the Cornish version of the English and Welsh St. Gwen, and is generally an early dedication, suggesting that there was early activity at this site. It is important to try and establish whether these ecclesiastical sites became foci within the landscape, and if they were constructed over existing focal sites.

Roads and droveways

As mentioned earlier, Warden Page (1895, 160) suggested that settlements were related to the main Hartland Road. The nucleation of settlement and occurrence of later enclosed moorland has affected the layout of the routeways in the Hartland Moors study area. The roads and tracks located on the Tithe Survey take an irregular form, cutting across the moorlands. The field pattern respects the line of the roads and adjoins them. It would appear that these fields were enclosed after the creation of the roads, infilling between them in small blocks, and Gregory (1950, v) suggests that the region was made more remote by the poor condition of these roads and tracks.

Droveways are particularly common within the Hartland Moors area indicating the pastoral economy known to be prevalent in the medieval period. Droves can be seen in the hamlet of Tredown in Hartland. The field listed in the nineteenth century in the Tithe Survey as the Common (343TA), shows evidence of a former droveway leading to a second area of common in this hamlet. Through oral history it is known that drovers came from Parkham, Holsworthy, Bradworthy, Stibb Cross and Torrington, driving the cattle to and from the sheep fair at Barnstable 'as far as they needed to be taken' (Shakespeare 1990, 56).

Evidence of industry

As discussed above, it is thought that the Hartland Moors area had a mixed economy in terms of agriculture, and in the later period incorporated fishing. Prior to the sixteenth century, pastoral farming (particularly fattening and dairying of cattle) would have made up a significant part of area's economy, as the droveways bear witness to. There was also a movement to the coast in the fourteenth and fifteenth centuries, and this can be seen as a move to alternative forms of employment, namely fishing and other coastal activities. The results

Parishes	Agriculture		Manufacture		All other people		Total	
Clovella	226	32%	133	19%	355	50%	714	100%
Hartland	363	23%	80	5%	1103	71%	1546	100%
Welcome	214	97%	6	3%	0	0%	220	100%
Woolfardisworthy	364	62%	23	4%	204	35%	591	100%

of this can be seen at the beginning of the nineteenth century in Hartland and Clovelly, when over half of the population were active in forms of employment other than agriculture and manufacture (see Table 4.5 and Chart 4.1). Thus, it can clearly be seen that in Clovelly and Hartland the ports were crucial parts of the economic structure, with fishing and trade being the prime monetary provider. Despite the number of people involved in the industry and the fact that in 1895 Clovelly was described as a 'great herring port' (Warden Page 1895, 152), there is evidence that in previous years this had not been the case. The vicar of Clovelly recorded a 'great fishery' in the 1740 parish records after many years of previous failure. His celebrations were short lived however, as he was to record in the six subsequent years a marked downturn in catches, after which he gave up recording the plight of the industry (Dickenson 1987, 57 in Fox 2001, 150). Along the same stretch of coastline the manor of Bucks (which later became the hamlet of Bucks Mill) also made fishing its main industry. As

TABLE 4.5: Table showing the percentage of population working in agriculture, manufacturing and other forms of employment in 1801 (after Vancouver: 1808, 405–409)

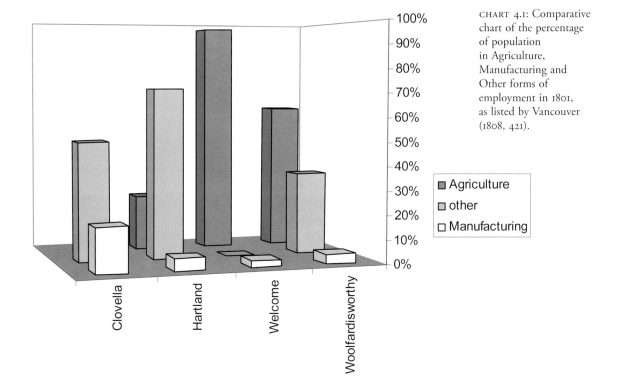

CHART 4.1: Comparative chart of the percentage of population in Agriculture, Manufacturing and Other forms of employment in 1801, as listed by Vancouver (1808, 421).

the only part of Woolfardisworthy parish which was at the coast this use of the resource is perhaps not surprising.

As a whole, Woolfardisworthy and also Welcombe parish are listed as having large scale agricultural employment in the nineteenth century, with 97 per cent of the working population employed in agriculture. This reflects the nature of the field pattern in Woolfardisworthy, as this was generally a mixed farming area.

This provides an interesting dichotomy between the parishes, in terms of use of the landscape in the medieval period. The high levels of employment in agriculture in Welcombe must be related to the location of the parish, and may in turn indicate the area's importance in the setup of the Harton Manor during the medieval period. Its more sheltered position in the river valley in combination with the soil structure, allows for an agricultural based economy to thrive compared to its exposed coastal neighbours. Even though Woolfardisworthy has relatively poor soil, its inland location and the maximisation of resources meant that the trend occurring in Welcombe was also the case within this parish, with other employment deriving from being accessible to the coast at Bucks Mill as mentioned above.

As previously discussed, other manufacturing resources were important within the study area and may have affected the estate and settlement structure. There is evidence of a number of lime kilns recorded (undoubtedly because of the region's coastal position for ease of access to raw material). Additionally, at Bucks Mill there were kilns related to the mill, with an associated quay and slipway that cut through the rocky coastline called The Gut used for landing the limestone (SMR SS32SE/55).

Concluding remarks

From the nineteenth-century landscape it can be seen that the Hartland Moors study area shares elements with the Blackdown Hills, in particular, the nature of the small nucleated hamlets and associated field systems. However, it can be suggested through the study of the historic landscape that the development of this area during the medieval period was distinctly different than that which occurred in the Blackdown Hills region of east Devon. The manner in which the moor was enclosed is an obvious difference, as is the lack of individual farmsteads. The dominance of the Harton manorial estate must be a factor in this, and this link between landholding and the historic landscape needs to be investigated in more depth. As such, the final study area, the South Hams, must now be considered in light of the analysis of the Blackdown Hills and Hartland Moors regions, with particular reference to the similarities and dissimilarities seen in the previous two chapters.

Notes

1   A Dane who was shipwrecked on the Hartland coast and caused trouble in the area

2   In the sixth century Saint Nectan moved to Hartland. Legend tells the henchmen of the Chieftain of Clovelly Dykes beheaded Nectan, and that he walked a mile back to the spring where he was a hermit holding his head, permanently staining the rock he placed it on (Burton 1953, 156).

3   Sir James Hamlyn Williams constructed this carriage road along the coast from Bucks Mill to Clovelly between 1811 and 1829 and is thought to be so called as it was Sir James' hobby.

4   See Chapters One and Five for a explanation of this settlement type.

CHAPTER FIVE

'A Desired Possession…'
– The South Hams

Introduction to the South Hams

In the preceding two chapters it was seen through the study of the historic landscape that there are similarities between the nucleated hamlets in the southern half of the Blackdowns and those occurring on the western coast of Hartland and at Bucks Mill in Woolfardisworthy. However, it is also clear that patterns of landownership, the nature of landscape enclosure and development during the medieval and post-medieval periods varied significantly between the two regions. Therefore, to serve as a comparison to the Blackdown Hills and Hartland Moors a third, smaller, case study is to be considered. The region of the South Hams was chosen from the five areas outlined by the CLP. The South Hams region comprises the lowland area to the south of Dartmoor, spanning from Torquay in the east to Plymouth and the boundary with Cornwall to the west. As with the other two case studies, an area comprising only a small part of the South Hams will be highlighted for study. This is to gain a representative sample of the region as a whole.

Climatically, the South Hams is milder than any other part of England. The combination of this, a moderate topography, and well-drained soils has allowed for a high proportion of good quality pasture (Vancouver 1808, 8–9; Shorter *et al.* 1969, 253). For example, the mix of coastal and estuarine environments in the South Hams provides a complex structure to the landscape, with the region divided by dissecting valleys and watercourses allowing for a diversification of land use. The eleventh-century Domesday survey suggests relatively intensive cereal cultivation from the number of plough teams listed for the holdings within the South Hams. This will be discussed later, but it is interesting that later commentators suggest a landscape which is more pastoral. Shorter *et al.* (1969, 253), for example, observe that the steep valley sides were traditionally left in permanent pasture or covered by woods, with arable cultivation occurring on the rounded slopes, and considerable tracts of the valley floor undergoing reclamation for meadow. Modern cultivation techniques however have allowed for arable growth on the steeper slopes.

H. Rider Haggard, writing in the early twentieth century, describes the landscape of south Devon, stating that '…the enclosures are small also, giving the idea that here the land is valuable, a desired possession, and surrounded, each of them, by straggling banks of stone and earth, in which grow tall straggling hedges' (Rider Haggard 1902, 175–6). During the sixteenth century, the South

Hams region was the second most densely populated region in Devon, with the highest mean assessment per head outside of the City of Exeter (Kew 1969, 32–3). Much of the area's wealth was a result of flourishing Totnes, but also the rich and fertile red sandstone led to a thriving land market (Kew 1969, 33).

Introduction to the South Hams study area

The sample area chosen for study focuses around the estuary of the river Avon. The river is also known as the Devonshire Avon, or by its earlier name, the river Aune (Fig. 5.1). As this study area is to act as a comparison, rather than digitising the Tithe Survey for entire parishes selected, areas have been chosen to answer specific questions.

Within this study area four parishes have been chosen for further study in order to get a representational picture of the area as a whole. The study area is divided into two by the river Avon, with the parish of Bigbury on the western side, and Thurlestone (containing Bantham Ham, see below), Churchstow, and South Milton parishes on the east. These four parishes have been chosen to fulfil different roles.

The parishes of Bigbury and Thurlestone have been highlighted to elucidate whether there is any difference in the management and arrangement of the historic landscape between the two sides of the estuary. The Tithe Survey for both areas will be sampled in order to answer this question, and those raised

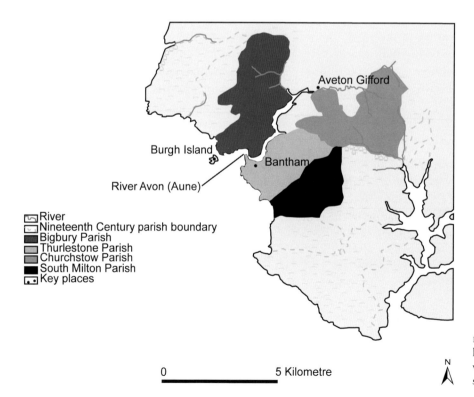

Key:
- River
- Nineteenth Century parish boundary
- Bigbury Parish
- Thurlestone Parish
- Churchstow Parish
- South Milton Parish
- Key places

0   5 Kilometre

N

FIGURE 5.1. Parishes highlighted for study within the South Hams study area

by the two earlier case studies. Churchstow has been highlighted in order to assess whether its inland position affects the nature of the evidence found there, and whether its link to the Abbey of Buckfast changes the nature of the historic landscape. This parish then provides the ideal comparison with those parishes within the Blackdowns and Hartland Moors which were influenced by Dunkeswell, Taunton, or Hartland Abbey. The parish of South Milton has also been chosen because of its coastal location, which is not influenced by the estuary. This is so comparisons can be made between it and the coastal parishes in the Hartland study area. Besides the four main areas the parishes of Loddiswell and Aveton Gifford will also be discussed to understand particular events or landscape management structures.

The topography of the South Hams study area slopes westwards from hilltops of 120 m, to the beaches along the coast. This area, like the Hartland Moors study area, is defined by a number of relatively steep cliff faces. Topographically the landscape is obviously influenced by the river Avon and the surrounding coastline which produces a series of sloping valleys. Turning to drainage, the valley in which Thurlestone is contained is bounded by two water courses, one being a brook which joins the sea at the small cove of Lea Foot Sand; the other the river Avon which ends at Bantham (Coupe 1920, 66). A number of small streams run from the settlements at Bigbury, South Milton and Thurlestone, where Buckland Stream divides the small settlements of West and East Buckland (a hamlet within the parish of Thurlestone), and feed into the Bigbury Bay. In turn, the small stream in Churchstow feeds the Kingsbridge Estuary. In terms of the solid and drift geology for the study area, blown sand is widespread along the coast, and this causes peat to develop on waterlogged moorland, as seen at Bantham Ham in Thurlestone (Edmonds *et al.* 1975, 81). This is particularly evident in the lowland areas of Thurlestone and South Milton where the river valleys meet the coast.

Introduction to the parishes

Within the South Hams parish sizes are generally more consistently regular in size than those which occur in the Blackdown Hills and Hartland Moors study areas. However, it can be seen from the Tithe Survey that there has been some fluctuation in the route of the boundaries, especially around the Bigbury area which has experienced a significant change in its borders over the last 160 years.

Recorded as *Bicheberie* in Domesday, Bigbury is thought to be taken from the OE for a stronghold of a man called Bica (Mills 1998, 37), although Hoskins (1954, 337) suggests it may have taken its name from *la Burgh* or Borough Island, a small island with a fifteenth-century chapel dedicated to St. Michael. The parish of Bigbury on the eastern side of the river Avon, was known locally for its fine sheep and barley, something which Polwhele (1793–1806, 465) attributes to the use of lime rather than sea-sand as manure, in contrast to neighbouring parishes. Indeed Polwhele (1793–1806, 465) describes the parish as having 'sixty eight farthings of land, each farthing consisting of 20 acres', and that Burgh Island contained 'about 10 acres [of] most excellent sheep pasture, which…has been tilled to great advantage'.

Across the river Avon lays the parish of Thurlestone. The earliest record for the name Thurlestone is recorded in King Æthelwulf's Charter of AD 847 as *ðyrelan stane or Thyrelanstane* (see Fig. 5.3), and is also recorded in Domesday as *Torlestan*. The parish is thought to take its name from the pierced (OE *thyrel*) stone located offshore (PND 1932, 312; Hoskins 1954, 494–5; Mills 1998, 346), which was used as a marker. As mentioned above, Thurlestone is located on the eastern side of the river Avon, and within the parish is the rock outcrop of Bantham Ham where there is evidence of an early medieval trading centre (see below). Situated as it is at the mouth of the Avon the place-name Bantham is descriptive, namely a dwelling place on the Bents (Fox 1953, 3). Bents are hardy perennial sea grasses which grow on the sand dunes which characterise this part of the south Devon coastline, and at Bantham such dunes rise to 15 m OD (Griffith and Reed 1998, 109).

Lying to the north of Thurlestone is the parish of Churchstow. The name Churchstow is not listed in Domesday, although a number of the estates which now lie within it were recorded. *Notone* (Norton), *Cumbe* (Combe Royal), *Lege* (Leigh) and *Surlei* (Sorley) are all listed in the Domesday survey. The first record of the name Churchstow occurs in the thirteenth century with the -stow suffix relating to the OE for assembly or holy place (Mills 1998, 406), and perhaps relates to the significance the Churchstow estate held in this area during the medieval period (see below). Polwhele (1793–1806, 468) provides us with a good description of the parish of Churchstow during the late eighteenth and early nineteenth centuries, stating that 'the grounds are all enclosed with hedges, planted with hazel, thorns, and various underwood'.

To the south-east of Thurlestone is the small parish of South Milton. Divided into two sections by a small spring and stream, South Milton faces the sea at Thurlestone Sands, a small stretch of sand surrounded by a series of rock outcrops; namely the Books and Thurlestone Rock. South Milton is named *Mideltone* in Domesday, and later Middleton, which was a common name relating to the middle farmstead or estate: OE *middletūn* (Mills 1998, 242). South Milton was held after the fourteenth century by the Carews, a family known from the Blackdown Hills, and prominent within Cornwall (Risdon 1811, 177).

Perception of landscape in the recent past

As discussed in Chapters Four and Five both Hartland and the Blackdown Hills had their fair share of myths and folklore attached to the landscape, and the South Hams is no exception. This is interesting as folklore is generally associated with (or surviving best in) more marginal areas.

Within the South Hams folk-beliefs that prevale into the present are mostly associated with pixies, witchcraft, the devil, and charms for curing illnesses. A good example is the fact that it was believed that the location of the present church in Thurlestone was thanks to pixies' intervention. The pixies are thought to have moved the church building materials from the original site at Channacombe Head to its present location in the town (Coupe 1920, 81). Grinsell (1937, 254) states that this phenomenon commonly indicates barrows on the intended site, and as will be discussed below, an earthwork with associated kitchen middens and hearths with occupation dating through the Iron Age, Romano-British and sub-Roman periods was found in the area. There are also flint scatters dating to the Mesolithic along the coast, and evidence of four bowl barrows (SMR SX64SE/10; /114; /98; /110) are present at Bantham Ham and along the coastline at Thurlestone. It is such relics that would allow stories to propagate of non-human groups living along the coast.

Because of the turbulent nature of the coastline, the wrecking of ships was frequent, especially before the construction of the Eddystone Lighthouse off Plymouth. It is recorded that until the early part of the twentieth century the 'wrecking' of these ships was a staple part of the local economy (Fox 1953, 4; Coupe 1920, 69). This is confirmed with a letter from a Dartmouth customs official in 1772 following the wreck of 300-ton ship in Bigbury Bay, describing the locals as 'barbarians' (Fox 1953, 4).

Previous archaeological research

Within the study area there has been a concentration of archaeological research, on Bantham Ham in Thurlestone (Fig. 5.2). Excavations in the 1950s by A. Fox (1955, 61) interpreted Bantham Ham as a trading site parallel with Tintagel in Cornwall. This is because of the presence of amphorae and soft-paste vessels. Later excavations undertaken in 1978 suggest that the fifth to seventh century AD saw temporary inhabitancy of the Bantham Ham (Silvester 1981, 112). The sheltered but short-lived camp site (with activity taking place on the exposed slope over the beach, and the marine resources supplying the staple diet with some hunting of red deer and hare) provided the ideal location for the Mediterranean traders to land. Further evidence of this is suggested by the presence of amphorae and other imported goods (Silvester 1981, 112–115).

Significantly, a principal issue raised from the research into faunal and marine remains during the 1978 excavations at Bantham is that the species represented within the samples largely reflect the various ecological zones which were available for exploitation in the post-Roman period (Silvester 1981, 114). This supports the documentary evidence. For example, the Exeter Domesday records that Bigbury manor held a salt-house (DB, 15,44), and also informs that salmon fishing on the river Avon was amongst the sources of revenue for the Manor of Loddiswell (DB, 17, 32; Fox 1953, 4).

In 1997, a second, smaller, excavation was undertaken at Bantham Ham

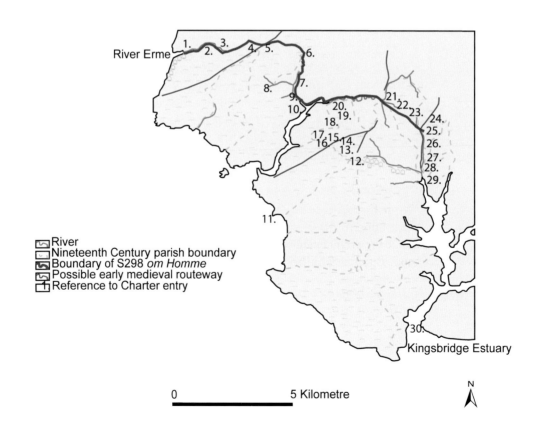

River Erme

River
Nineteenth Century parish boundary
Boundary of S298 *om Homme*
Possible early medieval routeway
Reference to Charter entry

Kingsbridge Estuary

0   5 Kilometre

N

FIGURE 5.2. Bantham
Ham from Burgh Island

ahead of the construction of a soakaway (Griffith and Reed 1998, 109). This small rescue excavation identified a roughly square enclosure comparable with other prehistoric or post-Romano-British enclosures found in the South-west (Griffith and Reed 1998, 124). Furthermore, the excavation supports earlier research at Bantham Ham that recovered a large volume of midden material alongside the enclosure, dating to the post-Roman period from about the fifth into the seventh or eighth centuries, and possibly into the medieval period (Griffith and Reed 1998, 125).

There has also been survey and excavation undertaken at Mount Folly in Bigbury-on-sea on two enclosures that were identified from aerial reconnaissance and geophysical survey (Wilkes 2004, 5). Although there were few artefacts recovered from the ditch fills, the pottery recovered from the 2003 excavation suggests that the enclosures were late Iron Age in date, although one sherd was early post-Roman in type (Wilkes 2004, 5).

It has been argued therefore, that in the sixth century Bantham Ham was a trading station, and this seasonal beach site drew trade with continental ships (Fox 2001, 9). This contact with the Mediterranean taking place at Bantham (and also areas such as Mothecombe further west along the coast. Sam Turner pers comm) around AD 500 and AD 700, can be indicated by the sherds of imported amphorae uncovered through excavation and coastal erosion (Burrow 1980, 66). Further archaeological evidence has been uncovered at Bantham that would indicate trade around the fifth and sixth centuries with France, Spain or Portugal (Fox 1955, 61–62). Imported early medieval amphorae, similar to the examples recovered from Tintagel, was uncovered from the eroded sand dunes, along with a bone comb, small iron spear-heads, and spindle whorls; there was also a later assemblage of pottery and bronze cooking vessels from the fourteenth and fifteenth centuries (*ibid.* 1955, 55–66).

Development and evolution of the South Hams landscape

Estate structure

We are fortunate that there are a number of charters relating to the South Hams area dating to the early medieval period that can provide us with information about the arrangement of land in the ninth and tenth centuries (Hooke 1990; 1994; Petter 1985). The first, mapped out in figure 5.3, is the South Hams (or *On Homme*) Charter s298, thought to have been drawn up in AD 847 during the reign of King Æthelwulf. The projected line of the charter boundary runs along the high ground, following a 100 m ridge from the river Erme to the Kingsbridge estuary, with the sea forming the southern boundary. Hooke (1990, 195, 198) suggests that the line follows the eastern boundary of the Manor of Combe Royal now located in the parish of Churchstow, and that the suggested area of the Clause also encompasses the required 20 hides of land, as listed in the document.

FIGURE 5.3. Early
medieval charter S298
om Homme, which
dates to the period of the
reign of King Æthelwulf
(Redrawing after Petter
1990, 195; 198)

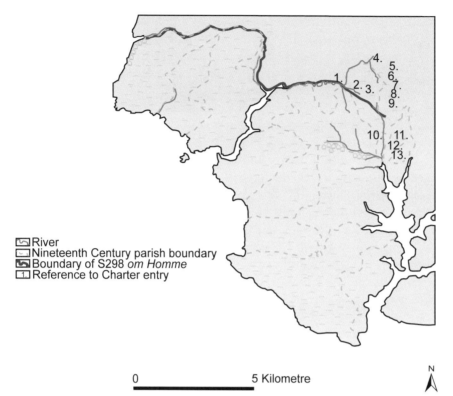

FIGURE 5.4. Early medieval charter S704 for Sorley an estate in South Hams (Redrawing after Hooke 1990, 199)

River
Nineteenth Century parish boundary
Boundary of S298 *om Homme*
Reference to Charter entry

0   5 Kilometre

N

The Sorley Charter is a later document, made as an accompaniment to a grant made by Edgar, and makes no reference to the earlier clause created by Æthelwulf (Hooke 1990, 198). It is thought that the Sorley boundary clause enclosed a greater area than the South Hams/*On Homme* Charter (Fig. 5.4), although excluding the northern half of the Sorley manor. Furthermore, whereas the charter of the South Hams or *Homme* used mainly natural features such as springs and valleys, the later clause used a number of archaeological features, many of which were barrows (Hooke 1990, 199). As can be seen, large areas of the nineteenth-century parish boundaries follow the projected line of the charters. As in the Blackdown Hills, this again suggests that elements within the historic landscape can be used to assist the determination of earlier landscape form.

As with the Hartland Moors and the Blackdown Hills, the Domesday survey provides the earliest comprehensive document source for the South Hams study area. Bigbury also included Burgh Island. During the nineteenth century Burgh Island was part of the Combe Barton Estate which is included in Aveton Gifford parish. It can be seen from the Domesday records (Fig. 5.5) that the holding of Bigbury (*Bichberie*) came under the ownership of the Count of Mortian (DB, 15,44), the half-brother of William, who benefited greatly from the redistribution, holding more land than any other of the king's followers (Thorn and Thorn 1980 vol. 2, 15; Willy 1955, 14). Bigbury was held by Reginald of Vautortes, which is a *département* of Mayenne, France, and suggests

FIGURE 5.5. Domesday
settlements for the South
Hams study area

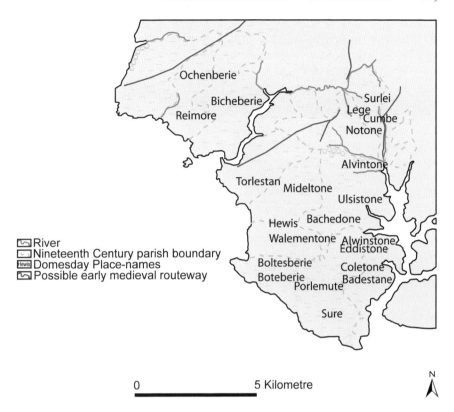

an absentee landowner. The Exon Domesday also states that in the hundred of Stanborough, 'Nine manors have been laid waste by Irishmen' (DB, 17,41), and highlights Thurlestone, Bagton, Collaton (in Malborough), South Huish, Galmpton (in South Huish), West Portlemouth, Ilton, Alston, and Soar as being possible candidates (Fig. 5.6). It is thought that these raids occurred in 1069 and were carried out by the two sons of Earl Harold who had taken refuge in Ireland (Thorn and Thorn 1980 vol. 2, 17, 41 general notes). South Huish and Bagton regained their values (25s and 15s respectively), but the others all saw a decline in value, with three (Soar, Collaton and Ilton) priced at a quarter of their former worth (Weldon-Finn 1967, 274).

Thurlestone is also listed in Domesday, as part of the holdings of Iudhael of Totnes. Within what is now the parish of Thurlestone was the Domesday holding of Buckland, which was added to the manor of Bolberry (now in the parish of Malborough to the south) held by the Count of Mortain, and was held freely by Edeva before 1066 (DB, 15,38). Buckland is now divided into east and west. East Buckland now only has two farms (Hoskins 1954, 495); while West Buckland could be described as a small hamlet with a number of smaller dwellings and a chapel.

Unlike in the Blackdown Hills and Hartland Moors study areas there is little information present from the thirteenth century TdN tax rolls for the estates in the South Hams study area (Table 5.1). Thurlestone, held within the Geld

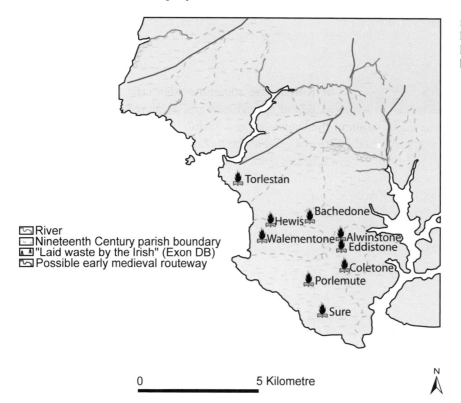

FIGURE 5.6. Domesday holdings suggested to have been raided in 1069 by the 'Irish'

list hundred of *Dippeforda* (Deptford), was held by William Buzun, paying fees to Reginald de Valle Tora [honour of Hurberton] (Whale 1898, index no 188). By the beginning of the fourteenth century the estate of Thurlestone was held by Stephen de Haccombe, still for a fee of 1 (Whale 1899, 15, index no 253). Furthermore, during the later medieval period, because of the South Hams' wealth, there was less evidence of sales of manorial holdings but what is evident within Thurlestone is that peasant farmers were able to purchase parts of their farms from the landlords, as was the case with William Cornish, and other land within the parish (Kew 1969, 33).

Like Thurlestone, the estate of Sorley in Churchstow was also held by Iudhael of Totnes, and as mentioned above, this estate along with Combe Royal (also in the parish) were significant parts of the ninth-century Charter boundary.

As mentioned previously, the manor of Churchstow was not listed in Domesday, but the survey does list the estates of Sorley, Combe Royal, Norton

TABLE 5.1. Listing from the thirteenth-century *Testa de Nevill*

Index no.	fees of…	Testa de Nevill name	Testa de Nevill holder	Testa de Nevill fee	Modern name & parish	Geld List Hundred
188	Reginald de Valle Tora [honour of Hurberton]	Thurleston	William Buzun	1	Thurlestone	Dippeforda

and Leigh which now lie within Churchstow Parish. The manor of Norton was held by the Church of Buckfast in Domesday and by Abbot Alwin before 1066 (DB, 6,9). This connection with the church continued, as the Abbot of Buckfast held the newly created manor of Churchstow, and from here he created his new borough of Kingsbridge sometime after 1220 (Hoskins 1954, 268). During the medieval period Churchstow manor played an important part in the organisation of the landscape, and Risdon (1811, 181) describes Churchstow as 'a parish highly situated', and as the 'ancient inheritance of Galfrid de Lisley'. Risdon (1811, 175) also states that Kingsbridge acknowledges Churchstow as its mother-church, and the location of the Kingsbridge burial ground was at the hamlet of Venn in the Churchstow parish (Polwhele 1793–1806, 470). The form of the parish boundaries also suggests Kingsbridge was created out of an earlier larger estate. The Domesday manor of Leigh also became a monastic cell called Buckfast, and later became the manor of the Abbot of Buckfast Abbey, with Norton remaining an estate (Hoskins 1954, 368).

South Milton is listed in Domesday as Mideltone by Alfred the Breton, and was held 'freely [and] jointly' by two thanes before 1066 (DB, 39,15). Within South Milton the manors of Horswell, Didwell and Holwell are all thought to date back to at least the thirteenth century, and perhaps earlier (Hoskins 1954, 435).

Elements of the historic landscape

The three sample areas chosen within the South Hams study area (Fig. 5.7) were highlighted because of the Tithe Survey field patterns. The three areas have also been chosen firstly to investigate a specific question: whether there are differences in landscape character on either side of the Avon estuary. This brings in to question the idea of small scale *pays* based at a settlement and parish level. It is clear from the discussion in Chapter Two that the South Hams is regarded to be a discrete *pays* region within Devon as a whole, particularly in terms of agricultural production, thinking in terms of large scale 'macro' *pays* which exist on a regional or parish scale, as oppose to the 'micro' *pays* which occur at settlement level. Therefore, the aim of highlighting two areas either side of the estuary is to establish whether further cultural differences, which can be seen through the historic landscape, can be identified.

A further aim of these sample areas is also to discuss the distribution of settlement within the South Hams. Sample Areas 1 and 2 are focused upon the main settlements within the parishes; Thurlestone and Bigbury respectively. Sample Area 3 is also located within Bigbury and is focused on the coastal zone of the parish which was, at the time of the Tithe Survey, an area of scattered farmsteads, but is where the present settlement of Bigbury-on-Sea is now located.

Sample Area 1 within Thurlestone parish encompasses Bantham, the now divided manor of Buckland, and the coastal zone between Warren Point and Bantham Ham on the eastern side of the estuary of the river Avon. A second

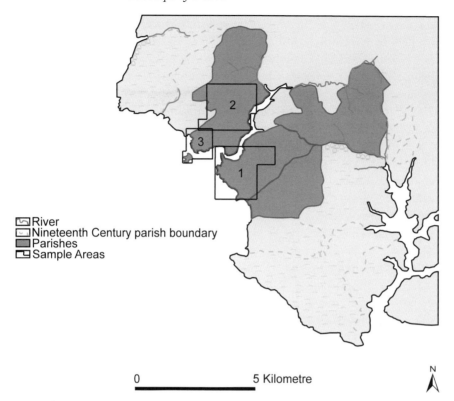

River
Nineteenth Century parish boundary
Parishes
Sample Areas

0   5 Kilometre

N

sample, Sample Area 2, has been identified in the parish of Bigbury. This zone covers a transect across the central area from the eastern parish boundary, across the settlement of Bigbury itself, and ending at the Avon Estuary and the parish boundary to the west. Finally, the third sample area also occurs within the parish of Bigbury. This is focused on an area of coastline on the western side of the river Avon, opposite Sample Area 1, and directly south of Sample Area 2.

Field systems

Sample Area 1, located in the parish of Thurlestone, has been isolated for study because of a combination of very different nineteenth-century field patterns. In particular, two areas of strip field can be seen on the Tithe Survey. The fields along the coast are large and regular, suggesting later enclosure, but on the steep sided valley of Buckland Stream there is a combination of narrow fields and small plots. Towards West Buckland there are a series of enclosed strips, which show a different landscape organisation to the fields to the south (Fig. 5.8).

The first area of strip fields is clustered around the settlement of West Buckland. There has been significant evidence for this type of field morphology within the other two study areas, and as was expected the landownership patterns showed fragmented ownership within this block of fields. It is clear that the boundaries of these strips continue across roads, and in some cases this

FIGURE 5.8. Sample Area
1 Tithe Survey

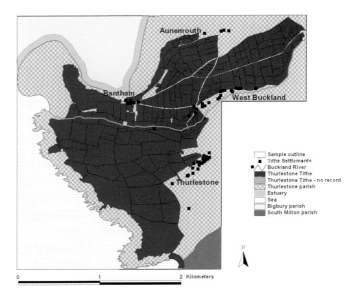

is mirrored by the pattern of Tithe Survey ownership, suggesting a large area of cultivation that predated the construction of the roadway. Ownership was held by six people, in varying combinations. The Earl of Devon held land with Richard Sheriff Jnr. John Square, (both of whom also held land individually), and Osmond Mordaunt. Land was also held in smaller quantities by William Toy and William Wakeham. A second defined area of strips can be seen on the eastern slopes of the river Avon near the settlements of Bantham and Aunemouth. These fields follow the direction of the contours, and also show a distinctly fragmented ownership. Again, as was seen in relation to Awliscombe and Buckerell in the Blackdown Hills, the nature of the ownership here differs from the fields surrounding West Buckland. Here ownership was again dominated by the Earl of Devon, shared with Joseph Earle, John Nicolas Petty, William Moore, and Richard Lydon.

The large regular fields that occurred to the south were all held by the Earl of Devon and William Robins, and make up the sole holding of this ownership partnership. Interestingly, in terms of estate holdings, this area is divided into two unequal holdings, the majority held under Farm, occupied by Squire Henry Rowe, the remaining 12 fields under West Downs with Roger Moore in occupancy. In the area of strip fields the estate holdings were again fragmented, showing a clear separation from the coastal area.

Over half of the fields sampled from the Thurlestone Tithe Survey were owned, at least in part, by the Earl of Devon (Fig. 5.9). This ownership is known to go back to at least the eighteenth century, as in 1777 the Earl carried out the 'Courtenay Survey' of his 900 acre estate (Oswald 1994, 24). This estate included the hamlets of Thurlestone, Bantham and Buckland, which all sit within Thurlestone parish. What is interesting is that the Earl held much of

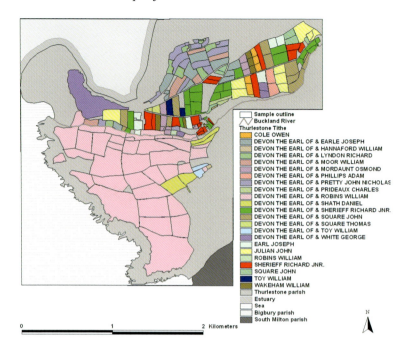

FIGURE 5.9. Sample Area 1 Tithe Survey Landownership

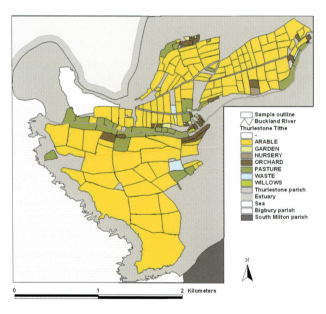

FIGURE 5.10. Sample Area 1 Tithe Survey land use

the land in partnership, which echoes Kew's statement about 'peasants' buying parts of estates from the landlord.

The Tithe Survey land use patterns for this selected area are markedly different to those seen within the Hartland and Blackdowns study areas (Fig. 5.10). Over half of the sample area was listed within the Tithe Apportionment as 'arable', with a defined band of pasture interspersed with some orchard and two

FIGURE 5.11. Sample Area
2 Tithe Survey

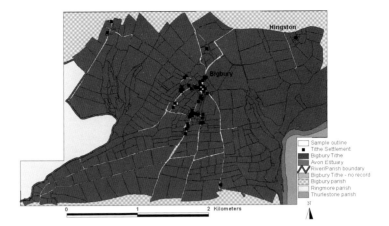

occurrences of 'willows' running along the steep side of the Buckland Stream valley. There is little waste and common (only seven fields within the sample area), and these are generally scattered.

In comparison, the final two sample areas are located on the western side of the river Avon. The first of the two zones in Bigbury, Sample Area 2, incorporates a number of visible elements for investigation, which will allow the hypothesis to be tested (Fig. 5.11). For example, if what has been seen within the other two study areas follows as a general rule, the row of strip fields lying to the west of the settlement of Bigbury should show multiple ownership (or in this case, leaseholders), and the ring-fenced enclosure surrounding the holding at Hingston would be a single holding. As described in Chapter One and seen in the Blackdown Hills and Hartland Moors case studies, a ring-fenced enclosure is a circular or oval field boundary with internal divisions, associated with an isolated farm or hamlet, held in severalty. It is apparent immediately that the field patterns that occur in Bigbury differ from the form of the historic landscape over the estuary in neighbouring Thurlestone. In Bigbury the fields are consistently larger, while there is evidence that many of these regular boundaries continued underneath the line of the roadways, suggesting an earlier layout.

Unusually for all three study areas, the Tithe Survey landholding class for Bigbury is divided into landowner [the 'overlord'], leaseholder [who holds the land], and occupier [the tenant inhabiting or working the holding] (Fig. 5.12 and Fig. 5.13). This is different from the other parishes in the South Hams study area, and also to those studied in the Blackdown Hills and Hartland Moors regions. This provides a clear difference in the structure of holdings in the Bigbury sample area. Landownership for the sample area is unequally divided between four owners and Glebe land. The majority is held by the Duke of Cleveland, with smaller holdings ascribed to Walter Prettejohn, Thomas Dave, and Thomas Pearce.

There is a clear physical boundary visible within the field patterns between the holdings of the Duke of Cleveland and Walter Prettejohn. Here a long

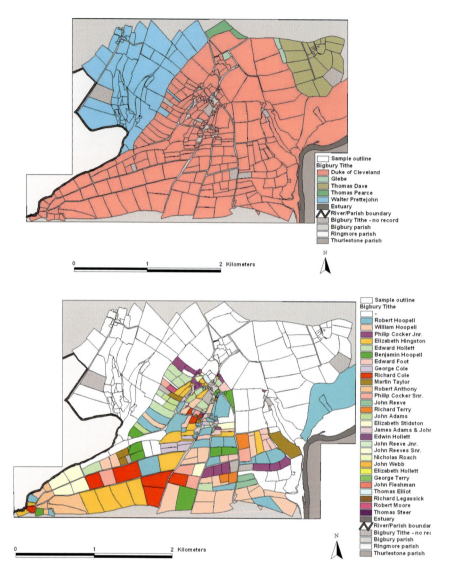

FIGURE 5.12. Sample
Area 2 Tithe Survey
landownership

FIGURE 5.13. Sample
Area 2 Tithe Survey
leaseholder

unbroken sinuous north-east to south-west boundary neatly demarcates the
two sets of holdings, with only three fields belonging to Prettejohn situated
within the block of strip fields to the west of Bigbury settlement held by the
Duke. The rest of the strips are held solely by the Duke of Cleveland, which is
not what was expected in terms of landownership patterns. The distribution of
Tithe Survey leaseholders in the strip fields is fragmented, which is more like
the expected pattern of ownership. Five of the seven leaseholders (Benjamin
Hoopell, William Hoopell, Edward Hollett, Martin Taylor and Phillip Cocker
Junior) also hold the strips in lease. The other two leaseholders, John Adams
and Robert Hoopell, have their strips occupied solely by John Saunders and
Robert Parraton respectively.

The land held by Thomas Dave, and occupied by Philip Trant forms the
Hingston estate, and follows the pattern of ring-fenced enclosures expected from
the Blackdown Hills and Hartland Moors study areas. Here there is an enclosed
area of fields, with the dwelling at the centre, with all land held by one person in
severalty, and occupied as such. This forms a direct comparison with the Model 4
shown in figure 1.4, which tends to occur in more upland areas of the county.

As a whole the distribution of leaseholders shows a much more irregular
pattern of holdings, dividing into small blocks or strips. There are several
suggestions that some holdings continued over roads, implying that these
divisions pre-date the road system. The blocks in the sample areas where there
are no leaseholders recorded were occupied in severalty. From this it can be seen
that the Tithe Survey occupier patterns are more reflective of landownership
patterns showing these cohesive blocks of occupancy, but also retaining the strip
structure of the western side of Bigbury (Fig. 5.14).

The patterns of Tithe Survey land use from the sample area shows
predominance of 'arable' (Fig. 5.15). There is a large quantity of orchards listed
around the main settlement of Bigbury, and also along the steep valley sides of
what is now known as Doctor's wood, a valley which runs down to the estuary.
Tithe field-name patterns show a large area with 'common' and 'brake' names
to the west of the Hingston estate (Fig. 5.16). As would be expected, the fields
which carry these names all contain straight divisions corresponding with later
enclosure.

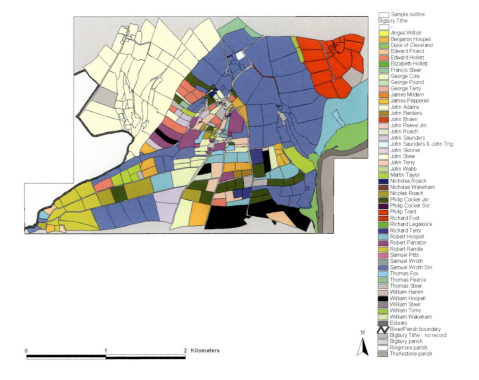

FIGURE 5.14. Sample Area
2 Tithe Survey occupier

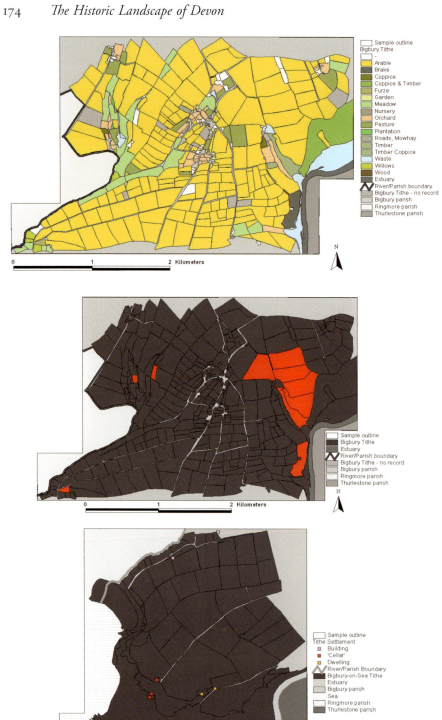

FIGURE 5.15. Sample Area 2 Tithe Survey land use

FIGURE 5.16. Sample Area 2 Tithe Survey distribution of 'common' and 'brake' field-names (red)

FIGURE 5.17. Sample Area 3 Tithe Survey

FIGURE 5.18. Sample Area 3 Tithe Survey landownership

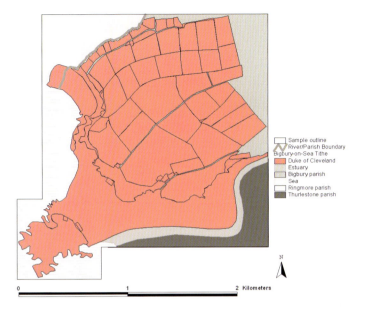

The third sample area (Fig. 5.17) is an area of coastline on the western side of the river Avon. This sample area aims to identify whether the coastal historic landscape mirrors the trends which occur in Thurlestone, and also if the fields occurring along the cliff tops follow the same rules as those in Hartland. Climatically the two areas are very different. However, the influences of the proximity of the sea have the same affect.

The fields within Sample Area 3 are large and regular, and different to the fields found around the settlement of Bigbury in Sample Area 2. All of the fields within Sample Area 3 are owned exclusively by the Duke of Cleveland following the trend of distribution seen in Sample Area 2, which is to be expected despite the dissimilarities of field morphology (Fig. 5.18). The Tithe Survey leaseholder patterns show discrete holdings held in severalty, with the only evidence of dispersed plots occurring along the border with Ringmore parish (Fig. 5.19). The Tithe Survey occupier patterns also mirror this distribution (Fig. 5.20).

Again, the pattern of Tithe Survey land use is as expected for an area within this type of topography and field morphology. The large regular fields which slope down to the sea are classed as 'arable', with the coastal edges listed as pasture. Along the length of the river bordering Ringmore parish the small square plots are recorded in the Tithe Apportionment as either meadow or willows, with gardens around the dwellings, and the tidal sandbank linking Burgh Island to the mainland as waste (Fig. 5.21 and Fig. 5.22). Although it is known that lime was used for fertiliser in this area, sanding of the agricultural land was believed to have been beneficial to cultivation during the medieval period, and Fox (2001, 66) states that within sixteenth century land surveys sand was said to 'increase the goodness...very much'.

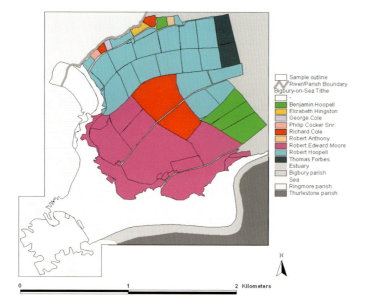

FIGURE 5.19. Sample Area 3 Tithe Survey leaseholder

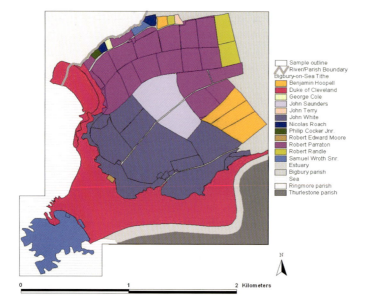

FIGURE 5.20. Sample Area 3 Tithe Survey occupier

It has been noted that medieval farming which occurred in the South Hams, and in particular within the Stanborough Hundred (which includes Churchstow, Thurlestone and South Milton), was very similar to that occurring in Cornwall, especially the Pydar hundred on the north-western coastline (Gray 1992, xix).

FIGURE 5.21. Sample Area 3 Tithe Survey land use

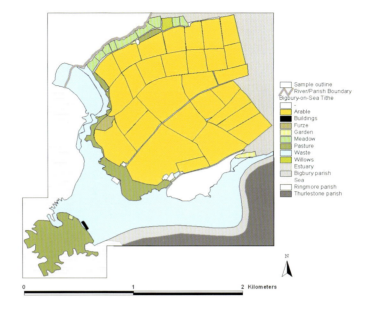

FIGURE 5.22. The Sandbar between Bigbury and Burgh Island

Summary

What these three sample areas reveal is contrasting organisation and landscape management despite their close proximity. It is perhaps not imprudent to suggest that the fields listed as 'arable' on the Tithe Survey may indeed represent cereal production. As a result of its rich soil, it has been suggested that medieval farming practices in the South Hams included considerable wheat and barley.

Also, because of its sheltered, warmer, and thus drier nature, there was also widespread fruit-growing and cider production (Cash 1966, 48; Gray 1992, xviii–xx).

The eleventh-century Domesday survey indicates the predominance of cereal cultivation in the South Hams through the number of plough teams listed. However, when comparing the number of ploughs against the other two study areas (see Table 5.2, and Chart 5.1) it can be seen that the highest number of

	ploughs	ploughs in lordship	Study area
Clayhidon	12	3	BH
Bolham (Water)	6	2	BH
Culm (Pyne)	4	2	BH
Hole	2	-	BH
Awliscombe	2	1	BH
Awliscombe	5	2	BH
Weston	2	1.5	BH
Awliscombe	1	-	BH
Mackham	1	-	BH
Ivedon	4	1	BH
Ivedon	0.5	-	BH
Combe Raliegh	8	3	BH
(Mohuns) Ottery	12	3	BH
Luppitt	6	2	BH
Greenway	5	3	BH
Shapcombe	4	1	BH
Bywood	3	1	BH
Awliscombe	3	1	BH
Awliscombe	4.5	2	BH
Awliscombe	3	-	BH
Culm (Davy)	4	3	BH
Shapcombe	3	-	BH
Hartland	110	15	HM
Clovelly	12	5	HM
Welcome	15	2	HM
Woolfardisworthy	4	-	HM
Noton	10	1	SH
Buckland	1.5	-	SH
Thurlestone	6	2	SH
Thurlestone	1	-	SH
Sorley	3	1	SH
Leigh	4	2	SH
Combe (Royal)	3	1	SH
Milton	12	2	SH

TABLE 5.2. Number of ploughs listed for Domesday Holdings in each study area

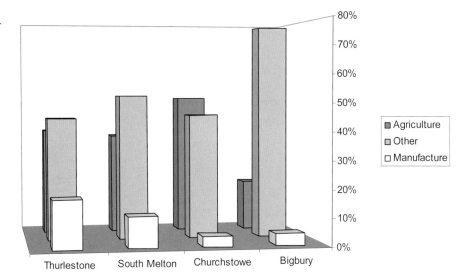

CHART 5.1. Comparative chart of the percentage of population in agriculture, manufacturing and other forms of employment in 1801, as listed by Vancouver (1808, 421).

ploughs listed is not in the South Hams but in the Hartland Moors region. The manor of Hartland itself is listed as having 115 ploughs, but even if this is discounted because of its size, the next highest amount occurs at Welcombe (15 ploughs), with South Milton third (13 ploughs). This is interesting in relation to the field morphology.

Nevertheless, it can be suggested that cereal cultivation was indeed high in this area the South Hams in the nineteenth-century. Furthermore, these patterns of land use, particularly within Sample Area 1 but perhaps also in the two sample areas in Bigbury, can be compared regionally to the eighteenth-century Courtenay Survey. In Sample Area 1, there are a number of small pasture fields along the banks of the Buckland River averaging an area of 1 acre. This confirms the distribution described in the Courtenay Survey of 1777. The Courtenay Survey describes an estate of over 900 acres which included the hamlets of Thurlestone, Buckland and Bantham. From this survey it is known that the pasture land was divided into 228 fields of approximately 1 acre, grouped into 48 farms, which were divided between 17 tenant farmers and further sublet into smaller holdings and allotments (Oswald 1994, 24).

Unlike the Blackdown Hills, there is no evidence in the historic landscape that the remaining land in the South Hams was used for convertible husbandry, although this practice was undoubtedly carried out in this region. Additionally, in all three sample areas there is very little waste recorded in comparison with the Blackdown Hills, and to a lesser extent, Hartland Moors. This must be to do with the greater quantities of improved pasture in the South Hams district than in east Devon and the Blackdown Hills because of topography and soil types (Fox 1975, 185). This improved pasture compensated for the small amounts of waste available in the South Hams and was priced at a rate between waste and the highly prized meadow (*ibid.* 1975, 185).

Field-names

The areas of this improved pasture and highly prized meadows can be elucidated from plotting the distribution of field-names. As with the landholding patterns seen for the three sample areas in the South Hams study area, it would be expected that the distribution of field-names and field morphologies will follow the same patterns seen in the two other areas.

Interestingly only 2 per cent of the fields within the three sample areas contained acre field-names. This may be a result of the nature of the sample areas chosen and may therefore not be representative, but the consistent lack of such field-name elements suggests that the enclosure of fields within the South Hams was relatively early.

However, park elements within the field-names were more greatly represented. Sample Area 1 in Thurlestone parish shows a high percentage of 'park' in the field names, with over 16 per cent of the 241 fields digitised within this sample area containing the element. These are distributed in blocks of regularly shaped fields relating to the settlements. Sample Area 2 located around the village of Bigbury also sees a high distribution, with just under 20 per cent of the fields containing the element 'park'. The distribution of these fields is interesting. The ring-fenced fields at Hingston have a clear concentration of park elements in their field-names, and there is also a clear correlation with the strip fields to the east of the village of Bigbury.

The occurrence of this pattern of field-names within the field system surrounding the farm at Hingston is noteworthy, and reinforces the ideas of ring-fenced enclosures being held as one cohesive unit. Moreover, the occurrence of field-names such as Church Park, which is frequently an early alternative to compass direction names (such as east or west) for the great field (Field 1993, 198). This is identifiable, because of its location in the ring-fenced enclosure at Hingston, as land being held by the church and suggests that the fields were enclosed relatively early.

The occurrence of Fogle or Fogwell Park names in the strips neighbouring Bigbury village is also illuminating, as the prefix may refer to land 'under fog'. This is an agricultural term which refers to land being left to feed cattle on standing grass, particularly coarse sedgy grass grown in wet places over winter, or grass which grows after the hay is harvested (Oglvie 1855; Elworthy 1886). The strips are located near to a river, and the occurrence of willow plots within, and adjacent to the strips, suggests wet ground.

In both cases the instances of these 'park' field-names do not respect roadways, echoing the field morphology. Even by the coast, at what is now Bigbury-on-Sea in Sample Area 3, the historic landscape study reveals a high percentage and a distribution of a discrete block of fields owned by the Duke of Cleveland and leased by Robert and Benjamin Hoopell.

There are very low occurrences of 'breach', 'brake' and 'moor' in the three sample areas of the South Hams study area. However, the South Hams study area sees a similar distribution to that visible in the Blackdown Hills of mead elements. Mead field-names had a high distribution throughout the South Hams study area. Sample Areas 1 and 2, which contain the nucleated settlements of Thurlestone and Bigbury see a percentage of around 7 per cent of fields containing this element. However, in Sample Area 3, which represents the areas now occupied by Bigbury-on-Sea, 15 per cent of fields contain mead elements, and correspond with a number of small square fields along the river valley and with the blocks of mead elements found in Sample Area 2.

Settlement

As with the patterns of Tithe Survey fields, the settlement distribution area has focused upon the three sample areas, with more general trends taken from other parishes within the wider area to gain a more complete picture.

Sample Area 1 shows that during the nineteenth century this area had a number of small nucleated settlements with little or no associated dispersed farmsteads (Fig. 5.23). Thurlestone was a relatively large nucleated settlement, with its church located at the eastern end of the village. For this settlement it seems correct to use the term village in its conventional sense as Thurlestone bears all the hallmarks of the 'classic' village morphology with other aspects such as service provision (e.g. a church), and communal management of the landscape (seen through the field morphology). West and East Buckland was a ribbon settlement spread along the high ground above the river Buckland. It is clear from the layout of the two settlements that West Buckland is the larger of the two, and this obviously accounts for its survival as a hamlet. Bantham also shows a degree of nucleation, clustered around the convergence of three roads on the banks of the river Avon. The settlement of Aunemouth shows three buildings neighbouring the manor house, and is perhaps the most dispersed settlement within the sample area.

The emphasis in Sample Area 2 is on the nucleated settlement of Bigbury and the resulting field systems which surround it. Further out from this centre are a number of smaller, more dispersed settlements. Polwhele notes that the village of Bigbury housed 'the cottages of the poor', with several other dispersed hamlets located to the north of the parish, mostly containing Coombe in their names (Polwhele 1793–1806, 465). It is clear from the Bigbury Tithe Survey that there has been a significant decrease in the number of houses within Bigbury village within the modern landscape (Fig. 5.24).

The settlement of Bigbury-on-Sea is a post nineteenth-century development. As mentioned previously, this area, included in Sample Area 3, was held by the Duke of Cleveland, and has only a few dispersed farmsteads. Alongside these dwellings, the Tithe Survey also lists the presence of 'houses or cellars'. The term cellar settlement is perhaps a misnomer, as these buildings were not for habitation, or at least not in their original forms. It is clear that there were no substantial or permanent settlements along the Devon coast line in the Middle Ages, and even by the late sixteenth century there were still no permanent settlements. The cellars were used seasonally as storage huts, and constructed

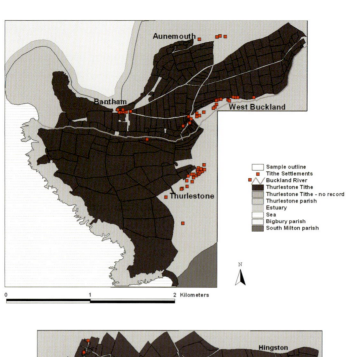

FIGURE 5.23. Sample Area 1 Tithe Survey settlement distribution

Legend:
- Sample outline
- Tithe Settlements
- Buckland River
- Thurlestone Tithe
- Thurlestone Tithe – no record
- Thurlestone parish
- Estuary
- Sea
- Bigbury parish
- South Milton parish

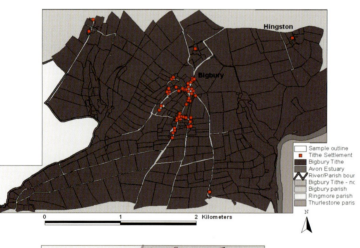

FIGURE 5.24. Sample Area 2 Tithe Survey settlement distribution

Legend:
- Sample outline
- Tithe Settlement
- Bigbury Tithe
- Avon Estuary
- River/Parish bour...
- Bigbury Tithe – n...
- Bigbury parish
- Ringmore parish
- Thurlestone paris...

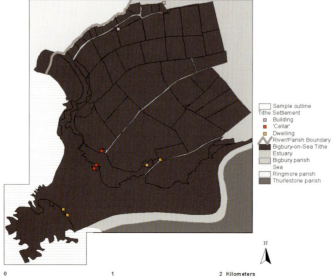

FIGURE 5.25. Sample Area 3 Tithe Survey settlement distribution

Legend:
- Sample outline
- Tithe Settlement
  - Building
  - 'Cellar'
  - Dwelling
- River/Parish Boundary
- Bigbury-on-Sea Tithe
- Estuary
- Bigbury parish
- Sea
- Ringmore parish
- Thurlestone parish

away from the shore in order to protect them from inclement weather (Fox 2001, 12). The Cellar settlements were constructed during the sixteenth century and were generally rented by tenant farmers who lived inland (Fox 1996b, 64–5). These buildings were a fundamental part of the sequence of pastoral farming in Devon during the later medieval period when fishing was a by-employment, interlocking the tasks inland with those on the shore, and the practice required cooperation between a number of farmers (Fox 2001, 12; 129–130). Fox (1996b, 62) notes that early records of south coast fishing villages are few, as they are rarely associated with the manorial centres. Indeed, he continues by suggesting that the earliest reference to such settlements is to Hallsands in 1347 but these are more to natural features than an occupation site (*ibid*. 1996b, 62).

The cellars in Sample Area 3 are located at the mean high and mean low water marks along the sandbank which runs to Burrow (now Burgh) Island (Fig. 5.25). They are thought to originate sometime during the sixteenth and seventeenth centuries, and during the same period it is thought that there was also a fishery located on Burgh Island. The cellars located on the mean low water mark are also part of the Burgh estate, and make up the only property within the sample area belonging to this estate. During these two centuries there was a flowering of seasonal cellar settlements followed by fisheries, fishing villages and ports along the South Hams coast, thus explaining the location of the later Bigbury-on-Sea (Fox 2001, 31) (Fig. 5.26).

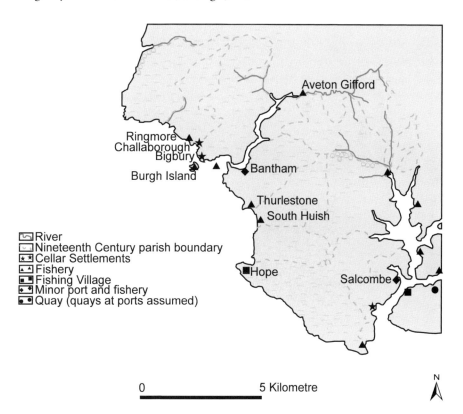

FIGURE 5.26. Sixteenth and seventeenth century fisheries and coastal settlements

The South Hams study area

Outside of the three sample areas, comprehensive recording of the parish of Churchstow for the beginning of the nineteenth century has given an insight into the structure of settlements in this region at this time. It can be seen that there were three 'villages': Churchstow town which had 20 houses with 132 occupants; Ven with 12 houses and 47 inhabitants; and Merrifield which contained six 'poor houses', housing 132 people (Polwhele 1793–1806, 468). The modern Ordnance Survey shows that Churchstow, as the main settlement within the parish, has undergone growth over the last two centuries; Venn has also remained as a hamlet, if severely reduced; but Merrifield is now only a single dwelling, as would be expected if this area contained poor houses as these would be the first to be cleared when such accommodation became politically unsuitable. This is interesting in relation to the three sample areas as it would appear that there has been little shrinkage in the size of settlements.

Summary

Taken as a whole, settlement pattern within the South Hams region is thought to show a more dispersed pattern than expected, with a number of hamlets dotted along the river valleys and onto the higher hills. The occurrence of the isolated farmstead that arises in the Blackdowns appears not to have occurred with such frequency within this area. Settlement seems to be grouped together in varying sized parcels rather than being spread across the landscape. This may be because of the nature of farming practices; the relatively high arable production may have meant that practical consideration of working the land required some kind of neighbourly co-operation. Again, this is echoed in the field systems of Sample Areas 1 and 2, when nucleated settlement occurred next to the associated strip fields.

Movement to coastal settlements during the sixteenth and seventeenth centuries must be taken into consideration for the decline in population in these areas. The construction of these coastal settlements marks a significant move in the landscape that is also evident also in the Hartland Moors area (for comparison see Chapter Four).

A further example can be seen from the parish of Loddiswell, which lies to the north of Churchstow. Within this parish it was thought that there were two villages, Loddiswell itself, and Staunton, lying 2 miles north (Michell and Common 1978, 21). The settlement of Loddiswell remains, but almost complete desertion is thought to have occurred at Staunton. The first reference to Staunton was in the thirteenth century, and by the middle of the eighteenth century there are 26 houses recorded (Michell and Common 1978, 21–22). Nevertheless, by the end of the eighteenth century it is suggested that the village was in decline. By the time of the Tithe Survey there were only eight buildings recorded as houses, and by the beginning of the twentieth century Staunton had almost completely disappeared (*ibid.* 1978, 22–23).

Comparison between the Tithe Survey and the modern aerial photographs suggests the extent of this settlement. A number of small plots, which would have been related to dwellings, can clearly be seen from the shape of the remaining fields on the OS, plus the cropmarks apparent on the aerial photography. Furthermore there is evidence of what could be described as furlong boundaries; sinuous reversed S-shaped fields located to the east of the settlement. This is what we would expect to be associated with a nucleated settlement.

What we are seeing here is a different phase of settlement desertion than that seen at places like Hendon in the Hartland Moors study area. This late desertion may have occurred for a number of reasons, but there is no conclusive evidence. Michell and Common (1978, 23) suggest that the increase in public transport and the coming of the railway, combined with an increase in mechanisation of agriculture, may have caused an outward movement in this area. If this is so, why is such abandonment not more widespread within this area? The decline in people may be to do with the location; Staunton was externally perceived as 'unhealthy'. During the latter part of the nineteenth century, people were warned not to go to the boggy Staunton Moor for 'there was disease there' (Michell and Common 1978, 22). Disease associated with marshland was a common occurrence and it is known from the Milles enquiry that after the marshes around Seaton and Powderham were drained the 'Ague' disappeared. The Ague is commonly attributed to malarial diseases.

Here it is valuable to compare the Devon examples with an area such as Canvey Island in Essex, where, during the same period, it can be seen that such infections were endemic. On Canvey Island it is known that malaria was as common to the inhabitants as modern infections of influenza. Locals suffered occasional incapacitation, but to visitors it was often fatal (Cracknell 1959, 26). Thus, it could be suggested that this type of illness was present in Staunton.

Roads and droveways

The Blackdown Hills and Hartland Moors study areas saw an irregular arrangement of droveways and sunken cart tracks criss-crossing the regions. Noticeably, this arrangement does not occur within the South Hams study area. There are a considerable number of roads which form linear routes from the settlement areas to the sea and estuary. Many of these roads appear to radiate from Churchstow. These tend not to follow contours, and present a possible indicator of former settlement where they cross.

Petter and Hooke (1990; 1994; Petter 1985) highlight a number of possible early medieval routeways (see Fig. 5.3), the lines of which are now fossilised in footpaths and minor roads. These early medieval roads cross the study area and run from the upland ridges to the coast, the river Avon at Bantham, or the Kingswear estuary. The roads cross through what are now the settlements of Churchstow, Loddiswell, Kingston and Kingsbridge.

It can be seen from all three of the sample areas within the South Hams study area that the roads, at least in the proper sense of the word, were later landscape features. From the field patterns gained from the Tithe Surveys it can be suggested that in many cases the field boundaries do not appear to respect the routeways. There is evidence that field-names and ownership patterns do not respect the boundaries made from the routeways either. Some of the tracks marked on the Tithe Survey for the sample areas are footpaths on the modern OS, which may suggest either that they were only minor roads during the nineteenth century, or that they have been usurped by later modern roads.

Evidence of industry

The types of industries which occurred in the South Hams differ from the types seen in the other two study areas. The Domesday survey indicates industries such as salt-houses, as seen listed as part of the estate of Bigbury. There are some similarities, for example as in the Hartland Moors study area, the banks of the Avon were also aptly situated for lime kilns, and there is a reference to a lime kiln in South Hams boundary clause of AD 847 (see Fig. 5.3). This practice occurred during the medieval period and continued to be transported by river to Averton Gifford at the end of the Avon estuary until the 1930s (Fox 1953, 5).

From the medieval period, however, the economy of this region has been based on corn production (Havinden and Stanes 1999, 282). As with the Blackdowns and Hartland, Vancouver (1808, 411) discusses the percentage of population employed in manufacturing and agriculture in 1806 for the parishes within the South Hams, and this is summarised in table 5.3.[1] Within the parish of Churchstow in 1806 112 people, or 51 per cent, were involved in agriculture, which its inland position would facilitate (Vancouver 1808, 411).

Bigbury had a high proportion of the population (333 people out of 430, or 77 per cent) not involved in either agriculture or manufacturing (Vancouver 1808, 411), which, when related to the evidence of fisheries associated with Bigbury discussed earlier, must account for this. In Bantham, pilchards were caught in large quantities off the coast and often used as manure because of the surplus (Coupe 1920, 68). However, in general terms the South Hams saw a decrease in the importance of fishing in the post-medieval period, with crabs and lobster-catching occurring at only a handful of settlements (Shorter *et al.* 1969, 256).

TABLE 5.3. Table showing number of people employed in agriculture, manufacturing or 'other' employment in the early nineteenth century (from Vancouver 1808, 411; 413)

Parish	Agriculture		Manufacture		All other persons		Total	
Bigbury	79	18%	18	4%	333	77%	430	100%
Churchstowe	112	51%	8	4%	99	45%	219	100%
South Melton	111	37%	33	11%	158	52%	302	100%
Thurlestone	138	39%	61	17%	157	44%	356	100%

Concluding remarks

Although it is clear that the management and structure of the South Hams differs from that for the Blackdowns and Hartland Moors simply as a result of the climate and topography, it would be unwise to suggest that there is complete synchronism between all three areas. However, what the Sample Areas have shown is that certain landscape signatures *can* be highlighted in all three areas.

The settlement patterns show marked differences to those found in the Blackdown Hills as a whole, but mirror the small hamlets seen at Awliscombe and Buckerell in the Blackdowns and those which occur along the western coast of the parish of Hartland. The occurrence of dispersed farmsteads was minimal, but where they did occur their associated field systems showed elements which would have not have been out of place in east Devon. In particular, the structure of the fields around the farmstead of Hingston showed clear traits of a ring-fenced enclosure, and this was mirrored in the patterns of landownership and occupier.

Desertion and shrinkage of settlements occurred much later in the South Hams study area then in the other two regions. The evidence presented by the Bigbury settlement and the hamlet of Staunton in the parish of Churchstow shows that in these cases the process did not occur until the late nineteenth century. This is in marked comparison to settlements such as Hendon in Hartland, which we know from documentary evidence went out of use during the late medieval period. It can be suggested that the building of the railway, and also the threat of illness, created pressures on the inhabitants of these small communities which did not occur in the Blackdown Hills and the Hartland Moors, and this may explain why the pattern of desertion is different here. This will be discussed more in Chapter Seven.

Finally, the difference in Tithe landownership patterns that occurred on either side of the Avon estuary is also an interesting consideration. The near complete dominance of the Duke of Cleveland shown in Sample Areas 2 and 3 is in sharp constrast to the fragmented nature of Sample Area 1.

Note

1   Spelling used in table 5.3 is as written by Vancouver (1808, 411–413).

CHAPTER SIX

Addressing Devon's Historic Landscape

Chapters Three, Four, and Five have discussed the nineteenth-century historic landscape of the Blackdown Hills, Hartland Moors, and South Hams with an emphasis on the relationship between field and settlement morphology and patterns of landholding, and the role of estates in the organisation and management of the land.

The nature of landownership and the distribution of field-names have also been explored alongside field systems and settlement patterns, and comparisons regarding the historic landscape have been made between areas. This chapter will elaborate on the study of the historic landscape and suggest reasons for the development of the landscapes of the three study areas, for example the impact of large manors in Hartland Moors, and pressure for buyable land in the Blackdown Hills.

The chapter has been divided into two parts to discuss issues relating to the origins and development of the historic landscape in Devon. The first part addresses the physical and mappable nature of the historic landscape, and explores the relationship between nineteenth-century field boundaries and settlement pattern with landholding, land use, and field-name distribution. The second section focuses on the ideas of *pays* regions and the alternative layers of information that can be added to the study of the historic landscape to understand more of the social and cultural elements.

PART ONE. THE HISTORIC LANDSCAPE

This book builds upon historic landscape studies that used morphology to examine field systems and settlement. The work undertaken at Stansted in Essex is of particular interest, as it shows models of field systems which are comparable to the field patterns seen in the Blackdown Hills and Hartland Moors study areas. The field patterns were identified by using the nineteenth-century Tithe Surveys and documentary sources within a GIS to highlight landscape signatures: the identifiable and frequently occurring patterns in field boundaries, settlement pattern and distribution of landholdings that are diagnostic of particular processes of formation and evolution.

The assumption that Devon's landscape relates to Rackham's Ancient Countryside or Highland Zones is at odds with the observation that the historic landscape shares similarity with the south-east of England. Devon is classically described by the likes of Rackham and others as an upland region of dispersed settlement and pastoral agriculture. The case study areas discussed in Chapters Three to Five add weight to the argument that this categorisation is too simplistic.

One of the original themes discussed in Chapter One was the examination of field morphology, particularly in reference to the extent of open field farming. As a county, Devon was thought to have been enclosed relatively early, and this included wastes and commons (Hoskins 1955, 84). Before 1550 the landscape consisted of scattered settlements and associated irregular field systems, with 'furze and heath' occurring alongside enclosed land (Hoskins 1943, 81–82). Reclamation and enclosure of the edges of Dartmoor was in evidence by the tenth century and continued for at least three centuries, creating a landscape of isolated farmsteads surrounded by irregularly shaped field boundaries (Taylor 1975, 99–100). By 1600, only 20 per cent of moorland and waste was still unenclosed, although in some higher uplands this figure could be as high as 50 to 60 per cent (Hoskins 1943, 84). Much of the field pattern in east Devon and the Blackdown Hills was defined by 1600, and remained unchanged until the nineteenth century and into the present (Fox 1972b, 6, 101). Finally, common land and royal woodlands were seen as waste or unimproved by the eighteenth- and nineteenth-century landed classes, and therefore these sensibilities justified the actions of landowners, who supported the expansion and improvement into the commons (Seymour 2000, 206–207).

This is a neat model of development and fits with the types of field systems illustrated in figures 1.3 and 1.4. The case study areas Blackdown Hills and Hartland Moors, however, suggest that this description is just one of many patterns of development.

The massive redistribution of former monastic lands during the sixteenth century instigated a change in land ownership not seen since the Norman Conquest. This eleventh century re-organisation was not equalled again until the break-up and sale of so many of estates during the agricultural depression in the late nineteenth and early twentieth centuries (Aston and Bettey 1998, 117). Both the Blackdown Hills and Hartland Moors study areas were heavily influenced by monastic houses during the medieval period, while the South Hams had links with the Abbey at Buckfast. The Blackdown Hills study area illustrates this clearly in the parish of Dunkeswell. The untitheable lands on the Dunkeswell Tithe Survey, and the concentrations of land held by the Simcoe family, who took over a number of granges belonging to Dunkeswell Abbey (see Figs 3.27; 6.3), illustrate the extent to which land belonging to ecclesiastical estates is still evident in the historic landscape. Figure 6.1 shows the distribution of Simcoe–held land in relation to the known holdings of Dunkeswell Abbey in the study area. The distribution of land held by the Simcoe family in the nineteenth century represents the former holdings of Dunkeswell Abbey, for example the land surrounding Wolverstone in Awliscombe and the Grange

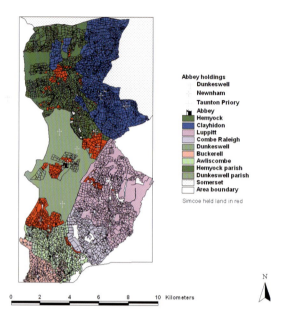

Abbey holdings
 Dunkeswell
 Newnham
 Taunton Priory
 Abbey
 Hemyock
 Clayhidon
 Luppitt
 Combe Raleigh
 Dunkeswell
 Buckerell
 Awliscombe
 Hemyock parish
 Dunkeswell parish
 Somerset
 Area boundary

Simcoe held land in red

0   2   4   6   8   10 Kilometers

N

FIGURE 6.1. Relationship between fields held by the Simcoe family and monastic holdings in the Blackdown Hills

Farm in Dunkeswell which was held by Drewe and Elizabeth Simcoe. These areas were held by the Crown for much of the remaining years of the sixteenth century. Other holdings of Dunkeswell Abbey fall predominantly in the areas which were non-titheable in the nineteenth century.

In Hartland the predominance of the lands held by Lewis William Buck in Hartland and Welcombe illustrate the extent of the coexisting estates of Harton and Hartland Abbey. Although not as clearly defined as the pattern of landholdings seen in the Blackdowns, it provides an interesting distribution. However, outside of the land held by Buck there were a number of small hamlets with associated fields not under his ownership. This indicates one of two things; either these small holdings grew up outside of the hold of the Harton estate and the Abbey of Hartland or, more likely, that with the Dissolution of the Abbey estate land was sold off to enterprising new landowners. Within the South Hams study area Buckland Priory made no obvious impact on the sample areas highlighted. However, it is clear that Buckfast Abbey was responsible for the creation of the neighbouring town of Kingsbridge.

Variations in landscape development can be seen in the Blackdown Hills and Hartland Moors case study areas. It is evident from the study of the nineteenth-century historic landscape of the Blackdown Hills that there is a significant differentiation between the lower-lying southern half and the upland fringes to the north of the study area. In the Hartland Moors regions, topography plays less of a part, with variations occurring through changes in estates and distinct patterns of settlement, for example land held by the former Harton manor.

Despite the differences in the field systems between the parishes of the south and those of the more northern parts of the Blackdown Hills, the relationship between fields and hamlets and isolated farmsteads mirrors what Finberg (1951, 33) expects for such communities. The fields nearest to nucleated settlements were tilled communally and relate to the small parallel-sided blocks of strip fields which can be seen near to the nucleation of settlement. These fields were interspersed with enclosed pasture and meadow surrounded by furze or moor, creating a three-tiered agricultural structure. Finberg (1951, 33) suggests in Devon and Cornwall these were called in-ground, middle-ground and out-ground, replacing the infield and outfield structure common in the Midlands landscape. The occurrence of field-names such as Furze ground, Inner ground, and Middle ground (as seen in Clayhidon, Hartland, Woolfardisworthy and Clovelly) may be evidence of this three-phased land management.

Open fields

Within east Devon the predominant form of enclosure occurred in the form of relic open fields with bundles of small strips creating a pattern of stripped and 'S'-shaped fields (Fox 1972a, 86). This enclosure was piecemeal and is considered to be an indicator or landscape signature of open field farming elsewhere in Devon. The 'S'-shaped field boundaries are generally associated with medieval fields as they are formed through ploughing with draught animals, especially oxen.

An example of relic open field surviving in the historic landscape occurs at Weston on the Awliscombe and Buckerell boundary border (Fig. 3.14). There is no doubt that this field pattern is associated with the hamlet of Weston, which was divided between the later ecclesiastical parishes of Awliscombe and Buckerell. It is also argued that this field pattern is suggestive of early manorial structure and evidence of some degree of cooperative farming. As discussed in Chapter Three, the division by the parish boundary of the hamlet and field system may suggest the landholding pattern dated from the period of the thirteenth to fifteenth centuries. The estate of Weston was held in two parts by the Pomeroy and Cheever families in the twelfth century, and later in the thirteenth to fifteenth centuries by the Abbot of Dunkeswell and 'others'. Some manors in east Devon began the process of enclosing open fields as early as the thirteenth century (Fox 1972a, 84), and so the Abbots of Dunkeswell have provided the impetus for the enclosure of the open field. In Awliscombe and Buckerell parishes a number of sinuous field boundaries (some following contours) are not respected by the parish boundary. These occur in relation to the mounds at Buckerell and Bushy Knap, which are suggested to be the sites of medieval fortifications or civil war defences, between the settlements of Buckerell and Awliscombe, and around Weston. This suggests that enclosure of Weston was undertaken before Awliscombe and Buckerell were divided into two parishes.

Within the parishes of Buckerell and neighbouring Feniton, strip fields indicating relic open field can also be identified, although not on the scale of those seen at Weston. In comparison, within the Hartland Moors study area perhaps the most distinctive areas of former open field are located near to the small hamlets along the western coast of Hartland parish (see Fig. 4.25). These small bundles of strip fields, with multiple owners and occupiers, mirror the pattern seen on a larger scale at Weston. In Hartland Moors the former open fields are situated in relation to the nucleated hamlets of South Hole, Hartisworthy, Milford and Meddon. This fits the models described by Roberts and Wrathmell and illustrated in figures 1.4 and 1.5. The fields which make up the relic open fields at Weston, South Hole, Hartisworthy, Milford and Meddon are different from the patterns seen in the rest of parishes of Hartland and Awliscombe and Buckerell.

Ring-fenced enclosures

Despite the number of relic open field systems that can be identified, these fields are at odds with the rest of the study areas and are not representative of the Blackdown Hills or Hartland Moors. The relic open field at Weston illustrates this perfectly. Indeed, outside of the parishes of Awliscombe and Buckerell there is no other trace within the historic landscape for such a field system. Neighbouring Combe Raleigh, although probably also enclosed early in the medieval period, contains no evidence of an open field structure, despite being under the landownership of one large estate (suggested by the blanket ownership of land by Mary Barnard in the nineteenth century; see below). Crucial to this area therefore is the pattern of nineteenth-century occupiers, which shows distinct compact tenement blocks associated with individual farmsteads and small hamlets.

The field pattern in Combe Raleigh has a series of small ring-fenced enclosures with regular internal divisions attached to individual farms, with later intake of the common and hill slopes, and clear post-medieval enclosure on the top of St. Cyres Hill. The occurrence of ring-fenced enclosures in Combe Raleigh is curious as these field systems are generally associated with upland areas (Roberts and Wrathmell 2002, 66; see figure 1.4). Ring-fenced enclosures are thought to indicate land that is held in severalty, and this is the case in Combe Raleigh (Fig. 3.16). This enclosure, although apparently contemporaneous, suggests a development which still occurred piecemeal and without the regimented community organisation seen at Weston only 2 km away.

Although ring-fenced enclosures are present in the lower-lying southern parishes of the Blackdown Hills, they are more common in the higher regions of the northern part of the study area. In particular ring-fenced enclosures are also present within areas of Parliamentary Enclosure (see Fig. 3.3). The occurrence of late Parliamentary Enclosure combined with small ring-fenced fields suggests a model for the upland fringe in this area. For example, the regular parallel-sided fields are evident in conjunction with the ring-fenced fields at Mays Farm, where there is evidence of shared ownership and possible convertible husbandry from the Tithe Surveys (see below). This provides a comparison to the small irregular fields located along the river valleys, which were enclosed earlier and which hold

Parish name (south to north)	Total number of 19th century fields digitised	Total number containing mead elements	Percentage of fields in parish	Overall Total of fields in study area
Buckerell	228	26	11.40%	
Awliscombe	970	113	11.65%	
Dunkeswell	246	14	5.69%	
Combe Raleigh	296	29	9.80%	
Luppitt	1128	144	12.77%	
Hemyock	1590	146	9.18%	
Clayhidon	2022	189	9.35%	
Total	6479	661		10.20%

Parish name (west to east)	Total number of 19th century fields digitised	Total number containing mead elements	Percentage of fields in parish	Overall Total of fields in study area
Hartland	3307	282	8.53%	
Welcombe	649	60	9.24%	
Woolfardisworthy	1329	67	5.04%	
Clovelly	692	82	11.85%	
Total	5977	491		8.21%

Parish name (west to east)	Total number of 19th century fields digitised	Total number containing mead elements	Percentage	Overall Total of fields in study area
Thurlestone	241	16	6.6%	
Bigbury	428	27	6.3%	
Bigbury-on-Sea	65	10	15.4%	
Total	734	53		7.22%

TABLE 6.1. Total number of digitised Tithe Survey fields containing mead elements in their field-names

a high percentage of mead elements in their field-names (Figs 3.33 and 4.24).

In models based on the Midlands zone, meadow, which the 'mead' elements within the fieldname represent, tends to be located along river valleys. This is due to the valleys' suitability for promoting rapid growth allowing for harvests between mid-May and mid-June (Williamson 2003, 163–4). Williamson (2003, 174) argues that in the Midland and East Anglian counties the more concentrated the meadow land the more nucleated the settlements were. Furthermore, Campbell (2000, 75–8) notes that his analysis of IPM places in east Devon (and therefore the Blackdown Hills) as part of a landscape zone where meadow was more consistently represented, in a landscape typography that stretched across the country to the Vale of Pickering. This landscape corresponds with what Roberts and Wrathmell and Rackham call the Midlands zone.

In the Blackdown Hills there is a high percentage of mead elements (Table 6.1). Their distribution does correspond with the river valleys which intersect

Parish name (south to north)	Total number of 19th century fields digitised	Total number containing park elements	Percentage of fields in parish	Overall Total of fields in study area
Buckerell	228	23	10.09%	
Awliscombe	970	54	5.57%	
Dunkeswell	246	0	0.00%	
Combe Raleigh	296	7	2.36%	
Luppitt	1128	12	1.06%	
Hemyock	1590	12	0.75%	
Clayhidon	2022	38	1.88%	
Total	6480	146		2.25%

Parish name (west to east)	Total number of 19th century fields digitised	Total number containing park elements	Percentage of fields in parish	Overall Total of fields in study area
Hartland	3307	424	12.82%	
Welcombe	649	80	12.33%	
Woolfardisworthy	1329	151	11.36%	
Clovelly	692	100	14.45%	
Total	5977	755		12.63%

Parish name (west to east)	Total number of 19th century fields digitised	Total number containing park elements	percentage	Overall Total of fields in study area
Thurlestone	241	40	16.6%	
Bigbury	428	83	19.4%	
Bigbury-on-Sea	65	6	9.2%	
Total	734	129		17.57%

the study area. A high percentage of field-names containing mead elements is present in the southern parishes of Awliscombe, Buckerell and Combe Raleigh. However, the highest percentage (12.77 per cent) of mead elements can be found in the parish of Luppitt, with just under 10 per cent occurring in Clayhidon and Hemyock. By comparison, the distribution of mead field-names in the Hartland Moors study area is far more fragmented, represented by small blocks of three or four fields. The parish with the highest percentage of mead elements within its field-names is Clovelly, corresponding with the nucleated settlement of Clovelly village.

The Hartland Moors study area sees a high proportion of 'park' elements in the Tithe Survey field-names (Figs 3.31 and 4.22). This corresponds to the lack of post-medieval 'acre' field-names in the historic landscape. As discussed in Chapters Three, Four and Five, the park element, meaning an enclosed piece of land, is derived from the Old English *pearroc*, and is particularly common

TABLE 6.2. Total number of digitised Tithe Survey fields containing park elements in their field-names

in South-Western field-names (Field 1993, 25). The highest percentage of park elements in the Tithe Apportionment field-names occurs in Clovelly parish (see Table 6.2). Here, 14.45 per cent of the fields digitised contain park elements, relating to small parallel-sided fields in blocks to the east of the parish. In the parish of Hartland, the occurrence of park field-names corresponds with the well-defined 'S'-shaped field boundaries associated with Brownsham on the northern coast.

If Field's (1993, 18) conclusion that those 'oven' or 'ofniman' elements derive from Old English and signify land removed from regulated common-field systems and rented for use as pasture is correct, then the occurrence of park names at Brownsham is useful. If it is assumed that the 'S'-shaped field morphology is evidence of medieval land management, and the Old English names are remnants of this earlier phase of activity, a chronology of development can be seen in this area of Hartland Moors.

Squatter camps and wastes and moors

Away from the ring-fenced enclosures and relic open fields the pattern of fields becomes less regular. It can be seen that the further into the heart of the Blackdown Hills, the more obviously piecemeal the enclosure becomes. The evidence of small irregular fields and encroachment on the moors and commons is particularly evident in the parish of Luppitt. Here small consolidations of land can be seen associated with squatter settlements on the common (discussed below). It has been argued that the occurrence of squatter settlement in east Devon and the Blackdown Hills was a response to a scarcity of land available to buy.

In the Blackdown Hills study area during the sixteenth century the hundreds of Hemyock, Colyton, and Axminster were important sheep-rearing areas, with urbanism concentrated around the small cloth producing settlements of Colyton and Honiton combining pastoral farming with domestic manufacturing (Thirsk 1967, *passim*; Kew 1969, 34; Fox 1973, 19). The district of East Devon was prosperous due to its relatively fertile soils and these cloth producing industries, but short of land for sale. Moreover, the region had more in common with Somerset and Dorset that the rest of Devon (Kew 1969, 34). Large manors were held by people of at least the rank of esquire, and a few freeholders, leading to an landownership pattern described as being of 'aristocratic character' (Kew 1969, 34–6). This lack of purchasable land created frustration amongst the yeomen and lesser gentry. It is argued that the shortage of buyable land led to an encroachment on to the moors and less agriculturally productive lands. This is visible in the historic landscape through the establishment of small individual farms like those seen on Hense Moor in Luppitt (Fig. 3.35). Stanes (1969, 46) draws attention to the Milles Enquiries of 1747–56 which notes that Hemyock was 'enclosed, except for the hills; the hills are very advantageous for pasture and for the poor cutting turf'.

Parish name (south to north)	Total number of 19th century fields digitised	Total number containing brake elements	Percentage	Overall Total of fields in study area
Buckerell	228	0	0.0%	
Awliscombe	970	0	0.0%	
Dunkeswell	246	0	0.0%	
Combe Raleigh	296	0	0.0%	
Luppitt	1128	4	0.4%	
Hemyock	1590	3	0.2%	
Clayhidon	2022	1	0.0%	
Total	6479	8		0.12%

Parish name (west to east)	Total number of 19th century fields digitised	Total number containing brake elements	Percentage	Overall Total of fields in study area
Hartland	3307	27	0.8%	
Welcombe	649	0	0.0%	
Woolfardisworthy	1329	3	0.2%	
Clovelly	692	5	0.7%	
Total	5977	35		0.59%

Parish name (west to east)	Total number of 19th century fields digitised	Total number containing brake elements	Percentage	Overall Total of fields in study area
Thurlestone	241	1	0.4%	
Bigbury	428	7	1.6%	
Bigbury-on-Sea	65	1	1.5%	
Total	734	9		1.23%

In the Hartland Moors study area it is clear that there is a lack of enclosure of moorland, with large tracts, such as Bursdon and Hendon unenclosed. The areas of unenclosed moorland and waste in Hartland present a different landscape character to that seen in the Blackdown Hills. However, from the work of Harold Fox, it is clear that Hendon in particular did see earlier occupation, but this settlement has since been lost. This will be discussed in more detail in this chapter.

It is important to consider the survival of the land use in field-names when discussing the enclosure of moorland and waste. This is because evidence of pre-enclosure land use can remain within field-names elements, for example, the occurrence of 'brake' elements within field-names is thought to be a good indicator of land broken up for cultivation (Taylor 1975, 104; Field 1993, 80). However, in the Blackdown Hills only eight out of 6479 fields digitised

TABLE 6.3. Total number of digitised Tithe Survey fields containing brake elements in their field-names

Parish name (south to north)	Total number of 19th century fields digitised	Total number containing breach elements	Percentage	Overall Total of fields in study area
Buckerell	228	0	0.0%	
Awliscombe	970	19	2.0%	
Dunkeswell	246	0	0.0%	
Combe Raleigh	296	7	2.4%	
Luppitt	1127	8	0.7%	
Hemyock	1590	19	1.2%	
Clayhidon	2022	39	1.9%	
Total	6479	92		1.42%

Parish name (west to east)	Total number of 19th century fields digitised	Total number containing breach elements	Percentage	Overall Total of fields in study area
Hartland	3307	0	0	
Welcombe	649	0	0	
Woolfardisworthy	1329	0	0	
Clovelly	692	0	0	
Total	5977	0		0.00%

Parish name (west to east)	Total number of 19th century fields digitised	Total number containing breach elements	Percentage	Overall Total of fields in study area
Thurlestone	241	1	0.4%	
Bigbury	428	0	0.0%	
Bigbury-on-Sea	65	0	0.0%	
Total	734	1		0.14%

TABLE 6.4. Total number of digitised Tithe Survey fields containing breach elements in their field-names

contained the element 'brake' (Table 6.1). These were located in the parishes of Luppitt, Hemyock and Clayhidon. In Hartland the number is little better, with 35 fields out of 5977 digitised. This may simply be an issue of linguistics, with this name not occurring in Devon despite being present in Somerset. The same may be true of 'breach' names, which are also common in Somerset. 'Breach' elements are a reference to clearing hitherto unused land (Field 1993, 80). As table 6.3 shows, there were no breach elements recorded in any of the fields digitised in the Hartland Moors study area, and less than 1 per cent of the total number of field-names in the Blackdown Hills. The highest percentage occurred in Combe Raleigh and Clayhidon. If for linguist reasons 'breach' and 'brake' names do not occur in Devon in large quantities then 'moor' and 'common' field-name elements may have been used instead (Figs 3.32/4.23).

'Common' elements are still sparsely distributed, but provide an interesting pattern where they do occur (Table 6.5). In all the parishes in the Blackdown

Parish name (south to north)	Total number of 19th century fields digitised	Total number containing common elements	Percentage of fields in parish	Overall Total of fields in study area
Buckerell	228	0	0.00%	
Awliscombe	970	9	0.93%	
Dunkeswell	246	0	0.00%	
Combe Raleigh	296	1	0.34%	
Luppitt	1128	4	0.35%	
Hemyock	1590	5	0.31%	
Clayhidon	2022	43	2.13%	
Total	6479	62		0.96%

Parish name (west to east)	Total number of 19th century fields digitised	Total number containing common elements	Percentage of fields in parish	Overall Total of fields in study area
Hartland	3307	9	0.27%	
Welcombe	649	5	0.77%	
Woolfardisworthy	1329	0	0.00%	
Clovelly	692	0	0.00%	
Total	5977	14		0.23%

Parish name (west to east)	Total number of 19th century fields digitised	Total number containing common elements	Percentage	Overall Total of fields in study area
Thurlestone	241	1	0.4%	
Bigbury	428	4	0.9%	
Bigbury-on-Sea	65	0	0.0%	
Total	734	5		0.68%

Hills study area, less than 1 per cent of fields contained 'common' names. The exception is Clayhidon, which sees 2 per cent of fields with this element. The occurrence of 'common' field-name elements correspond with the small regularly shaped fields on the boundaries between Clayhidon and neighbouring Hemyock and Wellington in Somerset. In the Hartland Moors study area there are no 'common' elements recorded in any of the fields digitised from the Woolfardisworthy and Clovelly Tithe Surveys. In Hartland and Welcombe parishes 'common' field-names occur in less than 1 per cent of fields.

The distribution of 'moor' elements in the Blackdown Hills study area follows an expected pattern with the three lower-lying southern parishes showing a small percentage of fields containing 'moor' in their field-name, whereas the element occurs in 5 per cent of the northern upland parishes. 'Moor' field-names occur in

TABLE 6.5. Total number of digitised Tithe Survey fields containing common elements in their field-names

Parish name (south to north)	Total number of 19th century fields digitised	Total number containing moor elements	Percentage	Overall Total of fields in study area
Buckerell	228	1	0.4%	
Awliscombe	970	17	1.8%	
Dunkeswell	246	12	4.9%	
Combe Raleigh	296	7	2.4%	
Luppitt	1128	62	5.5%	
Hemyock	1590	78	4.9%	
Clayhidon	2022	113	5.6%	
Total	6479	290		4.48%

Parish name (west to east)	Total number of 19th century fields digitised	Total number containing moor elements	Percentage	Overall Total of fields in study area
Hartland	3307	271	8.2%	
Welcombe	649	35	5.4%	
Woolfardisworthy	1329	169	12.7%	
Clovelly	692	87	12.6%	
Total	5977	562		9.40%

Parish name (west to east)	Total number of 19th century fields digitised	Total number containing moor elements	Percentage	Overall Total of fields in study area
Thurlestone	241	1	0.4%	
Bigbury	428	1	0.2%	
Bigbury-on-Sea	65	0	0.0%	
Total	734	2		0.27%

TABLE 6.6. Total number of digitised Tithe Survey fields containing moor elements in their field-names

a concentration around the settlement of Wolverstone in Awliscombe, creating discrete blocks of fields. Table 6.6 shows that in the Hartland Moors study area, 12 per cent of digitised fields in Clovelly and Woolfardisworthy contain 'moor' elements. In Hartland and Welcombe just over 8 per cent and 5 per cent respectively of fields have 'moor' field-names. In Hartland this percentage is distributed throughout the parish, but particularly concentrated on Tosbury Moor. The 'moor' names are also present in relation to the hamlets and associated strip fields of Milford, Hardisworthy and South Hole on the western coast. As seen in the case of Weston in the Blackdown Hills it can be argued that this set-up of strip fields and associated common mirrors on a smaller scale the model suggested by Roberts and Wrathmell in figure 1.4, where the open field strips are surrounded by larger fields used for pasture. The complete lack of common elements within the field-names of the Hartland moors may correspond with the presence of unenclosed land in the study area.

The combination of field morphology and documentary evidence suggests the enclosure of waste and common land occurred on a cyclical basis for convertible husbandry. The lack of 'brake' and 'breach' field-name evidence is, therefore, perhaps not wholly unexpected, especially when considering the high percentage of acre elements. Furthermore, the nature of the land management may also influence the survival of land clearance indicators. The conversion to moor or waste to arable or pasture once every eight years may not have formally enclosed the areas with permanent boundaries. When their shape was permanently enclosed with banks and hedges the fields were given the functional post-medieval acre field-names. This is particularly so in areas which experienced Parliamentary Enclosure.

Parliamentary Enclosure

Evidence of Parliamentary Enclosure is present in the Blackdown Hills study area, and can be also found at Parkham Ash to the east of Woolfardisworthy in the Hartland Moors study area. The landscape signature of Parliamentary Enclosure is distinguished by regular straight-sided fields. Fields of this type are identifiable not only in Devon but the whole of the country. Clear evidence of Parliamentary Enclosure can be seen in Clayhidon in the Blackdown Hills, and documentary evidence in the form of Enclosure Awards substantiates the field morphology. This is also confirmed by Nineteenth-century enclosure maps. The northern part of Clayhidon was enclosed from 1812 to 1822 as part of a 600 acre sweep across land held by the Duke of Wellington. This crosses over the Devon/Somerset border. Although there is some evidence from aerial photographs that this area was enclosed previously (perhaps during the later prehistoric or early medieval period, see Walls, 2004), the field morphology and the documentary evidence of the nineteenth-century enclosure suggest that this area was open for much of the medieval period.

The Parliamentary Enclosure of Clayhidon also confirms the use of 'acre' names as an identifier of later enclosure. Although there is some evidence of medieval field-names containing acre, they are generally thought to be modern (Field 1993, 125). This means that there are two types of 'acre' field-names; names such as Six Acre are generally associated with post-medieval enclosure, but names such as Birch Acre Close indicate an earlier field that has been enclosed. From querying the Tithe Apportionment dataset it can be seen that the majority of these Parliamentary enclosed fields contained acre field-names. In Clayhidon 'acre' names made up over 10 per cent of the total number of digitised fields.

The occurrence of the Parliamentary Enclosure landscape signature, the regular parallel-sided fields, and the combination of field and landownership patterns is important for both study areas and provides a model to be tested in the third case study area of the South Hams.

Testing landscape signatures and the Historic Landscape Characterisation for Devon

The third case study region, the South Hams, acted as a comparison to the Blackdown Hills and Hartland Moors, and was divided into three sample areas (see Fig. 5.7). The sample areas in the South Hams study area were chosen to test if the distinctive landscape signatures can be seen in other areas, and therefore other *pays* regions. In particular, the morphological models of ring-fenced enclosures (sub-circler enclosures with internal division held in severalty), and relic open fields (bundles of strip fields which fossilise possible furlong blocks with multiple ownership) are distinctive within the landscapes of the Blackdown Hills and Hartland Moors study areas. As discussed in Chapter Five, the South Hams experienced a process of enclosure which formed neater and more regular square fields than those seen in the Blackdown Hills or Hartland Moors study areas. This enclosure is thought to have occurred later, around the fourteenth and fifteenth centuries (Fox 1972a, 86; 1972b, 6).

Sample Area 1 focused on the nucleated settlement of Thurlestone and its associated fields and the coastline and estuary around Bantham Ham. The patterns of landholding, which did not respect routeways, indicate open field around the settlement of Thurlestone. This is important as it is indicating a land use which has been lost in later enclosures. Sample Area 2 was sited due to the occurrence of an oval enclosure which encompassed a single farmstead in a landscape dominated by strips, large regular fields, and the nucleated settlement of Bigbury. The field system of Hingston showed similarities to the ring-fenced enclosures seen in Combe Raleigh in the Blackdown Hills. In Combe Raleigh, these enclosures were held in severality, and these types of field system are generally associated with upland areas. The arrangement around the individual farmstead called Hingston provided the opportunity to test the hypothesis that the landscape signature for ring-fenced enclosures is that they would be held in severalty. This premise derived from the models discussed in Chapter Two. Roberts and Wrathmell (2002, 67) highlighted the patterns related to upland hamlets in the South-west. Fields occur as blocks or strips within a ring-fenced enclosure, which was enclosed in one phase and is usually associated with one landowner (Roberts and Wrathmell 2002, 67). The patterns of landownership and leaseholders did indicate that Hingston was held by one owner (see Figs 5.12 and 5.13). The third sample area was situated over Burgh Island and the area now covered by the settlement of Bigbury-on-Sea. This was an area of dispersed settlements and large later enclosed fields. The three sample areas in the South Hams study area confirm the landscape signatures associated with former open field and with ring-fenced enclosures, and do correspond with not only specific field patterns but also distinctive landownership patterns.

The explanation of the presence of particular patterns within the historic landscape can be tested by making comparisons between the Devon Historic Landscape Characterisation (HLC) and the historic landscape as seen through the nineteenth-century Tithe Surveys for all seven of the parishes in the

Blackdown Hills study area, and Hartland and Welcombe parishes in the Hartland Moors study area.

The Historic Landscape Characterisation (HLC) for Devon carried out by Sam Turner and Devon County Council was completed in late 2004. The purpose of the Historic Landscape Characterisation is to aid planning decisions through a better understanding of the previous and current land use by assigning a value such as 'enclosed land', or 'industrial'. The Devon HLC was completed using the modern (1999) and the 1890 Ordnance Survey maps. The HLC information for Clovelly and Woolfardisworthy was not available at the time of writing and therefore comparisons are only available for the parishes of Hartland and Welcombe.

There is little change recorded in the HLC between the 1890 Ordnance Survey and the characterisation using the 1999 Ordnance Survey, except for some areas of rough pasture that have been converted into 'enclosed land'. The areas of strip fields have also been incorporated into this blanket term of 'enclosed land' by this point. For this reason the modern characterisation is not included here.

This clearly defined change from open rough ground to enclosed areas does not incorporate the fluidity of the upland area, which saw seasonal and temporary enclosure. Obviously this categorisation of the historic landscape takes a broad brush approach, but there are some problems with the blanket use of the definition 'enclosure' which can miss differences in land management. The HLC, due to its nature, suggests that the historic landscape for the Blackdown Hills study area is generally regular and uniform in character, whereas this study has shown that there are significant differences occurring between the parishes.

Despite these small misgivings, which are slight when considering the scale at which the characterisation was carried out, the Devon HLC gives a good illustration of the development which occurred in the Blackdown Hills area. This can also be said for the Hartland Moors area. The 1890 characterisation defines the region as predominantly enclosed (approximately 47 per cent of 511 defined polygons), with rough pasture making up the second largest land use category. In terms of dating, the area is divided into three categories, Medieval, Post-medieval and Modern. The division between medieval and post-medieval is approximately 40 per cent to 70 per cent respectively. However, the HLC does not take into account the areas of relic open field on the western coast of Hartland parish. This is significant, as the identification of these areas have an impact on how the area is classified, and how the past landscape is understood.

The HLC uses field morphology in order to understand the antiquity of the landscape. It can be seen from the two previous sections (and the case studies in Chapters Three to Five) that by analysing field patterns a number of elements emerge which suggest the development of the landscape, for example the evidence of strip fields and ring-fenced enclosures. The landscape features (open field evidence *etc*) suggested by the HLC have been, for the most part, confirmed by the field-by-field landscape investigation. Nevertheless, it can be seen that the HLC does miss fundamental elements of the landscape and therefore its validity outside of planning applications needs to be questioned.

The validity of field-names as indicators of past landscapes

Having discussed field-names in relation to recognisable landscape signatures such as ring-fenced enclosure, it can be seen that the analysis of Tithe Survey field-names provides a further valuable layer of information. By spatially plotting their location, the occurrence of particular names can be assessed with the identified field patterns. A more comprehensive study of field-names can be seen in Appendix 1, tables 1–10, but only seven elements (acre, park, brake, breach, common, moor and mead) have been discussed in detail.

It is important to assess the usefulness of field-names through already identified landscape signatures. Firstly, to see whether names consistently occur in other areas, and secondly to identify other names which are present within these field systems and assess whether they also can be used elsewhere to locate the landscape signature.

Areas of relic open field seem an obvious starting point. Within the distinct blocks of strip fields associated with the settlement of Weston in the Blackdown Hills (see Fig. 3.15) a number of indicative names occur. Perhaps the most descriptive are the 'furlong' elements suggestive of former open fields. Furlong names occur in the strips of both parishes of Awliscombe and Buckerell, and literally mean length of a furrow; the division of a common field in which the furrows lie in the same direction (Field 1993, 14). This is exactly the type of name that would be expected in an area of former open field. Also occurring within the field strips are 'rag' elements. 'Rag', particularly in Wiltshire but also other southern counties, is thought to be indicative of small patches of woodland (Field 1993, 58). The occurrence of 'rag' fields names in this area of the Blackdown Hills may be indicative of two things. Firstly, a suggested land use, and secondly, descriptive of the size and nature of the fields. The existence of a number of field names such as Buckerell Lands may be indicative of open fields. The presence of these field-names in the former open field system provides information regarding landholding patterns. As discussed in Chapter Three, on the Tithe Surveys the fields around Weston were divided between the parishes of Buckerell and Awliscombe, and the occurrence of this name reinforced the cooperative nature of the relic open field.

Perhaps the most indicative field-name is 'landscore', which occurs in some of the strip fields in Awliscombe. Landscore is a corruption of OE *landscoru* meaning a division of land (OED 2nd ed. 1989). This element does not occur elsewhere in the Blackdown Hills study area, and its occurrence reinforces the argument that the small bundles of strip fields are the relics of open field farming.

'Acre' names, in forms such as Six Acre, are thought to be indicative of late enclosure and, therefore, are associated with post-medieval and Parliamentary Enclosure (Figs 3.30 and 4.21). It is clear that former land use and management patterns can be fossilised within the field-names, and the majority of these are thought to derive from the later medieval or post-medieval period as a product of enclosure (Laing and Laing 1996, 76). The occurrence of this type of 'acre' element within field-names provides a good example of this association between field-name and field morphology. Field-names containing the element 'acre' provide an interesting insight into the patterns of later enclosure, as the inclusion of acreage is the most common indicator of post-enclosure field-names.

The percentage and distribution pattern of 'acre' elements in the Blackdown Hills and Hartland Moors study areas is distinctly different (Table 6.7). Just under 10 per cent of fields digitised in the Blackdown Hills study area contained 'acre' elements in their field-names, with the highest percentages in the parishes of Clayhidon, Luppitt and Dunkeswell, on the hillslopes generally above 240 m.

The highest percentage of these 'acre' elements occurred in Luppitt, where the historic landscape is diverse in this parish. In Luppitt the spatial distribution of these field-names indicates the extent of the enclosure of the common. This fits the hypothesis that Luppitt was enclosed in a piecemeal way from the valleys up to the moorlands. The process of enclosure does not appear to be related to landholding patterns, as seen in Awliscombe, Buckerell and Combe Raleigh. Morphologically, the parallel-sided fields located to the east of Luppitt indicate later enclosure, confirmed by the predominance of acre names. This pattern continues into neighbouring Dunkeswell, where just under 23 per cent of fields digitised contain 'acre' the field-name element. However, this high percentage may be distorted as much of Dunkeswell was untitheable and therefore unmappable. Moreover, the fields that are present may represent land that was later enclosed and illustrates an unrepresentative picture of the parish as a whole.

The parish of Hemyock also shows a relatively high percentage of 'acre' names (7.17 per cent) corresponding with the idea that the uplands were enclosed later. However, the highest percentage occurs in Buckerell (7.46 per cent) which was not expected for a low-lying parish. Nevertheless, the distribution of these fields indicate that the acre names occur in groups of two or three fields located just below Hembury Hillfort to the north of the parish and in small blocks on the edges of the former open field at Weston, and the strips on the Feniton/ Buckerell border. The late enclosure names in this parish appear to indicate small areas of open common or waste ground surrounding these former open field structures. The long parallel boundaries would suggest brakes within the field structure, and may indicate the areas used for pasture, as seen in Roberts and Wrathmell's model discussed in Chapter One and illustrated in figure 1.4 and Roberts schematic model in figure 1.5. It is argued that the Blackdown Hills experienced a number of enclosure episodes that happened at different rates depending on their location. These enclosure episodes cumulate with the enclosure of the upland fringes to the north of the study area.

Parish name (south to north)	Total number of 19th century fields digitised	Total number containing acre elements	Percentage of fields in parish	Overall Total of fields in study area
Buckerell	228	17	7.46%	
Awliscombe	970	59	6.08%	
Dunkeswell	246	56	22.76%	
Combe Raleigh	296	16	5.41%	
Luppitt	1128	151	13.39%	
Hemyock	1590	114	7.17%	
Clayhidon	2022	203	10.04%	
Total	6479	616		9.51%

Parish name (west to east)	Total number of 19th century fields digitised	Total number containing acre elements	Percentage of fields in parish	Overall Total of fields in study area
Hartland	3307	127	3.84%	
Welcombe	649	10	1.54%	
Woolfardisworthy	1329	52	3.91%	
Clovelly	692	31	4.48%	
Total	5977	220		3.68%

Parish name (west to east)	Total number of 19th century fields digitised	Total number containing acre elements	Percentage	Overall Total of fields in study area
Thurlestone	241	0	0.0%	
Bigbury	428	9	2.1%	
Bigbury-on-Sea	65	2	3.1%	
Total	734	11		1.50%

TABLE 6.7. Total number of digitised Tithe Survey fields containing acre elements in their field-names

The Hartland Moors region shows a different distribution of 'acre' field-names. It is clear that there was not large scale Parliamentary Enclosure here but, crucially, there was significant late and post-medieval enclosure which is visible in the historic landscape. In the study area less than 4 per cent of the fields digitised in Hartland, Welcombe, Woolfardisworthy and Clovelly contain 'acre' elements within their field-names. The distribution of these names is dispersed and scattered, and does not form the distinct blocks seen in Luppitt, Clayhidon, or even Buckerell. Clovelly has the highest number of digitised fields containing the 'acre' element (just over 4 per cent), located in the east of the parish near to the border with Parkham parish

Therefore, 'acre' names which are related to size are indicative of later enclosure, and this is reinforced by field morphology. However, it is worth highlighting again that there are 'acre' names that do occur in fields which are not associated with later enclosure. Where they occur, the names tend to be added to seemingly earlier names. For example, Rabbit Clapp Five Acres in Dunkeswell, Clapper meaning warren or burrow created for keeping tame animals and common from the fifteenth century onwards (Field 1993, 74; OED 2nd ed. 1992), or Birch Acre Field in Hemyock. Rabbit Clapp Five Acres is a little strip-like field and Birch Acre Field is a small and irregular plot, and would not be classed as later enclosure by their morphological traits. They bear no relation to the large regular and parallel-sided fields such as those seen in Clayhidon.

These two examples illustrate that the use of field-names in combination with other elements of historic landscape studies, such as field shape and land use, can add a further dimension to the understanding of the processes and phases occurring in past landscapes.

The arguments for convertible husbandry and ley farming

The main evidence of convertible husbandry comes from documentary evidence. The evidence gained from the study of the Blackdown Hills historic landscape through field boundary morphology, field-names, land use and landholding patterns, is the manifestation of this form of agriculture. Convertible husbandry is a form of crop rotation, which occurs in approximately eight enclosed field compartments of around 3 to 4 acres closest to a farmstead. These small fields are used for both arable and pasture over a period of around 8 to 10 years. Fox (1991, 310) notes that convertible husbandry was well suited to the conditions that Devon experienced during the later Middle Ages, which were ideal for an amalgamation of arable and pastoral farming.

From the study of the nineteenth-century field patterns, it can be suggested that a distinctive landscape signature for ley or convertible husbandry can be seen in the Blackdown Hills study area. This is best illustrated in figure 3.24, the field morphology and nineteenth-century landownership pattern at May's Farm in the southern half of Clayhidon. As discussed in Chapter Three, to the north of May's Farm there is a block of seven fields which show evidence of ploughing through curved field boundaries, with associated moorland (Hole Moor) to the east. This example shows a lozenge shaped enclosure with a number of inverted 'S'-shaped field boundaries alternating between the Tithe Survey land use categories 'arable' and pasture and landownership of James Troake and John Pring. Even if the use of 'arable' refers to 'ploughable', rather than a straight description of land use, the suggestion that this land could have been used for convertible husbandry still applies.

A second occurrence of the distinct field morphology of ley or convertible husbandry can be seen at Cole Hill in Luppitt. Identified through Tithe Survey field pattern morphology, a block of six fields can be seen some with 'S'-shaped banks. A seventh field was added after the construction of a second cottage and garden plot. This field system lies on the southern edge of Hense Moor.

The later addition of a cottage and garden, held by John Searle on the Tithe Survey may indicate the temporary enclosure of waste, that later becomes fixed in the landscape as a permanent settlement or field system (Hoskins 1943, 87). This is something which has been alluded to in earlier chapters, and is a key to understanding how the historic landscape developed during the medieval period and resulted in the patterns visible on the nineteenth-century Tithe Surveys.

The number of fields in these two examples is significant. As discussed in Chapter One, Fox and Padel (2000, lxx–lxxi) suggest that convertible husbandry took place over a period of 6 to 8 years. The occurrence of seven fields at May's Farm, and six fields at Cole Hill would suggest that one field was enclosed for 1 or 2 years and then left fallow for the remaining years of the rotation.

The use of commons and moors was critical to how farming regimes such as convertible husbandry worked. It cannot be underestimated how important common land and waste were to the management and organisation of the landscape in the medieval period. Fox (1973, 30) discusses documentary evidence showing the practice of rent charges or fines for putting common wastes under tillage. It has been recorded that the waste land in the Blackdown Hills was used for outfield cultivation during the medieval period. Two disputes relate to Hackpen Hill to the east of the parish of Hemyock. In 1249 a disagreement was resolved with permission being granted to 'break up and cultivate' part of the hill, providing it was reverted back to pasture after the corn was harvested (Fox 1972a, 99). The second dispute, dating to 1301–2, was settled when it was agreed that 6 acres of waste could be cultivated yearly, so long as they were enclosed during cultivation and then opened again (Fox 1978, 99–100).

The examples seen in the Blackdown Hills study area are located in the more northerly parishes and relate to a landscape which contains a more dispersed settlement pattern. The signatures seen in the Blackdowns that can be associated with the practice of convertible husbandry do not occur in the historic landscape of Hartland Moors study area. The lack of such distinctive field patterns in the Hartland Moors study area suggests either that they have not survived, or that the field pattern does not occur here. If this is so, the lack of a distinct field morphology indicates that convertible husbandry was carried out in strip fields associated with nucleated settlements. This masks the identification of convertible husbandry in the Hartland Moors area through historic landscape studies. Furthermore, evidence of convertible husbandry practices are also not in evidence from the information gained from studying the nineteenth-century historic landscape in the third study area of the South Hams. This may be due to the better agricultural conditions in the South Hams, and the focus of land management of cereal cultivation.

The landscape signatures, the blocks of distinct fields associated with a dwelling, sub-divided with alternating patterns of land use seen in the Blackdown Hills are not prevalent in the Hartland Moors study area. However, in the Hartland Moors area, the occurrence of the Tithe Survey land use classification 'arable occasionally…' is interesting as it is suggestive of a process similar to ley or convertible husbandry. This suggests that the signature of the distinct pattern of field boundaries seen in the Blackdown Hills and Tithe Survey land use patterns are not transferable to all other areas of Devon, unlike the morphologically identifiable ring-fenced enclosures or straight-sided fields of Parliamentary Enclosure.

Suggesting a chronology of landscape development

The discussion so far has addressed field morphology, land use, landholding patterns, and field-names in a holistic way to create a picture of the development of the historic landscape. The addition of landholding and field-names as layers of information to historic landscape studies moves interpretation of past landscapes away from purely morphologically driven research. Combining this information allows a tentative relative chronology of development to be suggested for the Blackdown Hills and Hartland Moors study areas.

The earliest visible phase of enclosure within the nineteenth-century historic landscape of the Blackdown Hills is located in the lower-lying sheltered valleys which dissect the southern part of the study area. Field morphology and patterns of landholding suggest piecemeal enclosure that was undertaken in two different ways. The relic open field at Weston indicates early enclosure by around the thirteenth century. The field pattern here suggests that the medieval open strips were enclosed by agreement more or less at the same time, but in a piecemeal arrangement, fossilising their form in the later field boundaries. Fields in the southern parishes of Buckerell, Awliscombe and Combe Raleigh also fit the description of the earliest phases of enclosure in east Devon, dating to around the thirteenth century. Piecemeal enclosure occurs in the centre of the study area (and conversely the Blackdown Hills as a whole) and is interspersed with later more regular enclosure. This suggests areas which are left open after enclosure and may indicate pasture land used for convertible husbandry and seasonal grazing. Around Dumpdon Hillfort in Luppitt it can be argued that some of these larger and more regular fields started life as earlier irregular plots, which had been opened up to make them more agriculturally favourable. These larger fields occur on the higher ground, illustrating the expansion onto the moors and waste land, and correspond with the types of fields seen in figures 1.4 and 1.5. Finally, there is the easily identifiable post-medieval enclosure, culminating the sweep of Parliamentary fields occurring in Clayhidon which dates to the years 1812–1822. Dating can only be tentatively suggested as there is little tangible evidence to fix precise timescales, but there are clear indications that the origins of the nineteenth-century landscape lay partly in the Middle Ages.

The Hartland Moors study area underwent a different process of enclosure to that seen in the Blackdown Hills. The process of enclosure is more complex than in the Blackdown Hills despite its regularity in field morphology. As discussed in Chapter Four, there is significant evidence to tie the development of the medieval landscape in the Hartland Moors region with the manor of

Harton. There is evidence from field-names and field morphology of large areas of enclosure which are seemingly contemporary, but landholding patterns indicate a number of fragmentary holdings. The presence of relic open field on the western edge of Hartland parish, and the oven field-names at Brownsham indicate pockets of earlier enclosure along the coasts. Field-name evidence indicates that moorland was enclosed in the late medieval or post-medieval periods. However, many moors are not enclosed and there is no Parliamentary Enclosure (other than the area at Parkham Ash mentioned earlier) within the study area.

Tithe Survey landownership: regressive approaches

Landholding patterns have proven crucial in interpreting the development of the nineteenth-century historic landscape. Combined with field morphology, land use and field-names, landholding patterns have informed a chronology of landscapes and suggested, for the Blackdown Hills in particular, that the nineteenth-century historic landscape has its origins in the medieval period. How far the individual patterns of landholding can be confidently traced back is fundamental to the validity of historic landscape studies.

Perhaps the most obvious starting point of the nineteenth-century Tithe Survey landownership pattern is relic open fields. The alternation of multiple landowners (and in many cases occupiers) in strips can be argued to be indicative of a medieval open field structure and is present in all three of the study areas. The makeup of landownership indicates how land was farmed before enclosure, with some owners holding individual strips scattered over a wide area. With enclosure these patterns become fields and survive into the nineteenth century. This pattern is further supported by field morphology, the distinct strips forming bundles, and also by field-name evidence, which indicates the possible presence of furlong blocks and divisions of land.

These patterns of landownership can then inform areas where field systems do not survive. The occurrence of land held in severalty in association with ring-fenced enclosures (see Fig. 1.4) is also indicative of an earlier landscape, as seen at Hington in Sample Area 2 in the South Hams (Fig. 5.12). Furthermore, in the case of Clovelly in Hartland and Combe Raleigh in the Blackdown Hills, patterns of nineteenth-century occupiers can provide evidence of tenement farms associated with individual farmsteads or settlements. These well-defined field systems are associated with distinctive types of landholding. Using field morphology and documentary evidence, it can be suggested that relic open field systems were enclosed around the thirteenth century. Regression of landownership can be tentatively taken back to this date. It is probable that this pattern could illustrate a pre-thirteenth-century landscape, but this cannot be confidently suggested, and would be more speculation.

It is clear that the pattern of landholding gained from the nineteenth-century Tithe Survey does add an important layer to the study of the historic landscape. This is especially so when landownership distributions do not respect nineteenth-century field morphology operating as indicators for former practices that cannot be accessed by the analysis of field systems alone. In particular, this analysis of Tithe Survey landholding relates to the later medieval period after the eleventh century when where there was a distinct change in the nature of which land was held and managed. Aston and Bettey (1998, 117) note that such a transition in ownership could hardly fail to have profound effects upon the landscape, the economy, and society in general.

It is noted that by discussing patterns of Tithe Survey landownership only the top layers of the hierarchical scales are being considered. However, it is important that this type of landholding information is discussed as it allows for further questions about how communities work within these estate centres. Important to this is how land and settlements were distributed, and the role of nucleated centres of occupation and the individual farmstead.

The apparent continuity between the nineteenth-century patterns of landholding and earlier estates provides an interesting hypothesis that elements of the historic landscape can be used to assess medieval landscapes. Perhaps this should not be so surprising, after all we embrace the use of parish boundaries within landscape studies as elements that are supposed to be relatively unchanging from the areas defined by the twelfth centuries. For example, Bettey (2000, 35) notes when discussing the chalk downlands of southern England, that parish boundaries are a 'lasting legacy of the Saxon period'. Any movement of parish boundaries would be much less frequent than the changes in landownership. However, despite these boundaries being mostly in place by the twelfth century, such as in the South Hams study area where they follow the route of the early medieval Charters, in many cases they were not mapped until the nineteenth century.

Unlike parish boundaries, landownership patterns cannot be traced back to the Conquest and the early medieval period. For example, although seemingly apparent in the nineteenth-century Tithe Surveys the extent of Domesday estates suggested by Reichel (discussed in Chapter Two) cannot be reached through the historic landscape without doubt being cast on the methods applied. The case study by Ransom also illustrates the problems of regressing landownership back beyond the twelfth and thirteenth centuries. Any similarities between Tithe Survey landownership patterns and Domesday acreage is speculative, and can only provoke questions regarding the formation of such landscapes.

Caution must be taken when using sources such as IPMs as areas given can be estimates rather than exact measurements (Fox 1972a, 89). The problem of 'Devon acres' must also be taken into account, as the discrepancies in what an acre is means that even seemingly exact measurements could vary from region to region (see Chapter Two).

Understanding settlement patterns

In this section I seek to address how field systems and patterns of landholding are altered by, and affect, settlement distribution. As a simple explanation, the three study areas show contrasting patterns of settlement structure which are more complicated than previous categorisations have allowed for.

Hoskins (1943, 89) states that the creation of new farms can be particularly seen within the Blackdown Hills in the sixteenth and seventeenth centuries, through the appearance for the first time of farm-names within the documents. Caution must be taken with such an assumption, just because the name only appears for the first time in the records in the post-medieval period does not mean that the settlement does not have an earlier antecedence. However, by using field morphology, landholding patterns and field-names, a picture can be established which does suggest a post-medieval origin for many farmsteads.

In Hemyock parish, for example, 50 per cent of its farm-names had appeared by 1500. In Clayhidon parish 40 per cent of farm-names were present within the documents by this date (Hoskins 1943, 89). Table 6.8 shows the change in population figures from the eleventh to the nineteenth century, and appendix 2 and figure 6.2 illustrate the estimated establishments of the settlements in the Blackdown Hills as taken from the Devon place-name volumes, and show the spread of the first recorded instances of the estates and farms within the study area. It is noted that there is doubt to the legitimacy of some of the dates given to settlements, as they are derived simply from personal names from the lay subsidies. The southern parishes of the study area show the greatest number of settlements recorded in the thirteenth, fourteenth and fifteenth centuries. Settlements located in the parishes in the north of the study area in the heart

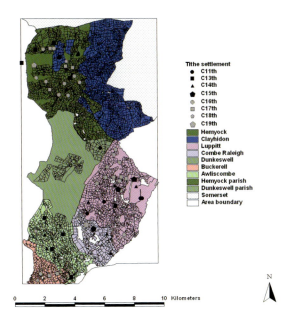

FIGURE 6.2. Distribution of earliest recorded dates for settlements listed in the Blackdown Hills

Parish	Domesday	Lay subsidy 1332	Lay subsidy 1544 & 1545	Polwhele 1793–1806	Vancouver 1808
Awliscombe	50	16	65	-	426
Buckerell	-	16	35	-	280
Clayhidon	48	24	67	-	690
Combe Raleigh	15	-	38	270	237
Hemyock	18	32	48	-	1020
Luppitt	48	-	79	-	675
Bigbury	24	28	60	*c.*370	430
Churchstow	-	15	48	283	219
South Milton	15	23	44	-	302
Thurlestone	35	15	44	-	356
Clovelly	37	24	61	-	714
Hartland	135	49	219	1200	1546
Welcome	25	26	32	-	-
Woolfardisworthy	8	20	68	-	591

TABLE 6.8. Population numbers from Domesday, Lay Subsidies, Polwhele and Vancouver

of the Blackdown Hills show a higher percentage of sixteenth and seventeenth century names recorded than in the southern parishes of Awliscombe, Buckerell, and Combe Raleigh. In the nineteenth century there are few new settlement names recorded anywhere in the study area.

As a whole, the Blackdown Hills contain a number of very different settlement types depending on their location, and their related estate structures. The nucleation at Weston on the Awliscombe and Buckerell border presents a different form to the nucleated settlement to that at Wolverstone in the north of Awliscombe. On the nineteenth-century Tithe Survey the settlement of Wolverstone shows evidence of shrinkage, seen through aerial photographs. A number of fields form small garden plots that exist without associated buildings, but show a similar form to the other plots within Wolverstone itself. It is interesting that this settlement, held during the medieval period by Dunkeswell Abbey, suffered shrinkage when Weston and Awliscombe only a mile to the south did not.

The settlements in the southern parishes of Buckerell and Awliscombe are largely nucleated and the majority can be classed as hamlets (see Fig. 3.34), with the exception of Buckerell and Awliscombe (which have the service facilities, e.g. churches, which allow the classification as a village). Further into the heart of the Blackdown Hills smaller hamlets are also present, but in association with isolated farmsteads, something not seen in the south. As discussed previously the number of individual farmsteads increases the further north into the study area, with less nucleated settlements.

An example of this is the early nineteenth-century settlement of Jacob's City in Clayhidon. The creation of this settlement was driven by the short supply of land, and was founded on the former common land after the 1822 enclosure of this part of Clayhidon. The settlement consists of a number of small dwellings and irregular garden plots, which are at odds with the large rectangular enclosed fields. Jacob's City bares little similarity to the neighbouring settlement of Wiltown, which is thought to have been set up by the fourteenth century. Wiltown is a small hamlet of three farms neighbouring a lozenge-shaped ring-fenced enclosure. This enclosure is surrounded by later parallel-sided fields containing acre names. Jacob's City was finally abandoned before the Tithe Survey, but the buildings are still plotted.

Different types of settlement morphologies are present in the Hartland Moors study area. Hoskins (1952a, 290) explains this by stating that this pattern had more in common with the nucleated settlements seen in the parishes of the Midland zone. The distribution of nucleated settlements and associated relic open fields, and the concentration of dwellings around the chapels founded in the fourteenth century all seem to support this view. Fox (1983, 40) suggests that this occurrence of nucleated settlements is due to the control exerted by the Dynham estate. It can be seen that the distribution of these nucleated settlements corresponds with areas under Dynham control. However, there are also nucleated settlements on the western coast of Hartland, which may indicate that smaller estates regulating and controlling their own hamlets and open fields could have the same effect.

The Hartland Moors study area has a number of distinct landscape signatures. For example, there is evidence at Bursdon for a signature which indicates a settlement located on the edge of moorland, with a clear pattern of irregular fields associated with it. There is evidence for the complete removal of the hamlet of Hendon in the parish of Hartland (Fox 1989, 50). A combination of documentary evidence and local tradition points to this hamlet's size and location, as there are few visible traces of this lost hamlet. At Wolverstone in the Blackdown Hills, in contrast, field morphology, combined with crop- and soilmarks, indicate the extent of the earlier settlement. However, a number of small plots combined with larger outfields show similarities with those in neighbouring Bursdon and this does provide a significant clue to Hendon's location and the presence of former settlement. This provides an interesting hypothesis that within the nineteenth-century historic landscape there are distinct landscape signatures which can be tested.

It is immediately clear that the landholding and estate structure of the Blackdown Hills and Hartland Moors bears little comparison, inspite of both areas being considered 'marginal' by 'traditional' ideas of *pays* regions, and landscape zones such as 'Ancient Countryside'. The two areas also show different landscape signatures in the nineteenth century. Despite this there are a number of similarities between the Blackdown Hills and Hartland Moors, particularly in relation to nucleated settlements and strip fields.

The medieval estate structure of the Blackdown Hills shows a large number of small-scale estates, with Dunkeswell Abbey playing a relatively small part. The estates visible in the nineteenth-century historic landscape are mirrored through the patterns of Tithe Survey landownership and occupier within the study area. The southern parishes of the Blackdowns see a number of small cohesive blocks of landownership, which are commonly mirrored by the patterns of occupiers. Two obvious exceptions to this rule are Combe Raleigh with one landowner, and the area of relic open field adjacent to the nucleated hamlet of Weston, which sees a distinctive and classable pattern of strips with multiple owners. The northern parishes of the Blackdown Hills see a more dispersed pattern of landownership.

In comparison, the Hartland Moors study area was dominated by the Dynham family and the Abbey of Hartland. This is especially apparent in the parishes of Hartland, Welcombe and Woolfardisworthy. Hoskins (1952a, 290) stated the 'settlements of Hartland correspond to 'Midlands' style settlements with a central lord overseeing a system which included open field systems, the so-called 'big village set-ups". In turn, Fox (1983, 40) noted that such nucleation occurred around Harton, the manor of the Dynham lords. However, by the time of the nineteenth-century Tithe Surveys the patterns of landownership within Hartland, Woolfardisworthy and Welcombe are more fragmented. It is suggested that the distribution of fields held by Lewis William Buck is a further indication of the extent of the large Harton estate. In comparison, Clovelly parish, like Combe Raleigh in the Blackdown Hills is thought to have been under the control of one large estate. This is supported by the pattern of nineteenth-century Tithe landownership.

The location of the former settlement of Hendon in Hartland, through the distinctive field system seen at Bursdon, is perhaps the most compelling signature to be tested in the South Hams study area. The South Hams study area shows the greatest degree of nucleation, and therefore makes an ideal location to assess whether the patterns of fields and farmsteads seen at Hendon and Wolverstone are signatures of shrunken or abandoned settlement. In the South Hams study area dwellings are grouped together, with often only two or three nucleated settlements within a parish. The three sample areas in the South Hams show very little evidence for individual farmsteads. Where they do occur, the individual farmsteads are located on the coast or estuary edge. From the descriptions discussed in Chapter One, it is clear that these South Hams settlements do correspond to what would generally be described as a hamlet. Many, like Bigbury, occur around a central green, but they have no service facilities, such as churches, and they are under the control of larger estates. In the post-medieval period both Hartland Moors and the South Hams areas saw migration towards the coast and the establishment of fishing sites (Fox 2001, 17, 162).

Movement and transhumance in the historic landscape

In the medieval and post-medieval periods, although communities were under the control of a landowner they would have their own dynamics, interacting with each other on a day-to-day level. This interaction manifests itself in the way that wastes and commons were utilised, and the movement of animals visible through droveways. Austin (1985, 73) mentions that the documentary evidence for movement is sparse but not absent, for example, oral history sources suggest that such practices were widespread throughout the county (Shakespeare 1990, *passim*).

Routeways and droveways were stable elements within the historic landscape, and provide an insight into the management of the areas. Movement is also visible through land use indicators, or field-names. It is generally assumed that the late medieval accounts of stock movement to and from the uplands reflect more ancient customs (Austin 1985, 73). Fox (1989, 60–62) discusses specialism occurring within regions of Devon during the later Middle Ages, and as a result of this, the movement of animals between these areas. Fourteenth and fifteenth century manorial accounts give a tentative representation of such movements occurring in Devon, as figure 6.3 indicates. This map must represent only a fraction of the movement that took place during the later Middle Ages but the practice appears to have been widespread. The movement is divided into three types: summering of cattle, focused on Dartmoor (a practice which oral history seems to suggest continued into the modern period, see below); rearing

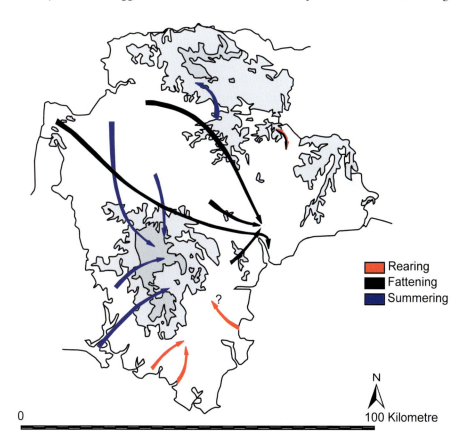

FIGURE 6.3. Suggested cattle transhumance routes across Devon (Redrawing after Fox 1996a, 9)

of young stock, sent from coastal manors; and finally, the fattening of cattle. This is suggested through documents, with movement from east Devon parishes to the meat and leather markets of Exeter (Fox 1989, 62–3).

The Blackdown Hills also show evidence of transhumancy going back into the medieval period, both on a local and inter-regional level. As mentioned in earlier chapters there was movement of cattle from Taunton Priory to Middleton Barton in Clayhidon for grazing during the twelfth and thirteenth century. This shows the types of relationships that occurred between the different areas of the Blackdown Hills, and more importantly highlights a network which spanned the Devon/Somerset border.

In the thirteenth century Welsh Black cattle were shipped across the channel to Minehead and then driven south across the Blackdown Hills to the livestock fair at Chard in Somerset (Toulson 1999, 57). The South Hams also saw movement of young cattle for rearing. As figure 6.3 shows, the eastern side of the Avon Estuary around the parish of Thurlestone saw contact between these lowlands and the inland pastures on the edge of Dartmoor. Transhumancy between Dartmoor and the fertile fields of the South Hams is known through oral history, with cattle brought down to graze in the winter (SRA, n.d, tape 297, side 1). As Herring (1996, 35) indicates, such seasonal movement of sections of stable agricultural societies must have involved fragmentation of these communities and divisions of households for part of the year. Therefore, this type of movement must represent interdependence between regions (Fox 1996a, 9).

Finally Hartland and other parts of north-west Devon saw contact with the Exe Estuary, a cross county link of 40 miles. Cattle movement can generate fairs (Fox 1996a, 15), and Hartland drovers would meet at the sheep fair at Barnstaple, and drove the cattle from there across the landscape (Shakespeare 1990, 56).

This long distance movement of animals was seasonal and driven by markets or the fattening of cattle. It is clear that within Devon's enclosed landscape, there was also movement *within* townships and parishes, with animals being moved over shorter distances, droved from field to field (Fox 1996a, 10). Devonian John Hooker described this movement of animals within estates around the 1600s. Hooker noted that livestock was moved from one field to the next through a number of small closes; 'by their often changes they feed still as it were upon a new springing grass' (Blake Hooker's Synopsis Chorographical n.d, 344; Fox and Padel 2000, lxxi). Fox and Padel (2000, lxxi) suggest this type of movement was suitable for dairy cattle and moving young animals. This movement and stalling of animals can be seen in the historic landscape through field-names such as Lamb Close. This type of movement can also be seen in the Blackdown Hills at Bywood farm which lies on the Dunkeswell/Hemyock border, where the platforms surveyed by the CLP have been identified as pound-like structure (Hawkins 2004, 14). The platforms and their associated field boundaries are situated on the edge of the river valley of the tributary of the Madford river, and below the platforms is rough boggy ground. The field where the platforms are located is named in the Tithe Apportionment as Little Calves Plot, and is neighboured by Calves Plot. As Fox and Padel stated, these field-names are indicative of the penning of animals, seasonally, or for internal transhumance of the young cattle.

Such field-names are visible at Bywood but as a whole occur in only 28 fields in the Blackdowns study area. In the Hartland Moors study area there is also less than 1 per cent of fields containing this calves element within their names. In the South Hams sample areas these names do not occur at all, which is interesting in relation to oral history which records movement from Dartmoor, but may be due to the size of the sampled area rather than the absence of the field-names. However, as discussed in Chapter Five, the field-name evidence in the South Hams of fogle or fogwell may illustrate the seasonal grazing of livestock not only from long distances, but also in relation to smaller estates or holdings.

In Clayhidon, there is also evidence of animal movement through field-names and field morphology. Like much of the former waste and moor in Clayhidon, Hole Moor experienced late enclosure which can be seen by the straight divisions commonly associated with post-medieval enclosed landscapes. The Tithe Survey Apportionment land use and field-name lists three watering plots at either end of the moorland; two evident through the land use category, the third occurring as a field-name recorded under pasture. The watering plot lying on the southern edge of Hole Moor appears to be fed from a spring which in turn becomes the source of a tributary of Bolham river, and all of the watering plots listed on the Tithe Survey are located at the top of valleys. These fields, identified through the Tithe Apportionment and located near to Newcott Barton, Wiltown and Hole Moor, correspond with field morphology of routeways. Fields with evidence of funnels such as those seen relating to droveways, suggest that they were part of the network of animal movement across the Blackdown Hills. In relation to these fields there are also two other interesting field-names, Horse Pool, and Cowbridge. These names reinforce the argument for the movement of animals in this area. It is interesting that these watering plots only appear in the Tithe Survey of Clayhidon. There is also evidence for cattle being drawn together on Clayhidon Hill to the north of Clayhidon to drive them inland in reaction to the Napoleonic threat (Toulson 1999, 57). The announcement made in May 1798 gave the routes as Holly Lane, Rosemary Lane and Bar Park Lane and then on to Castle Neroche and Ashill to the east and finally resting at the wide valley grazing grounds beneath Somerton in Somerset (Toulson 1999, 57).

The three study areas, therefore, show three very different approaches to transhumance and the use of waste and moorland. The South Hams saw movement which links two very different landscapes together in order to get the best pasture land for cattle. The Hartland Moors region also saw long distance movement across Devon, but also internal transhumance to fairs, which worked in an informal communal nature when the need arose. The Blackdowns saw a complex pattern of movement which in the medieval period linked fragmented estates together, and movement from other areas of the country.

Fleming (1998, 45) draws attention to the idea of an 'intricately interwoven 'community', whose members interact frequently in the performance of daily tasks or rituals, there dispersed in a seamless web across the land'. Although discussing prehistoric territory, the argument Fleming (1998, 45) raises is equally applicable to the medieval and post-medieval landscape in Devon. It is obvious that the medieval and post-medieval landscape is more enclosed, and divisions of ownership and tenure are more evident than in the prehistoric period, but when discussing the movement in and between farms and estates in the Middle Ages the idea of interwoven communities is as equally valid.

PART TWO. THE TEXTURED LANDSCAPE

The issue highlighted by Fleming presents the complexities of studying the historic landscape, and this section attempt to discuss how these complexities manifest themselves within the landscape, and how archaeologists may be able to access them.

The social effects of enclosure

Archaeologically, a key factor in understanding the ways in which people perceived their environments can be gained from a study of the impact of common land enclosure carried out throughout the medieval and post-medieval periods. The clearest example of this relates to the Blackdown Hills on the Devon/Somerset border. The area around the Devon parish of Clayhidon and the Somerset parish of Wellington saw a dramatic decrease in common access between 1812 and 1821. In this area 600 acres of common access was reduced to a mere 40 acres of turbary. Gallagher (1993, 221) argues that people's thinking about the natural environment developed in the medieval period, with the stretches of 'untamed' European wildernesses regarded as living symbols of chaos and danger that teemed with demons and monsters. In later centuries this improvement was accelerated through economic imperative created by the bourgeoisies, and in the eighteenth- and nineteenth-century commons and royal woodlands were seen as waste and unimproved by the landed classes (Gallagher 1993, 221). Thus, during an age where improvements and expansions were taking place in all areas of life for the glory of God and Country, people had the right to subdue the wilds, and it was this perception that was used to justify the actions of the landowners who supported the Act of Parliament. Such is the case in the Blackdowns example. It was the Duke of Wellington himself who personally supported the enclosure of his common land and open fields, although he had never actually visited his Devon and Somerset estate.

Williamson (2000, 57) suggests that landscape historians over-emphasise economic arguments when discussing enclosure of this kind, and that ideological and psychological influences have been downplayed. Such agricultural improvements undoubtedly have a significant physical impact on landscapes (in many cases a dramatic one), as large tracts of land were enclosed within a matter of 20 years in rural areas that had seen little in the way of large scale engineering projects. However, perhaps more fundamentally, the process of enclosure had a profound social effect on the people who lived and worked in these rural areas, namely the sudden and enforced restriction of movement through a landscape that would, in many cases, have been open for centuries. Thus, the improvements undertaken at the end of the eighteenth century by way of progressive farming techniques and enclosure were intensely felt by the workers whose landscapes were in many cases dramatically transformed (Seymour 2000, 207). The diversity of post-medieval enclosure was used as an instrument of ideological and economic change, causing deeper structural shifts in mentalities within rural locations and altering the rhythm of day to day life (Johnson 1996, 44–96; Williamson 2000, 57).

Many of the acts of resistance against these acts of enclosure involved what Johnson (1996, 58) calls elements of symbolic inversion. By this, he means local communities, (often led by women) continued to engage in rituals such as 'beating the bounds' as acts of defiance, taking farm implements to destroy obstacles such as hedges and ditches (Johnson 1996, 58; Kelley 1990, *passim*; Thomson 1991, 307–8).

A number of examples of the problems and outcomes of enclosure of common lands can be cited in Devon and the surrounding countryside. In the seventeenth century there were arguments (and possible regrets) between neighbouring farmers in Rackenford about the parcelling up of common lands (Child 2001, 22–5), and in the nineteenth century we see physical evidence of how people's day to day lives were altered by enclosure at the site of Jacob's City in the parish of Clayhidon.

Jacob's City, situated on the northern edge of Clayhidon parish, is another prime example of the after effects of blanket enclosure of common land mentioned above, with a small group of houses (in a sense a squatter settlement) built by Jacob Hutchings and his family on the remaining turbary. As mentioned above, this settlement was not in use for long, as by the Tithe Survey many of the houses were deserted. These acts and reactions to this domestic change in the landscape of the upland fringes may also have been influenced by social decisions and the following pages will discuss this in relation to wider cultural regions or *pays*.

The indentification of cultural *pays* in Devon, and social influences on the landscape

Previous chapters have introduced the concept of *pays* as cultural units which are defined by physical and social conditions, for example topography, type of industry, or extent of population. These cultural units have varied in size from a few parishes to whole counties. However, I have tried to argue that by only looking at a parish scale further *pay* units are being overlooked. For example, Jones and Page (2003, 71) discuss the medieval landscape of Wittlewood in terms of *pays*, but importantly they state that the area they are studying is not large enough to be classified in its own right as a *pay* region. The decision not to try and identify smaller-scale variations in landscape character is unfortunate and an opportunity was missed. By sticking with the categorisation of *pays* being large units defined by the traditional classes of woodland and champion landscapes, the local diversity of this area, which the authors highlighted, is undervalued.

The analysis of cultural patterns involves exploring the way the landscape developed with regard to the characteristics of field patterns, settlement layout and morphology (Bell 1999, 295). These designations of *pay* regions allow for explanation of physical trends within the historic landscape to be discussed. However, the identification of *pays* through these geographical and topographical constructs should allow further questions to be asked about the differences in attitude and 'ways-of-life' between these regions. For example, Woolgar (1999, 132) draws attention to the regional differences of diet within the medieval period due to the produce of each *pay* being different. This is more akin to the French understanding of the term of *pays*. Cosgrove (1984, 29) draws attention to Vidal de la Blanche's description of *Pays de la Beauce* which he suggests 'evokes both a powerful visual image of landscape and a sense of the functional rhythms of its daily life'. Indeed, Braudel (1988, 41) discussed the French notion of *pays*, stating that 'the vital thing for every community is to avoid being confused with the next tiny '*patrie*', to remain '*other*'.

When discussing a landscape characterised predominantly by dispersed settlement like Devon this idea of a sense of community 'otherness' within regions is interesting. In the modern day Blackdown Hills a key statement which encapsulates this idea comes from the chairman of the Clayhidon Local History Group, who argues that 'people living together in a community, regardless of how scattered that community might be, create their own history' (Wakeling 1999, 5). In an area such as the Blackdown Hills, especially in the northern half of the study area (that has a distinctly dispersed settlement); the relationship between community and place has to be strong and one in which each reinforces the identity of the other (Relph 1976, 34). An early medieval example of this sense of communal identity despite spatial separation comes from an Anglo-Saxon context, and can be seen archaeologically through the morphology of longhouses (Bourdieu 1990; Hamerow 2002, 51). Here the idea of social capital is discussed, where over generations obligation and prestige are accumulated through services rendered and gifts given. Geographer Yi-Fu Tuan (1977, 136) notes that in terms of our neighbours, distance is a meaningless spatial concept; 'here' can impose different spatial orders. Thus the idea of communities still working as a unit even though they were spread out across the landscape defines an alternative way of thinking about *pays*. It is clear from the preceding discussion about transhumance, that in the medieval landscape of Devon holdings were linked through droveways for many miles, and contacts kept across the county.

Within regions, forms in the landscape instigate specific responses; these may be due to aesthetics, economic variability, accessibility, and so on, but in turn these observations create the essence of the landscapes themselves. Individuals look upon the landscapes that they inhabit with regard to social and cultural factors. Perceptions of places (both positive and negative) that manifest themselves in folklore, traditional stories and general opinion (such as the Blackdown Hills as marginal for example), create attachments to regions through memories and actions, and initiate the creation of landscapes. Thus, landscapes are the meanings ascribed by people to their cultural and physical surroundings which arise within life and memory and changes between individuals and communities (Hirsch 1995, 1; Humphrey 2001, 55).

Tanner (1991, 21) suggests that within many cultures space is the basis of classification systems; used as a philosophy of social order rather than a model of it, itself being a 'natural phenomenon' that people use as a template to classify ideas that reflect society. This 'space' is thought to become 'place' through human intervention and manipulation (Thomas 2001, 171), and Ingold (1993, 155) makes a case that 'a place owes its character to the experiences it affords to those who spend time there – to the sights, sounds and indeed smells that constitute its specific ambience'. Moreover, our immediate perceptions of the places we encounter are in terms of 'what it affords for the pursuit of the action in which we are currently engaged' (Ingold 1992, 44). Put another way, it is this relationship between place and person that allows landscapes to become apparent, stopping them from being a blank background to life, but instead a meaningful environment with which we have an intimate and familiar connection. Thus, it is these culturally created places which become the *pays* that we identify within the landscape.

Discussion of *Pays* and the study areas

Despite evidence of consistent landscape signatures seen in this study, the fundamental statement in regard to the three study areas is that the landscape is not one of shared typology or influences. In order to study the landscape of Devon it is important not to look simply at regional *pays* but also at parish level and even in some cases at individual villages or hamlets.

We have seen that there was significant movement of animals through the landscape echoed in the field morphology and field-names in the historic landscape and reinforced, as noted above, by a system of interdependence between regions (Fox 1996a, 9). Fox (1996a, 4) also states that it was common during the medieval period for landowners to hold property in different *pays*, consisting of different qualities; for example, grassland or growing seasons which facilitated the movement of animals from manor to manor. As noted in

Chapter Three, the accounts from around the twelfth and thirteenth centuries at Middleton discuss the movement of cattle from Taunton to the estate in Clayhidon. As mentioned previously, examples are known from oral history for drovers moving animals across from Parkham parish in Hartland to Barnstaple, and from Dartmoor to the South Hams for seasonal grazing (Shakespeare 1990, 56).

As noted in Chapter One, an important aspect of landscapes is the cultural identity of places constructed by those living and working within them. Therefore, how these *pays* embody social as well as physical aspects of landscape needs to be considered. Stanes (1969, 63–5) discusses the evidence from the Milles Enquiries of the mid-eighteenth century of regional differences in terms of agriculture, in particular that of the South Hams. Within this region there is evidence for a 'South Hams breed' of cattle and later sheep. The area had a distinct agrarian character, from the measurement of its crop (in sacks) and land (farthings); it brewed its own beer (white ale), and perhaps most importantly, it had the recognition by its people of a distinct archaic name thought to date back to the ninth century (Stanes 1969, 65). This is significant as *pays* are by definition cultural constructs that are not only governed by physical traits. As Austin and Thomas (1990, 48) point out, we cannot adequately discuss houses, field-systems and artefacts 'without considering their creation by (and consequently their role in the creation *of*) human subjects'.

The notion of *pays* reinforces the argument that landscapes are, by definition, socially constructed entities. Although human agency is needed to shape and manage them, landscapes rely on what Children and Nash (1997, 1) call the 'mechanics of the mind' to give them meaning and structure. This structure varies depending upon the individual or group: the *pay*.

Following on from this we can argue that *how* people perceived the world around them depends on their experience within it, both positively and negatively. This perception can change and be altered through time, crucially by ideas associated with particular places. People bond with the landscapes they dwell within, they make places culturally alive (Taçon 1994, 135). Thus, places become vested with an identity (good or bad, sacred or profane, focal or marginal) through physical and social experiences, such as crop failure, war, plague, religious ritual, and so on (Ucko 1994, xviii).

The enclosure of commons and waste discussed above is a good example of this. Many of the rhythms of day to day life would have been altered by the enclosure of the commons. It is known from oral history that on Dartmoor peat could only be collected from the common lands if the 'hearth' (or settlement) was listed in Domesday, although in later years a shilling a year could be paid for this right (SRA n.d, tape 296). Practices such as these would have had significant antecedence, and would have occurred in areas such as the Blackdown Hills. We see evidence of this surviving in the way in which the Luppitt Commoners Committee divide out their commons each year by a ritual using candle (*pers comm* Graham Smith). Every commoner has a pin, which is stuck into a lit candle. As the candle melts pins fall out and this identifies how much land is allocated to each person. This division of common land in Luppitt survives only through the lack of enclosure in this part of the parish.

From this it can be seen that there are a number of histories layered within the historic landscape. These narratives of agricultural traditions and social hierarchy combine with the physical elements recorded in the landscape; the field morphology, and the temporary traces of scattered settlements and former boundaries on the commons and moorlands. This combination of elements, both physical and ephemeral, creates a landscape history which is like a 'soup pot' which is 'always boiling, and to it have continually been added new bits…' (Tolkien 1947/1983, 110). This is especially so when narratives become a stable element within communities for a number of generations, eventually changing and shaping the course of the accepted histories (Braudel 1980, 31). These elements eventually embody what in the present we accept as truth (Children and Nash 1997, 1).

These ideas again draw on the idea of perception that areas defined as being agriculturally marginal are also perceived as socially marginal. These therefore attract stories and views which emphasise a different type of otherness than the one discussed by Braudel. The physical entities such as enclosure (or lack of it) and field-names can promote and fossilise such ideas.

Imagined landscapes – the creation of alternative ways of seeing

The ideas of perception in landscape, and the stories and folklore which are subsequently ascribed to them, presents an interesting challenge. One of the aims of this research is to add further layers of information to the study of the historic landscape. This was done by studying the relationship between landholding patterns, and field and settlement morphology, and discussing field-name evidence. It can also be suggested that further information can be added, by looking at more cultural aspects of landscapes, particularly perceptions of landscape through oral history and folkloric evidence. The three study areas provide good examples of the alternative layers available for historic landscape studies. Archaeological features act as markers within the landscape, either political or cultural, therefore serving as powerful mnemonics. These stories help to give an area a strong spatial identity, ordering the landscape in a personal way, serving to create a recognisable and understandable world in a period where maps were not readily accessible.

The correlation between folklore and reality situates fictitious myth into the flow of people's day to day lives (Propp 1984, 49), and it can be seen how particular places, especially within rural areas, could develop a number of identities with different sectors of the community. Devon provides the perfect example of Propp's idea. Whitlock (1977, 13) suggests that Devon's topography, the 'maze' of steep hills and long valleys, acts as a barrier between neighbouring Somerset and Dorset, and as a result created the external view of a 'secretive, half-tamed countryside'. Such opinions held by those on the periphery helped to foster the idea that something 'different' was occurring within these remote communities. Oral historians describe this as 'linguistically appropriating the landscape'; an act where people and their surroundings become indivisible (Patricia Partnow *pers comm* in Green 2000, 26). The humanly created landscapes of these areas are bound up in deep-seated cultural beliefs; stories that are topographically and socially based.

As a result, stories and metaphors were (and still are) used by people in order to make sense of, and explain, the world around them, creating divisions, and revealing the underlying heart of communities (Lévi-Strauss 1966; Gosden 1999, 113). This can be further reinforced when discussing the Blackdown Hills. The idea of marginality is particularly potent for the Blackdown Hills region. Straddling the border between Devon and Somerset, the Blackdown Hills are externally considered as an isolated place, and associated with things wild and sinister. As a result, this area is blanketed in myths and suspicion.

As mentioned in Chapter Three, many of the roads and tracks within the Blackdown Hills have remained unchanged from the Tithe Survey, and may suggest much earlier routes. It should then fit that many of these roads, both in Devon and Somerset, had sinister reputations (Tongue 1965, 97). Within the study area, the Hemyock road between Broad Street in Clayhidon and Cityford (Churchinford) in Somerset was said to be haunted (*ibid.* 1965, 97). This road runs along the former common of Ridgewood at Bolham Water, which was enclosed through Act of Parliament leaving only a small section open, listed in the Tithe Survey as 'unenclosed land'. In the creation of alternative landscape narratives, significance is partially attributed to wilderness such as moor or common as at Ridgewood. These areas were particularly thought of as the haunting grounds of ghosts, demons and other spirits, and many of the supernatural encounters occurred either at night or as the mist comes in.

The idea of these useful and economically needed areas becoming no-go areas after dark is an interesting one. As seen in previous chapters, the areas of open waste and common were intrinsic to the management of medieval and post-medieval landscapes, for grazing and also conversion to arable land.

Within the Blackdown Hills stories of lost souls wandering the Blackdown Hills are common and many bandits and thieves traded on the superstition and fear which surrounded the area in order to move through the landscape unchallenged. The following example was recorded in the Western Circuit on 2 October 1690. It details the 'Bewitching' of Mr Jacob Seley in the Blackdown Hills en route to Taunton after an evening at a Public House. Mr Seley stated to a judge that he was set upon by the ghosts of 'Monmouth's Men... hang'd on the sign post', and that the ghosts went on to steal his horse (Coxhead, 1954, 145–6). It was generally thought he had been told the stories of hauntings by locals in the pub over dinner (and no doubt a few drinks), and that the thieves had followed him from the inn in order to trade on his fear.

It is known that many men from the local communities joined the

Monmouth rebel army in 1685 and camped on Luppitt Common. Local stories state that many of these men were executed on Black Down Common which lies on the border with Hemyock in Uffculme. Hence the belief that these men still wandered the commons trying to get home. The wastes and moors of the Blackdown Hills were also believed to be haunted by Spunkies or Will-o'-the Wisps, which throughout Devon were thought to be the souls of unbaptised children.

To medieval communities the night became home to imagined horrors, with the unexplainable playing an important role in these stories, being in temporal terms both real yet indistinct; known, but containing unknowns (Young and Harris 2003, 135–138).

The the fear of wilderness may also derive from more everyday concerns, such as being ambushed by outlaws. The organisation of the landscape, and the fear of those who dwell beyond the 'civilised' boundaries of the settlements and tracks, helps to create this perception. Furthermore, Harte (2003, 186–7) draws attention to the fact that although the association between monsters and wilderness is common, many 'demonic' experiences also occurred on route-ways close to home and on the outskirts of towns and villages.

As mentioned earlier, Hartland Point (the westernmost tip of Hartland Parish) and the earthwork at Clovelly Dykes provide a good example of what Tolkien describes as the 'soup bowl'; the mixing of ideas which was always boiling and to which new things were added ((Tolkien, 1974/1983, 110). Hartland Point, also known as Hercvlis or Hercules Promontory, is one of the few sites within Devon to have a known Romano-British name which survives to the present. In the late eighteenth century, both the antiquarian Camden and Polwhele (1793–1806, vol. 1, 136) stated that the name arose from Hercules coming to Britain to fight giants, and suggests an origin of Phoenician sailors trading with the Devon coast (cited in Pearse Chope, 1940, 6). Although the Phoenician origin is doubtful, the legend of the giants on Hartland Point, which is also the site of a Cliff-Castle, is an interesting one and reinforces the general trend for such creatures to be associated with these monuments. Therefore, it is easy to see how myths of Hercules could be updated to Arthur and moved 6 miles inland to Clovelly Dykes (Franklin 2006, 155), which, as mentioned in Chapter Four was thought to be Camelot. The existence of such stories within the landscape further colours the external perception of places and leads to the cultural regions such as those suggested for Bucks Mill in Woolfardisworthy. The passing down of such stories means that the meanings change, like Chinese Whispers, and propagates alternative histories for regions.

An example of this is the story of Gereint, a tribal leader in the Arthurian stories that are attributed to Clovelly Dykes who was wounded with an incurable wound to his leg (Lauder and Williams, 1982, 17), a fate which is said to have befallen Oberon, the king of the fairies, during the battle between the Devonian Pixies and Fairies (Bray 1853, 11–12). Oberon is the name of a demon that was said to be frequently conjured by fifteenth and sixteenth century wizards, and later, Shakespeare's King of the fairies in Midsummer Nights Dream (Thomas 1971, 727–728; Kittredge 1929, 110, 208, 210). Such myths indicate how stories were changed and manipulated to fit the landscape in which they were set (Franklin 2006, 155).

Consequently, myths are something whose origins are unknown, but which are always present within a community or group. It is this perpetuation which is important to their validity, creating an idea of identity, not only of how communities envisage themselves, but also of how others see them; this in turn constructs landscapes which are engrained with meaning. Tuan (1977, 86) suggests two kinds of mythical space; one is a 'fuzzy area of defective knowledge surrounding the empirically known', and this is an extension of the familiar and day to day. The second is '…the spatial component of world view, a conception of localised values within which people carry on their practical lives' and functions as a world view or cosmology, is better articulated, and more consciously held (*ibid.* 1977, 86, 88).

It is not just the seemingly marginal areas which attract folkloric activity. There was a strong belief in pixies within the parish of Thurlestone. The community here believed that the pixies moved the foundations of their new parish church overnight to its present position further inland as the construction was located on pixy dwellings (Coupe 1920, 84–5). Grinsell (1937, 254) states that this phenomenon commonly indicates barrows on the intended site. The coast of Thurlestone around Bantham Ham (itself the site of a significant earthwork) where the church was to be situated is associated with kitchen middens, hearths and occupation evidence dating to the Iron Age, Romano-British and post-Roman periods. There are also flint scatters dating to the Mesolithic along the coast, and evidence of four bowl barrows (SMR SX64SE/10; /114; /98; /110). A landscape of this type, filled with the remains of hearths, evidence of food preparation, and flints associated with barrows, would allow stories to propagate of non-human groups living along the coast.

I have argued elsewhere that it is possible that the belief structure present in the South Hams is due in part to the proximity to Dartmoor, and that the acts of transhumance between the two areas allowed for folkloric stories to spread between communities (Franklin 2006, 153).

This is an important factor in how landscapes gained meaning and significance in the medieval period. With these connections between the moors and the lowland areas, information, stories and ideas can be passed between settlements, helping to foster alternative narratives as explanations for events. Thus, myths get perpetuated and eventually become truths within local history.

Summary

> 'sticklers for the truth and scientific accuracy should ignore the subject of folklore...
> for folklore by its very nature is compound of inaccuracies'
>
> (St. Leger-Gordon 1965, 11)

Despite the difficulties, it is not impossible to access folkloric and mythological elements in past landscapes. Where research previously treated folklore as a form of historical science, and attempted to recreate the mythical past through organised and regimented analysis (Krappe 1930, xv; Phythian-Adams 1975, 6–7), as this study has attempted to show, the importance and potential of folktales within medieval landscape studies has not been appreciated fully especially as this is a period where we are still essentially dealing with a written record that is restricted to legal or religious documents (Franklin 2006, 149). These communities have a rich repertoire of symbols and meanings for all parts of life, and practices that had not changed for decades. Therefore, folktales can be regarded as the 'literature' of the rural communities (Yeats 1888, xii).

When discussing landscapes the documentary sources are varied, providing a number of different avenues to investigate. In particular, post-medieval documentary evidence is key to undertaking any such research, as these documents provide the 'voice' of the communities which are being discussed, and can reflect earlier communities. The local myths, superstition and folklore that underlie landscapes can be accessed through oral history, documentary sources, and place- and field-name studies. Folklore, like any other archaeological source, needs to be treated with care in order not to impose modern perspectives on the medieval period. Nevertheless, methodologically combining such cultural elements with past landscapes is a valid exercise.

It is clear that more work needs to be carried out (by combining documentary, archaeological and folkloric evidence) than this chapter can allow, but from these examples it is hoped that the potential of such a holistic methodology to create a more layered narrative of the past can be illustrated. It has been argued that on their own, documents can only record a thin slice of life; but when they are combined with the archaeological research and elements such as folklore and myth a more comprehensive view can be attained (Caunce 1994, 13).

Returning to the St. Leger-Gordon quotation that heads this section, folklore may be full of inaccuracies, but I feel that through this statement she is missing the point about the nature of the subject. It may be wild and contradictory, but it is a product of the landscapes in which stories were, and are, told and retold, and therefore provide an insight into the communities of which they are part (Franklin 2006, 158). Myths and stories reveal not facts about the past but the significance of it (Gazin-Schwartz and Holtolf 1999, 13). Therefore I argue that the information acquired from folklore, combined, as it is here with more 'conventional' landscape tools, can provide a link to the environments of past communities (Franklin 2006, 158).

Both Part One and Part Two of this chapter aim to show the complexities associated with studying Devon's historic landscape. By creating a series of overlapping layers which inform and can be queried, a better picture of the development of the medieval and post-medieval landscape can be elucidated. Landscape archaeology relies not only on a fleeting glance at a map, and the odd walk in the landscape, but on a number of interconnecting quantitative and qualitative approaches (Children and Nash 1997, 2). Therefore, as I have noted elsewhere, when approaching the medieval period in a holistic manner, this form of enquiry can add to the more formal methodology conventionally used within landscape archaeology (Franklin 2006, 158).

Part One was used to illustrate how a number of layers of information can be collated together as a study of the historic landscape in order to produce a impression of the origins and development of the landscape of Devon during the medieval period (especially from the Dissolution to the nineteenth century).

The use of landholding patterns which, as the example of the Galsworthy family at Moors Farm in Hartland proves, can be successfully traced back to the sixteenth century is of particular significance. This information provides a link between the physical elements seen through the Tithe Surveys, such as field systems and settlement patterns. The layers of this historic landscape study perform two different roles; to inform but also to query. The querying of the Tithe Apportionment field-names illustrates the importance and use of this. By discussing and mapping the distribution of field-name elements and contrasting their occurrence with the field morphology, land use, and landholding patterns a greater insight into the historic landscape can be seen.

Final remarks

It is clear that without the use of GIS the scale to which the data within this study was manipulated and queried could not have been attempted. The resultant patterns of landholding, field and settlement morphology, and field-name analysis which have been identified through the nineteenth-century Tithe Surveys have allowed different types of landscapes which may be present to emarge. In particular, the extent of open field systems identified in this way adds a spatial dimension to the documentary evidence.

It is clearly demonstrated that the historic landscape can, and has been used, in two ways; firstly as a source to provide morphological evidence and resource to gain information about landholding patterns; and secondly as a means of interrogating other evidence, for example field-names. This evidence can be furthered by looking at folklore, to create a totally holistic study of the historic landscape.

TABLE 1. Total number of digitised Tithe Survey fields containing furze or furzy elements in their field-names

Parish name (south to north)	Total number of 19th century fields digitised	Total number containing furze or furzy elements	Percentage of fields in parish	Overall Total of fields in study area
Buckerell	228	3	1.32%	
Awliscombe	970	12	1.24%	
Dunkeswell	246	2	0.81%	
Combe Raleigh	296	3	1.01%	
Luppitt	1128	13	1.15%	
Hemyock	1590	34	2.14%	
Clayhidon	2022	28	1.38%	
Total	6479	95		1.47%

Parish name (west to east)	Total number of 19th century fields digitised	Total number containing furze or furzy elements	Percentage of fields in parish	Overall Total of fields in study area
Hartland	3307	23	0.70%	
Welcombe	649	6	0.92%	
Woolfardisworthy	1329	22	1.66%	
Clovelly	692	9	1.30%	
Total	5977	60		1.00%

Parish name (west to east)	Total number of 19th century fields digitised	Total number containing furze or furzy elements	percentage	Overall Total of fields in study area
Thurlestone	241	4	1.7%	
Bigbury	428	2	0.5%	
Bigbury-on-Sea	65	0	0.0%	
Total	734	6		0.82%

TABLE 2. Total number of digitised Tithe Survey fields containing gratton elements in their field-names

Parish name (south to north)	Total number of 19th century fields digitised	Total number containing gratton elements	Percentage of fields in parish	Overall Total of fields in study area
Buckerell	228	0	0.00%	
Awliscombe	970	0	0.00%	
Dunkeswell	246	0	0.00%	
Combe Raleigh	296	0	0.00%	
Luppitt	1128	0	0.00%	
Hemyock	1590	0	0.00%	
Clayhidon	2022	0	0.00%	
Total	6479	0		0.00%

Parish name (west to east)	Total number of 19th century fields digitised	Total number containing gratton elements	Percentage of fields in parish	Overall Total of fields in study area
Hartland	3307	2	0.06%	
Welcombe	649	2	0.31%	
Woolfardisworthy	1329	0	0.00%	
Clovelly	692	0	0.00%	
Total	5977	4		0.07%

Parish name (west to east)	Total number of 19th century fields digitised	Total number containing gratton elements	percentage	Overall Total of fields in study area
Thurlestone	241	0	0.0%	
Bigbury	428	1	0.2%	
Bigbury-on-Sea	65	0	0.0%	
Total	734	1		0.14%

Parish name (south to north)	Total number of 19th century fields digitised	Total number containing ham elements	Percentage of fields in parish	Overall Total of fields in study area
Buckerell	228	2	0.88%	
Awliscombe	970	17	1.75%	
Dunkeswell	246	0	0.00%	
Combe Raleigh	296	4	1.35%	
Luppitt	1128	12	1.06%	
Hemyock	1590	20	1.26%	
Clayhidon	2022	20	0.99%	
Total	**6479**	**75**		1.16%

Parish name (west to east)	Total number of 19th century fields digitised	Total number containing ham elements	Percentage of fields in parish	Overall Total of fields in study area
Hartland	3307	31	0.94%	
Welcombe	649	7	1.08%	
Woolfardisworthy	1329	18	1.35%	
Clovelly	692	11	1.59%	
Total	**5977**	**67**		1.12%

Parish name (west to east)	Total number of 19th century fields digitised	Total number containing ham elements	percentage	Overall Total of fields in study area
Thurlestone	241	7	2.9%	
Bigbury	428	5	1.2%	
Bigbury-on-Sea	65	0	0.0%	
Total	**734**	**12**		1.63%

TABLE 3. Total number of digitised Tithe Survey fields containing ham elements in their field-names

Parish name (south to north)	Total number of 19th century fields digitised	Total number containing hayes elements	Percentage of fields in parish	Overall Total of fields in study area
Buckerell	228	3	1.32%	
Awliscombe	970	2	0.21%	
Dunkeswell	246	3	1.22%	
Combe Raleigh	296	0	0.00%	
Luppitt	1128	1	0.09%	
Hemyock	1590	1	0.06%	
Clayhidon	2022	3	0.15%	
Total	**6479**	**13**		0.20%

Parish name (west to east)	Total number of 19th century fields digitised	Total number containing hayes elements	Percentage of fields in parish	Overall Total of fields in study area
Hartland	3307	1	0.03%	
Welcombe	649	0	0.00%	
Woolfardisworthy	1329	0	0.00%	
Clovelly	692	1	0.14%	
Total	**5977**	**2**		0.03%

TABLE 4. Total number of digitised Tithe Survey fields containing hayes elements in their field-names

TABLE 6.5. Total number of digitised Tithe Survey fields containing worthy elements in their field-names

Parish name (south to north)	Total number of 19th century fields digitised	Total number containing worthy elements	Percentage of fields in parish	Overall Total of fields in study area
Buckerell	228	0	0.00%	
Awliscombe	970	0	0.00%	
Dunkeswell	246	0	0.00%	
Combe Raleigh	296	0	0.00%	
Luppitt	1128	0	0.00%	
Hemyock	1590	0	0.00%	
Clayhidon	2022	0	0.00%	
Total	6479	0		0.00%

Parish name (west to east)	Total number of 19th century fields digitised	Total number containing worthy elements	Percentage of fields in parish	Overall Total of fields in study area
Hartland	3307	15	0.45%	
Welcombe	649	0	0.00%	
Woolfardisworthy	1329	4	0.30%	
Clovelly	692	4	0.58%	
Total	5977	23		0.38%

Parish name (west to east)	Total number of 19th century fields digitised	Total number containing worthy elements	percentage	Overall Total of fields in study area
Thurlestone	241	0	0.0%	
Bigbury	428	0	0.0%	
Bigbury-on-Sea	65	0	0.0%	
Total	734	0		0.00%

TABLE 6. Total number of digitised Tithe Survey fields containing ton or don elements in their field-names

Parish name (south to north)	Total number of 19th century fields digitised	Total number containing ton/don elements	Percentage of fields in parish	Overall Total of fields in study area
Buckerell	228	4	1.75%	
Awliscombe	970	8	0.82%	
Dunkeswell	246	0	0.00%	
Combe Raleigh	296	6	2.03%	
Luppitt	1128	14	1.24%	
Hemyock	1590	9	0.57%	
Clayhidon	2022	13	0.64%	
Total	6479	54		0.83%

Parish name (west to east)	Total number of 19th century fields digitised	Total number containing ton/don elements	Percentage of fields in parish	Overall Total of fields in study area
Hartland	3307	46	1.39%	
Welcombe	649	12	1.85%	
Woolfardisworthy	1329	5	0.38%	
Clovelly	692	5	0.72%	
Total	5977	68		1.14%

Parish name (west to east)	Total number of 19th century fields digitised	Total number containing ton/don elements	percentage	Overall Total of fields in study area
Thurlestone	241	1	0.4%	
Bigbury	428	1	0.2%	
Bigbury-on-Sea	65	1	1.5%	
Total	734	3		0.41%

excluding barton, or stone(s) where it occurs as an individual word (is included as suffix)

Parish name (south to north)	Total number of 19th century fields digitised	Total number containing barton elements	Percentage of fields in parish	Overall Total of fields in study area
Buckerell	228	1	0.44%	
Awliscombe	970	10	1.03%	
Dunkeswell	246	8	3.25%	
Combe Raleigh	296	3	1.01%	
Luppitt	1128	5	0.44%	
Hemyock	1590	11	0.69%	
Clayhidon	2022	3	0.15%	
Total	6479	41		0.63%

Parish name (west to east)	Total number of 19th century fields digitised	Total number containing barton elements	Percentage of fields in parish	Overall Total of fields in study area
Hartland	3307	7	0.21%	
Welcombe	649	2	0.31%	
Woolfardisworthy	1329	0	0.00%	
Clovelly	692	6	0.87%	
Total	5977	15		0.25%

TABLE 7. Total number of digitised Tithe Survey fields containing barton elements in their field-names

Parish name (south to north)	Total number of 19th century fields digitised	Total number containing aller elements	Percentage of fields in parish	Overall Total of fields in study area
Buckerell	228	0	0.00%	
Awliscombe	970	5	0.52%	
Dunkeswell	246	2	0.81%	
Combe Raleigh	296	5	1.69%	
Luppitt	1128	4	0.35%	
Hemyock	1590	5	0.31%	
Clayhidon	2022	1	0.05%	
Total	6479	22		0.34%

Parish name (west to east)	Total number of 19th century fields digitised	Total number containing aller elements	Percentage of fields in parish	Overall Total of fields in study area
Hartland	3307	0	0.00%	
Welcombe	649	0	0.00%	
Woolfardisworthy	1329	0	0.00%	
Clovelly	692	0	0.00%	
Total	5977	0		0.00%

TABLE 8. Total number of digitised Tithe Survey fields containing aller elements in their field-names

Parish name (south to north)	Total number of 19th century fields digitised	Total number containing leas elements	Percentage of fields in parish	Overall Total of fields in study area
Buckerell	228	0	0.00%	
Awliscombe	970	5	0.52%	
Dunkeswell	246	1	0.41%	
Combe Raleigh	296	0	0.00%	
Luppitt	1128	8	0.71%	
Hemyock	1590	14	0.88%	
Clayhidon	2022	17	0.84%	
Total	6479	45		0.69%

Parish name (west to east)	Total number of 19th century fields digitised	Total number containing leas elements	Percentage of fields in parish	Overall Total of fields in study area
Hartland	3307	2	0.06%	
Welcombe	649	0	0.00%	
Woolfardisworthy	1329	0	0.00%	
Clovelly	692	2	0.29%	
Total	5977	4		0.07%

TABLE 9. Total number of digitised Tithe Survey fields containing leas elements in their field-names

TABLE 10. Total number of digitised Tithe Survey fields containing calves or calf elements in their field-names

Parish name (south to north)	Total number of 19th century fields digitised	Total number containing calves/calf elements	Percentage of fields in parish	Overall Total of fields in study area
Buckerell	228	1	0.44%	
Awliscombe	970	3	0.31%	
Dunkeswell	246	0	0.00%	
Combe Raleigh	296	1	0.34%	
Luppitt	1128	4	0.35%	
Hemyock	1590	7	0.44%	
Clayhidon	2022	12	0.59%	
Total	6479	28		0.43%

Parish name (west to east)	Total number of 19th century fields digitised	Total number containing calves/calf elements	Percentage of fields in parish	Overall Total of fields in study area
Hartland	3307	9	0.27%	
Welcombe	649	2	0.31%	
Woolfardisworthy	1329	3	0.23%	
Clovelly	692	4	0.58%	
Total	5977	18		0.30%

TABLE 11. Total number of digitised Tithe Survey fields containing ground (or pleasure ground) elements in their field-names

Parish name (south to north)	Total number of 19th century fields digitised	Total number containing ground elements	Percentage of fields in parish	Overall Total of fields in study area
Buckerell	228	0	0.00%	
Awliscombe	970	2	0.21%	
Dunkeswell	246	0	0.00%	
Combe Raleigh	296	4	1.35%	
Luppitt	1128	0	0.00%	
Hemyock	1590	4	0.25%	
Clayhidon	2022	2	0.10%	
Total	6479	12		0.19%
Parish name (west to east)	**Total number of 19th century fields digitised**	**Total number containing ground elements**	**Percentage of fields in parish**	**Overall Total of fields in study area**
Hartland	3307	57	1.72%	
Welcombe	649	5	0.77%	
Woolfardisworthy	1329	18	1.35%	
Clovelly	692	22	3.18%	
Total	5977	102		1.71%
Parish name (west to east)	**Total number of 19th century fields digitised**	**Total number containing ground elements**	**percentage**	**Overall Total of fields in study area**
Thurlestone	241	0	0.0%	
Bigbury	428	2	0.5%	
Bigbury-on-Sea	65	0	0.0%	
Total	734	2		0.27%
Parish name (south to north)	**Total number of 19th century fields digitised**	**Total number containing pleasure ground elements**	**Percentage of fields in parish**	**Overall Total of fields in study area**
Buckerell	228	0	0.00%	
Awliscombe	970	5	0.52%	
Dunkeswell	246	0	0.00%	
Combe Raleigh	296	2	0.68%	
Luppitt	1128	0	0.00%	
Hemyock	1590	0	0.00%	
Clayhidon	2022	0	0.00%	
Total	6479	7		0.11%
Parish name (west to east)	**Total number of 19th century fields digitised**	**Total number containing pleasure ground elements**	**Percentage of fields in parish**	**Overall Total of fields in study area**
Hartland	3307	0	0.00%	
Welcombe	649	0	0.00%	
Woolfardisworthy	1329	0	0.00%	
Clovelly	692	0	0.00%	
Total	5977	0		0.00%

APPENDIX 2

Earliest recorded occurrence of settlement names in the Blackdown Hills (from PND)

Parish	PN	Earliest documented name	Date	Possible earlier names
Awliscombe	Cottason Fm	Cotterilleshayes Fm 1622	C17th	
Awliscombe	Godford	Codefort 1206/Godeford 1227	C13th	
Awliscombe	Ivedon Ho	Evedon 1228	C13th	
Awliscombe	Waringstone or Weston	Weringeston 1227	C13th	
Awliscombe	Bennettshayes	Bennettshayes 1700	C18th	pers name Benet 1330
Awliscombe	Birds Fm	pers name Beard 1330*	C13th	
Awliscombe	Hamlin's Park	pers name Hamelyn 1330	C14th	
Awliscombe	Hunthayes	pers name Honte 1330	C14th	
Awliscombe	Marlecumbe	Marlecumbe 1227	C13th	
Awliscombe	Ridgeway Fm	Rigweye 1330	C14th	
Awliscombe	Smallicombe	Smalecumbe 1244	C14th	
Awliscombe	Wadhays	Wadehegh 1238	C13th	
Awliscombe	Woverstone	Wolveston 1262	C13th	
Buckerell	Avenhayes	Avenhayes 1765	C18th	
Buckerell	Colhayes	Coleheia 1238	C13th	
Buckerell	Combe Hayes	pers name cumbe 1310	C14th	
Buckerell	Deerpark	Deereparke 1663	C17th	
Buckerell	Sowton	Sutheton Juxta Fineton 1298	C13th	
Buckerell	Splatts	Splatts 1524	C16th	
Buckerell	Treaslake	Treslake 1694	C17th	
Clayhidon	Bolham Water	Boleham 1086	C11th	
Clayhidon	Hole	Holna1086	C11th	
Clayhidon	Newcott Fm	Nonicote1242	C13th	
Clayhidon	Batten	pers name Batten 1823	C19th	
Clayhidon	Bellett's Fm	pers name Ballett 1810	C19th	
Clayhidon	Caller's Fm	pers name Calwe 1330*	C14th	
Clayhidon	Cordwent's Fm	pers name Cordewente 1615	C17th	
Clayhidon	Dungreen Fm	pers name Dunn1670	C17th	
Clayhidon	Garlandhayes	pers name Garlaund 1333	C14th	
Clayhidon	Holmes Hill	pers name Home 1330*	C14th	
Clayhidon	Jenning's Fm	pers name Jennynge1587	C16th	
Clayhidon	Lockyer's Fm	pers name Lockyear 1774	C18th	
Clayhidon	Palmer's Fm	pers name le Palmere 1319	C14th	
Clayhidon	Searles	pers name Searle 1613	C17th	
Clayhidon	Shackles Cross	pers name Shackell 1586*	C16th	
Clayhidon	Shepherd's Fm	pers name Shepherde 1525	C16th	
Clayhidon	Smith's Fm	pers name Smith 1660*	C17th	
Clayhidon	Troake's Fm	pers name Troke 1548	C16th	
Clayhidon	Trood's Cottage	pers name Trod 1333	C14th	
Clayhidon	Valentine's	pers name Valentine1699	C17th	
Clayhidon	Heazle Fm	Hesele 1330	C14th	
Clayhidon	Wiltown	Wille 1330*	C14th	
Clayhidon	Applehayes	Aplynshayes 1566	C16th	
Clayhidon	Bridge Ho	Birchouse 1765	C18th	
Clayhidon	Forches Corner	Forges Cross 1765	C18th	
Clayhidon	Gladhayes	Clodeheis 1330	C14th	
Clayhidon	Gollick Park	Gollakecoote 1566	C16th	
Clayhidon	Gotleigh Moor	Goteleye 1274	C13th	
Clayhidon	Graddage Fm	Greatediche 1566	C16th	Graddich 1330
Clayhidon	Hidewood Lane	Huydewood 1566	C16th	
Clayhidon	Lillycombe Fm	Lyllecombe 1566	C16th	
Clayhidon	Longham Fm	Langham 1543	C16th	
Clayhidon	Middleton Barton	Middelton 1244	C13th	
Clayhidon	Ridgewood Fm	Riggewode 1521	C16th	Riggewode 1227?
Combe Raleigh	Crook	Cruke 1330	C14th	
Combe Raleigh	Ellishayes Fm	Alysheys 1420	C15th	

Parish	PN	Earliest documented name	Date	Possible earlier names
Combe Raleigh	Carpenter's Hill	pers name Carpenter 1643	C17th	
Combe Raleigh	Hutchingshayes	pers name Huchyn 1481	C15th	
Combe Raleigh	Scotchayes	Skottysheghys 1468	C15th	pers name Scot 1353*
Combe Raleigh	Aller	Aller 1629	C17th	
Combe Raleigh	Stonehayes	pers name atte Stone 1330*	C14th	
Combe Raleigh	Woodhaynes	Woodhays 1620	C17th	
Dunkeswell	Bywood Fm	Biuda 1086	C11th	
Hemyock	Alexanderhayes	Alysandreshayes 1423	C15th	
Hemyock	Culm Davy	Comba 1086	C11th	
Hemyock	Culm Pyne Barton	Colun 1086	C11th	
Hemyock	Gorwell	Gorwilla 1086	C11th	
Hemyock	Mackham	Madecomb 1330	C14th	
Hemyock	Mountshayne Fm	Maundeuillesheghs 1330	C14th	
Hemyock	Pen Cross	Penn 1718	C18th	
Hemyock	Simons Burrow	Simundesbergha 1190	C12th	
Hemyock	Browning's Fm	pers name Browninge 1610	C17th	
Hemyock	Buncombe's Cottage	pers name Bunkombe1699	C17th	
Hemyock	Churchills	pers name Churchyll 1524	C16th	
Hemyock	Clement's Fm	pers name Clements 1814	C19th	
Hemyock	Crocker's Fm	pers name le Crokker 1330	C14th	
Hemyock	Ellis Fm	pers name Ellis 1657	C17th	
Hemyock	Goodall's Fm	pers name Goodhale 1524	C16th	
Hemyock	Hartnell's Fm	pers name Hartknoll/Hortknoll 1524	C16th	
Hemyock	Jewell's Fm	pers name Jewell/Juel 1672	C17th	
Hemyock	Lemon's Fm	pers name Lemon/Leaman 1633/36	C17th	
Hemyock	Lugg's Cottages	pers name Lugg 1692	C17th	
Hemyock	Pike's Cottages	pers name Pike 1636	C17th	
Hemyock	Potter's Fm	pers name Pottere 1333*	C14th	
Hemyock	Toogood's Cottages	pers name Toogood 1583	C16th	
Hemyock	Blackaller Fm	pers name Blakeallre 1244	C13th	
Hemyock	Burrow Hill Fm	pers name atte Burgh 1333	C14th	
Hemyock	Coomeshead	pers name Cumbesheved 1244*	C13th	
Hemyock	Hill Fm	pers name atte Hulle 1340*	C14th	
Hemyock	Moorhayes Fm	pers name atte More 1333*	C14th	
Hemyock	Pitt Fm	pers name de la Putte 1244*	C13th	
Hemyock	Thorn Fm	pers name atte Thorne 1333*	C14th	
Hemyock	Ashculm	Aysshcomb 1330	C14th	
Hemyock	Castle Hill	Castell Mote 1566	C16th	
Hemyock	Collinshayne	Collinshayes 1752	C18th	
Hemyock	Combe Hil	Culmehill 1605	C17th	
Hemyock	Conigar Fm	Cunniger 1667	C17th	
Hemyock	Culmbridge Fm	Columbrugg 1281	C13th	
Hemyock	Deepsellick Fm	Deepsellacke 1624	C17th	
Hemyock	Hackpen Hill	Hackependowne 1605	C17th	
Hemyock	Holcombe Ho	Holcombe Wood 1566	C16th	
Hemyock	Hurcombe	Hertecombe 1330	C14th	
Hemyock	Madford	Madresford 1281	C13th	
Hemyock	Millhayes	Millesheghes 1330	C14th	
Hemyock	Newton Fm	Newton 1566	C16th	
Hemyock	Oxenpark Fm	Oxenparke Wood 1566	C16th	
Hemyock	Pound Ho	Pounde 1566	C16th	
Hemyock	Shuttleton Fm	Sheteldoune 1566	C16th	
Hemyock	Tedburrow Fm	Tedborough 1566	C16th	
Hemyock	Westown	Weston 1566	C16th	
Hemyock	Windsor Fm a	Wynsore 1566	C16th	
Luppitt	Dumpdon Hill	Dumpton 1690	C17th	Ryngburghe 1344

Parish	PN	Earliest documented name	Date	Possible earlier names
Awliscombe	Cottason Fm	Cotterilleshayes Fm 1622	C17th	
Awliscombe	Godford	Codefort 1206/Godeford 1227	C13th	
Awliscombe	Ivedon Ho	Evedon 1228	C13th	
Awliscombe	Waringstone or Weston	Weringeston 1227	C13th	
Awliscombe	Bennettshayes	Bennettshayes 1700	C18th	pers name Benet 1330
Awliscombe	Birds Fm	pers name Beard 1330*	C13th	
Awliscombe	Hamlin's Park	pers name Hamelyn 1330	C14th	
Awliscombe	Hunthayes	pers name Honte 1330	C14th	
Awliscombe	Marlecumbe	Marlecumbe 1227	C13th	
Awliscombe	Ridgeway Fm	Rigweye 1330	C14th	
Awliscombe	Smallicombe	Smalecumbe 1244	C14th	
Awliscombe	Wadhays	Wadehegh 1238	C13th	
Awliscombe	Woverstone	Wolverston 1262	C13th	
Buckerell	Avenhayes	Avenhayes 1765	C18th	
Buckerell	Colhayes	Coleheia 1238	C13th	
Buckerell	Combe Hayes	pers name cumbe 1310	C14th	
Buckerell	Deerpark	Deereparke 1663	C17th	
Buckerell	Sowton	Sutheton Juxta Fineton 1298	C13th	
Buckerell	Splatts	Splatts 1524	C16th	
Buckerell	Treaslake	Treslake 1694	C17th	
Clayhidon	Bolham Water	Boleham 1086	C11th	
Clayhidon	Hole	Holna1086	C11th	
Clayhidon	Newcott Fm	Nonicote1242	C13th	
Clayhidon	Batten	pers name Batten 1823	C19th	
Clayhidon	Bellett's Fm	pers name Ballett 1810	C19th	
Clayhidon	Caller's Fm	pers name Calwe 1330*	C14th	
Clayhidon	Cordwent's Fm	pers name Cordewente 1615	C17th	
Clayhidon	Dungreen Fm	pers name Dunn1670	C17th	
Clayhidon	Garlandhayes	pers name Garlaund 1333	C14th	
Clayhidon	Holmes Hill	pers name Home 1330*	C14th	
Clayhidon	Jenning's Fm	pers name Jennynge1587	C16th	
Clayhidon	Lockyer's Fm	pers name Lockyear 1774	C18th	
Clayhidon	Palmer's Fm	pers name le Palmere 1319	C14th	
Clayhidon	Searles	pers name Searle 1613	C17th	
Clayhidon	Shackles Cross	pers name Shackell 1586*	C16th	
Clayhidon	Shepherd's Fm	pers name Shepherde 1525	C16th	
Clayhidon	Smith's Fm	pers name Smith 1660*	C17th	
Clayhidon	Troake's Fm	pers name Troke 1548	C16th	
Clayhidon	Trood's Cottage	pers name Trod 1333	C14th	
Clayhidon	Valentine's	pers name Valentine1699	C17th	
Clayhidon	Heazle Fm	Hesele 1330	C14th	
Clayhidon	Wiltown	Wille 1330*	C14th	
Clayhidon	Applehayes	Aplynshayes 1566	C16th	
Clayhidon	Bridge Ho	Birchouse 1765	C18th	
Clayhidon	Forches Corner	Forges Cross 1765	C18th	
Clayhidon	Gladhayes	Clodeheis 1330	C14th	
Clayhidon	Gollick Park	Gollakecoote 1566	C16th	
Clayhidon	Gotleigh Moor	Goteleye 1274	C13th	
Clayhidon	Graddage Fm	Greatediche 1566	C16th	Graddich 1330
Clayhidon	Hidewood Lane	Huydewood 1566	C16th	
Clayhidon	Lillycombe Fm	Lyllecombe 1566	C16th	
Clayhidon	Longham Fm	Langham 1543	C16th	
Clayhidon	Middleton Barton	Middelton 1244	C13th	
Clayhidon	Ridgewood Fm	Riggewode 1521	C16th	Riggewode 1227?
Combe Raleigh	Crook	Cruke 1330	C14th	
Combe Raleigh	Ellishayes Fm	Alysheys 1420	C15th	

Bibliography

Manuscript Sources

Crown Pleas of the Devon Eyre of 1238 (Summerson, 1985)

Devon Monastic Lands: Calendar of Particulars for Grants 1536–58 (Young, 1955)

Domesday Book and Exon Domesday Book 1086 (Thorn & Thorn, 1980)

Feet of Fines 1190–1272; 1272–1369

Feudal Aids 1303 (Deputy Keeper of Records, 1879)

Inquisitiones post mortem (IPM) various dates from 13th to 16th century

Lay Subsidies 1334; 1544–45

Rotuli Hundredorum (Record Commission 1812–1818, 2 vols. i pp.73b, 89b)

Tax Roll 1302; 1303

Tax Roll of 'Testa de Nevill' 1234–42 (L'Estrange Ewen, 1939)

Printed Works

Allan, J. 1994 Medieval Pottery and the dating of Deserted Settlements on Dartmoor. *Devon Archaeol Soc Proc* 52. 141–147.

Altenberg, K. 2001 Marginal Life. Experiencing a Medieval Landscape in the Periphery. *Current Swedish Archaeology* 9. 93–113.

Altenberg, K. 2003 *Experiencing Landscape: A Study of Space and Identity in Three Marginal Areas of Medieval Britain and Scandinavia*. Stockholm.

Andresen, J., Madsen, T. and Scollar, I. (eds) 1993, *Computing the Past – Computer Applications and Quantitative Methods in Archaeology*. CAA 92 Aarhus.

Astill, G. 1988a Rural Settlement: the Toft and the Croft. In *The Countryside of Medieval England* (eds G. Astill and A. Grant). Oxford. 36–61.

Astill, G. 1988b Fields. In *The Countryside of Medieval England* (eds G. Astill and A. Grant). Oxford. 62–85.

Astill, G. and Grant, A. (eds), 1988 (1994). *The Countryside of Medieval England*. Oxford.

Aston, M. 1983 Deserted Farmsteads on Exmoor and the Lay Subsidy of 1327 in West Somerset. *Proc Somerset Archaeol Nat Hist Soc* 127. 71–104.

Aston, M. 1998b Land Use and Field Systems. In *Aspects of the Medieval Landscape of Somerset* (ed. M. Aston). *Contributions to the Landscape History of the County*. Bridgewater. 82–97.

Austin, D. 1985 Dartmoor and the Upland Village of the South-West of England. In *Medieval Villages: A review of current work* (ed. D. Hooke). Monogr number 5, Oxford. 71–79.

Austin, D. and Alcock, L. (eds), 1990 *From the Baltic to the Black Sea: studies in Medieval Archaeology*. London.

Austin, D. and Thomas, J. 1990 The 'Proper study' of medieval archaeology: a case study. In *From the Baltic to the Black Sea: Studies in Medieval Archaeology* (eds D. Austin and L. Alcock). London. 43–78.

Austin, D. and Walker, M. J. C, 1985 A new landscape context for Houndtor, Devon. *Medieval Archaeology* 29. 147–52.

Bell, S. 1999 *Landscape pattern, perception and process*. London.

Bettey, J. 2000 Downlands. In *Rural England: An Illustrated History of the Landscape* (ed. J. Thirsk). Oxford. 27–49

Blomē, B. 1929 *The Place-Names of North Devonshire*. Uppsala.

Bodman, M. 2003 *Watermills and other water powered sites in Devon*. Unpub Devon SMR.

Bradley, R. 2000 Mental and Material Landscapes in prehistoric Britain. In *Landscape the richest historical record* (ed. D. Hooke). The Society of Landscape Studies Supplementary Series 1. 1–11.

Braudel, F. 1980 *On History*. (Trans S. Matthew) London.

Braudel, F. 1988 *The Identity of France Volume 1: History and Environment*. (Trans S. Reynolds) London.

Brown, A. P. 1977 Late Devensian and Flandrian Vegetational history of Bodmin Moor, Cornwall. *Phil. Trans Royal Soc London*.

Burrow, I. 1980 Dark Age Devon: The Landscape AD 400–1100. In Devon County Council (ed.) *Archaeology of the Devon Landscape*. Exeter.

Burton, S. H. 1953 *The North Devon Coast. A Guide to its Scenery and Architecture, History and Antiquities*. London.

Caseldine, C. J. 1999 Environmental Setting. In *Historical Atlas of South-West England* (eds R. Kain and W. Ravenhill). Exeter. 25–34.

Cash, M. (ed), 1966 *Devon Inventories*. Torquay.

Caunce, S. 1994 *Oral History and the Local Historian*. London.

Chandler, J. 1996 John Leland in the West Country. In *Topographical Writers in South-West England* (ed. M. Brayshay). Exeter. 34–49

Chapman, H. 2006 *Landscape Archaeology and GIS*. Stroud.

Children, G. and Nash, G. 1997 Establishing a Discourse: The Language of Landscape. In *Semiotics of Landscape: Archaeology of Mind* (ed. G. Nash). BAR Int Ser 611, Oxford. 1–4.

Child, S. 2001 Common Fields Enclosed and Regretted: A Seventeenth century argument among North Devon Farmers. *The Devon Historian* 62. 22–25

Chrystall, F. and McCullagh, R. 2000 The Classification of field systems by shape and function. In *Townships to Farmsteads: Rural Settlement Studies in Scotland, England, and Wales* (eds J. A. Atkinson, I. Banks, and G. MacGregor). Oxford. 117–129.

Clayden, B. 1971 *Memoirs of the Soil Survey of Great Britain, England and Wales: Soils of the Exeter District*. Harpenden.

CLHG (ed.) 1999 *Clayhidon: A Parish on the Blackdowns*. Clayhidon.

Cooper, G. 2002 Fieldname Survey. In *The South Cadbury Environs Project Fieldwork report 1998–2001* (ed. R. Tabor). Bristol. 15–25.

Coupe, F. E. 1920 *Thurlestone Church and Parish*. Kingsbridge.

Cope, J. 1998 *The Modern Antiquarian. A Pre-Millennial Odyssey through Megalithic Britain*. London.

Cosgrove, D. E. 1984 *Social Formation and Symbolic Landscape*. Wisconsin.

Coxhead, J. R. W. 1954 *Legends of Devon*. Westwood Ho!.

Cracknell, B. E. 1951 *Canvey Island: The History of a Marshland Community*. Leicester.

Darby, H. C., Glasscock, R. E., Sheail, J, and Versey, G. R. 1979 The Changing Geographical Distribution of Wealth in England 1086–1334–1525, *Journal of Historical Geography*, 5(3). 249–56.

The Deputy Keeper of Records, 1879 *Inquisitions and Assessments relating to Feudal Aids; with other Analogous Documents Preserved in the Public Record Office. AD 1284–1431. Volume 1*. London.

Downes, J. 1998 *A Guide to Devon Dialect, formerly entitled A Dictionary of Devon Dialect*. Padstow.

Dyer, C. 2000 *Everyday Life in Medieval England*. London.

Everitt, A. 2004 Founders: W. G. Hoskins. *Landscapes* 5(1). 5–17.

Everson, P. and Williamson, T. (eds), 1998 *The Archaeology of landscape. Studies presented to Christopher Taylor*. Manchester.

Fairclough, G., Lambrick, G. and Hopkins, D. 2002 Historic Landscape Characterisation in England and a Hampshire case study. In *Europe's Cultural Landscape: Archaeologists and the Management of Change* (eds G. Fairclough, S. Rippon, and D. Bull). Exeter. 69–83

Field, J. 1993 *A History of English Field-Names*. London.

Finberg, H. P. R. 1951 *Tavistock Abbey, a Study in the Social and Economic History of Devon*. Cambridge.

Finberg, H. P. R. 1952 The making of a Boundary. In *Devonshire studies* (eds W. G Hoskins and H. P. R. Finberg). London. 19–39.

Finberg, H. P. R. 1952 The Open Field in Devon. In *Devonshire studies* (eds W. G Hoskins and H. P. R. Finberg). London. 265–288.

Finberg, H. P. R. (ed.) 1967 *The Agrarian History of England and Wales* IV, 1500–1640. Cambridge.

Findlay, D. C., Colborne, G. J. N., Cope, D. W., Harrod, T. R., Hogen, D. V. and Stains, S. J. 1984 *Soils Survey of England and Wales. Bulletin No. 14 Soils and their use in South West England*. Harpenden.

Fischer, P. F. 1999 Geographical Information Systems: Today and Tomorrow? In *Geographical Information Systems and Landscape Archaeology* (eds M. Gillings, D. Mattingly, and J. van Dalen). Oxford. 5–12.

Fleming, A. 1998 Prehistoric landscape and the quest for territorial pattern. In *The Archaeology of landscape. Studies presented to Christopher Taylor* (eds P. Everson and T. Williamson). Manchester. 42–66

Fleming, A. and Ralph, N. 1982 Medieval settlement and land use on Holne Moor, Dartmoor: the landscape evidence. *Medieval Archaeology* 26, 101–37. 107–9.

Fox, A. 1955 Some evidence for a Dark Age Trading site at Bantham. *Antiquaries Journal* 35. 55–67.

Fox, C. 1953 *Exhibition of Village History. Bantham 2000 BC – 1953 AD*. Unpublished Catalogue.

Fox, H. S. A. 1972a Field Systems of East and South Devon. Past I: East Devon. *Trans Devonshire Ass vol.* 104. 81–135.

Fox, H. S. A. 1972b The Study of Field Systems *The Devon Historian* 4. 3–11.

Fox, H. S. A. 1973 Outfield Cultivation in Devon and Cornwall. In *Husbandry and Marketing in the South-West 1500–1800* (ed. M. Havinden). Exeter. 19–38

Fox, H. S. A. 1975 The Chronology of Enclosure and Economic Development in medieval Devon. *The Economic History Review Second Series* xxviii(2). 181–202.

Fox, H. S. A. 1986 Contraction: Desertion and Dwindling of Dispersed Settlement in a Devon Parish. *Medieval Village Research Group Annual Report* 31. 40–42.

Fox, H. S. A. 1989 Peasants, farmers, patterns of settlement and *pays*: transformations in the landscapes of Devon and Cornwall during the later Middle Ages. In *Landscape and Townscape in the South West* (ed. R. Higham). Exeter Studies in History No. 22. Exeter: University of Exeter. 41–73.

Fox, H. S. A. 1996a Introduction: Transhumance and Seasonal Settlement. In *Seasonal Settlement Vaughan Paper No. 39* (ed. H. S. A. Fox). Leicester. 1–24.

Fox, H. S. A. 1996b Cellar Settlements along the south Devon Coastline. In *Seasonal Settlement Vaughan Paper No. 39* (ed.

H. S. A. Fox). Leicester. 61–69.

Fox, H. S. A. (ed.), 1996 *Seasonal Settlement Vaughan Paper No. 39.* Leicester.

Fox, H. S. A. 1999 Medieval Farming and Rural Settlement. In *Historical Atlas of South-West England* (eds R. Kain and W. Ravenhill). Exeter. 273–280.

Fox, H. S. A. 2001 *The Evolution of the Fishing Village: Landscape and Society along the South Devon Coast,* 1086–1550.Oxford.

Fox, H. S. A. and Padel, O. J. 2000 *The Cornish Lands of the Arundells of Lanherne, Fourteenth to Sixteenth Century.* Devon & Cornwall Record Society, NS vol 41. Exeter.

Franklin, L. 2006. Imagined Landscapes. Archaeology, Perception and Folklore in the Study of Medieval Devon. In *Medieval Devon and Cornwall: Shaping an Ancient Countryside.* Cheshire. 144–161

Fyfe, R. M., Brown, A. G. and Rippon, S. J. 2003 Mid- to late-Holocene vegetation history of Greater Exmoor, UK: estimating the spatial extent of human-induced vegetation change. *Vegetation History and Archaeobotany* 12(4). 215–232

Gaffney, V. and Stančič, Z. 1991 *GIS approaches to regional analysis: a case study of the island of Hvar.* Oxford.

Gelling, M. 2000 *Place-Names in the Landscape.* London.

Gerrard, C. 2000 The Shapwick Project 1989–99. In *Somerset Archaeology Papers to mark 150 years of the Somerset Archaeological and Natural History Society* (ed. C. J. Webster). Taunton. 31–38.

Gerrard, C. 2003 *Medieval Archaeology.* London

Gillard, M. J. 2000 The Exmoor Region in the medieval period: rural settlement. In North Devon and Exmoor: report and Proceedings of the 146th Summer Meeting of the Royal Archaeological Institute (ed. B. Dix). *Archaeol J* 157. 416–422.

Gillard, M. J. 2002 *The Medieval Landscape of the Exmoor region: Enclosure and Settlement in an upland Fringe.* Unpub PhD. Thesis, Univ of Exeter.

Gillings, M. 1995 Flood Dynamics and settlement in the Tisza valley of north-east Hungary: GIS and the Upper Tisza Project. In *Archaeology and Geographical Information Systems: A European Perspective* (eds G. Lock and Z. Stančič). 67–84

Gillings, M. and Wise, A. 1999 *Archaeology Data Service GIS Guide to Good Practice.* Oxford.

Gillings, M., Mattingly, D. and van Dalen, J. (eds), 1999 *Geographical Information Systems and Landscape Archaeology.* Oxford.

Glover, J. E. B., Mawer, A. and Stenton, F. M. 1932 *The English Place-Name Society Volume IX: The place-names of Devon. Parts 1 and 2.* Cambridge.

Gosden, C. 1999 *Anthropology and Archaeology. A changing relationship.* London.

Graham, B. 2000 The past in place: historical geographies of identity. In *Modern Historical Geographies* (eds B. Graham and C. Nash). Harlow. 70–99

Graham, B. and Nash, C. (eds), 2000 *Modern Historical Geographies.* Harlow.

Gray, T. (ed.), 1992 *Harvest Failure in Cornwall and Devon.* Plymouth.

Green, A, 2000 Coffee and Bun, Sergeant Bonnington and the Tornado: Myth and place in Frankton Junction. *Oral History* 28(2). 26–34

Gregory, I. N. and Southall, H. R. 2002 Mapping British Population History. In *Past Time, Past Place: GIS for History* (ed. A. K. Knowles). Redlands California: 117–130

Griffith, F. M. and Reed, S. J. 1998 Rescue Recording at Bantham Ham, South Devon, in 1997. *Devon Archaeol Soc. Proc.* 56. 109–131.

Griffith, F. M. and Weddell, P. 1995 Ironworking in the Blackdown Hills. In *Iron for Archaeologists. A review of recent work in the archaeology of early ironworking sites in Europe. Abstracts* (eds P. and S. Crew).

Griffith, F. M. and Weddell, P. 1996 Ironworking in the Blackdown Hills: results of Recent Survey. In *The Archaeology of Mining and Metallurgy in South-West Britain. Mining History: The Bulletin of the Peak District Historical Society Vol.* 13 (ed. P. Newman). Hist Metallurgy Soc Special Pub 27–34.

Grøn, O., Engelstad, E. and Lindblom, I. (eds), 1991 *Social Space Human Spatial Behaviour in Dwellings and Settlement.* Odense.

Hall, D. 1982 *Medieval Fields.* Aylesbury.

Hallam, H. E. 1981 *Rural England 1066–1328.* London.

Harvey, D. C. 2000 Landscape Organisation, Identity and Change: territoriality and hagiography in medieval west Cornwall. *Landscape Research* 25(2). 201–212.

Havinden, M. 1969 Agricultural History in the South-West. In *The South-West and The Land* (eds M. A. Havinden and C. A. King). Exeter. 7–18

Havinden, M. (ed.) 1973 *Husbandry and Marketing in the South-West 1500–1800.* Exeter.

Havinden, M. A. and King, C. A. (eds), 1969 *The South-West and The Land.* Exeter.

Havinden, M. and Stanes, R, 1999 Agriculture and rural Settlement 1500–1800. In *Historical Atlas of South-West England* (eds R. Kain and W. Ravenhill). Exeter. 281–293.

Havis, R. and Brooks, H. 2004 *Excavations at Stansted Airport,* 1986–91. East Anglian Archaeology reports no. 107.

Hawken, S. 2005 Community Landscape Report Bushy and Buckerell Knap. Unpub. Rep. Univ. of Exeter.

Hawkins, M. J. *Sales of Wards of Somerset 1603–41 1965.* Somerset Record Society 67. Frome.

Herring, P. 1996 Transhumance in medieval Cornwall. In *Seasonal Settlement Vaughan Paper No. 39* (ed. H. S. A. Fox). Leicester. 35–44

Hey, D. 2000 Moorlands. In *Rural England: An Illustrated History of the Landscape* (ed. J. Thirsk). Oxford. 188–209

Hirsch, E. 1995 Landscape: between place and space. In *The Anthropology of Landscape: Perspectives on Place and Space* (eds E. Hirsch and M. O'Hanlon). Oxford. 1–30.

Hobbs, S. J. 1995 Harton Town Trust. Unpub Talk

Hooke, D. (ed.), 1985 *Medieval Villages: A review of current work*. Monogr number 5, Oxford.

Hooke, D. 1990 Studies on Devon Charter Boundaries. *TransDevonshire Ass* 122. 193–211.

Hooke, D. 1994 *Pre-Conquest Charter-Bounds of Devon and Cornwall*. Woodbridge.

Hooke, D. (ed.), 2000 *Landscape the richest historical record*. Soc Landscape Studies Supplementary Series 1.

Hoskins, W. G, 1952b Galsworthy. In *Devonshire Studies* (eds W. G. Hoskins and H. P. R. Finberg). London. 78–93.

Hoskins, W. G. 1954. *A New Survey of England: Devon*. London.

Hoskins, W. G. 1954 (2003) *Devon*. Chichester.

Hoskins, W. G. 1955 (1985) *The making of the English Landscape New Edition*. London.

Hoskins, W. G. 1959 *Devon and its People*. Exeter.

Hoskins, W. G. and Finberg, H. P. R. (eds), 1952 *Devonshire studies*. London.

Humphrey, C. 2001 Contested Landscapes in Inner Mongolia: Walls and Cairns. In *Archaeologies of Landscape Contemporary Perspectives* (eds W. Ashmore and A. B. Knapp). Oxford. 55–68.

Ingold, T. 1992 Culture and the perception of the environment. In Bush Base: Forest Farm. Culture, environment, and development (eds E. Croll and D. Parkins). London. 39–56.

Ingold, T. 1993 The Temporality of the Landscape. *World Archaeology* 25(2). 155–173.

Jewell, A. 1981 Some Cultivation Techniques in the South-West of England. In *Agricultural Improvement: Medieval and Modern* (ed. W. Minchinton). Exeter.

Johnson, M. 1996 *An Archaeology of Capitalism*. Oxford.

Jones, R. and Page, M. 2003. Characterizing Rural Settlement and Landscape: Whittlewood Forest in the Middle Ages. *Medieval Archaeology* xlvii. 53–83.

Kain, R. J. P. 1984 The Tithe Files of Mid-Nineteenth Century England and Wales. In *Discovering Past Landscapes* (ed. M. Reed). London. 56–83

Kain, R. J. P. and Oliver, R. R. 2001 *The Historic Parishes of England and Wales: an electronic map of boundaries before 1850 with a gazetteer and metadata*. Colchester.

Kain, R. and Ravenhill, W. (eds), 1999 *Historical Atlas of South-West England*. Exeter.

Kew, J. 1969 Regional Variations in the Devon Land Market, 1536–1558. In *The South-West and The Land* (eds M. A. Havinden and C. A. King). Exeter. 27–43.

Knowles, A. K. (ed.), 2002 *Past Time, Past Place: GIS for History*. Redlands California.

Laing, L. and Laing J. 1996 *Medieval Britain. The Age of Chivalry*. London.

Lambourne, A. 2004 *'According to the Logic of the Landscape'. A Critical Examination of the Significance of the Dartmoor Reaves for the wider Devon Landscape of Today*. Unpublished

MA Dissertation, Univ of Exeter.

Langdon, J. 1982 The Economy of horses and oxen in medieval England. *Agricultural History Review*. 30. 31–40.

Leach, P. and Tabor, R. 1996 The South Cadbury Environs Project. *Proc Somerset Archaeol Nat Hist Soc* 139. 47–57.

L'estrange Ewen, C. 1939 *Devon Taxation Returns in 1334*. Paignton.

Levi-Strauss, C. 1966 *The Savage Mind*. Chicago.

Lewis, C., Mitchell-Fox, P. and Dyer, C. 2001 *Village, Hamlet and Field. Changing Medieval Settlements in Central England*. Macclesfield.

Llobera, M. 1996 Exploring the topography of mind: GIS, social space and archaeology. *Antiquity* 70. 612–622.

Lock, G. R. and Harris, T. M. 1996 Danebury revisited: an English Iron Age Hillfort in a digital landscape. In *Anthropology, Space, and Geographical Information Systems* (eds M. Aldenderfer and H. D. G. Maschner). Oxford. 214–240.

Lock, G. and Stančič, Z. (eds), 1995 *Archaeology and Geographical Information Systems: A European Perspective*. Bristol

McLure, J. T. and Griffiths, G. H. 2002 Historic Landscape Reconstruction and Visualisation, West Oxfordshire, England. *Trans in GIS* 6(1). 69–78

Michell, C. and Common, M. 1978 Staunton – A Deserted South Hams Village. *The Devon Historian* 16. 21–23.

Mills, A. D. 1998 *A Dictionary of English Place-Names* (second edition). Oxford.

Minnitt, S, 1982 Farmers and Field Monuments 4000–2000 BC. In *The archaeology of Somerset: a review to 1500 AD* (eds A. Aston and I. Burrow). Taunton. 23–28.

Muir, R. 2001 *Landscape Detective: Discovering a Countryside*. Macclesfield.

Oswald. N. C. 1994 The Ownership of Farms and Farmlands in Thulestone and the South Hams in Recent Times. *The Devon Historian* 49. 24–27

Padel, O. J. 1999 Place-names. In *Historical Atlas of South-West England* (eds R. Kain and W. Ravenhill). Exeter. 88–94.

Parker, A. J. 2001 Maritime Landscapes. *Landscapes* 1. 22–41.

Pearce, S. 1985 The Early Church in the Landscape: the evidence from North Devon, *Archaeol J* 142: 255–75

Pease Chope, R. 1902a *The Story of Hartland*. Hartland.

Pearse Chope, R. 1902b The Early History of the Manor of Hartland. *Trans Devonshire Ass* Vol. xxxiv. 418–454.

Pearse Chope, R. 1940 *The Book of Hartland*. Torquay.

Petter, H. M. 1985 A Charter of King Aethelwulf. *The Devon Historian* 80, 21–24

Phythian-Adams, C. (ed.), 1993 *Societies, Cultures and Kinship, 1580–1850*. London.

Phythian-Adams, C. 1998 *ELH: punching above its weight*. http://www.le.ac.uk/elh/elhist1.html.

Phythian-Adams, C. 2000 Frontier Valleys. In *Rural England. An Illustrated History of the Landscape* (ed. J. Thirsk). Oxford. 236–262

Polwhele, R. 1793–1806 (1977) *The History of Devonshire in*

Three Volumes. Volumes 1–3. Exeter.

Propp, V. 1984 *Theory and History of Folklore. Theory and History of Literature, Volume 5*. (trans by A. Y. Martin and R. P. Martin). Manchester.

Rackham, O. 1986 *The History of the Countryside*. London.

Ransom, B. 2004 Domesday Ilsington. *The Devon Historian* 68. 7–12.

Ray, B. C. 2002 Teaching the Salaam Witch Trials. In *Past Time, Past Place: GIS for History* (ed. A. K. Knowles). Redlands California. 19–34.

Reichel, O. J. A. 1894a Some Suggestions to Aid Identifying the Place-Names in the Devonshire Domesday. *TransDevonshire Ass* 26. 133–67.

Reichel, O. J. A. 1894b The Hundred of Hartland and the Geldroll. *Trans Devonshire Ass* 26. 416–418.

Relph, E. 1976 *Place and Placelessness*. London.

Rippon, S. 1991. Early Planned Landscapes in South-East Essex. *Essex Archaeology and History* 22. 46–60.

Rippon, S. 1996b *The Gwent Levels: The Evolution of a Wetland Landscape*. CBA Res Rep 105, London.

Rippon, S. 1997 *The Severn Estuary Landscape Evolution and Wetland Reclamation*. London.

Rippon, S. 2000 Landscapes in transition: the later Roman and early medieval periods. In *Landscape the richest historical record* (ed. D. Hooke). Studies Supplementary Series 1. 47–61. London

Rippon, S. 2007 Historic Landscape Characterisation. Its Role in Contemporary British Archaeology and Landscape History. *Landscapes* 2. 1–14.

Risdon, T. 1811 *The Chorographical or Survey of the County of Devon*. London.

Roberts, B. K. 1996. *Landscapes of settlement: prehistory to the present*. London

Roberts, B. K. and Wrathmell, S. 2000 An Atlas of Rural Settlement in England. London

Roberts, B. K. and Wrathmell, S. 2002 *Region and Place. A study of English rural settlement*. London.

Rowse, A. L. 1977 *The History of Devonshire by Richard Polwhele*. Volumes 2 and 3. Dorking.

Ruggles, C. L. N., Medyckyj-Scott, D. J. and Gruffydd, A. 1993 Multiple Viewshed analysis using GIS and its archaeological applications: a case study in Northern Mull. In *Computing the Past – Computer Applications and Quantitative Methods in Archaeology* (eds J. Andresen, T. Madsen, and I. Scollar). CAA 92 Aarhus. 125–132

Seymour, S. 2000 Historical geographies of landscape. In B. Graham and C. Nash (eds) *Modern Historical Geographies*. Harlow. 193–217

Shakespeare, L. 1990 *The Memory be Green: On Oral History of a Devon Village* [*Littleham*]. Littleham.

Short, J. R. 1991 *Imagined Country Environment, culture and society*. London.

Shorter, A. H., Ravenhill, W. L. D. and Gregory, K. J. 1969 *Southwest England*. London.

Silvester, R. J. 1981 An Excavation on the Post-Roman Site at Bantham, South Devon. *Devon Archaeol Soc Proc* 39. 89–118.

Stanes, R. 1969 Devon Agriculture in the Mid-Eighteenth Century: The Evidence of the Milles Enquiries. In *The South-West and The Land* (eds M. A. Havinden and C. A. King). Exeter. 43–65.

Summerson, H. (ed), 1985 Devon and Cornwall Record Society Ns Volume 28. *Crown Pleas of the Devon Eyre of 1238*. Torquay.

Taçon, P. S. C. 1994 Socialising landscapes: the long-term implications of signs, symbols and marks on the land. In L. Head, C. Gosde, and J. P. White (eds) *Social Landscapes*. Archaeology in Oceania 29, 3. 117–29. Sidney

Tanner, A. 1991 Spatial organisation in social formation and symbolic action: Fijian and Canadian examples. In *Social Space Human Spatial Behaviour in Dwellings and Settlement* (eds O. Grøn, E. Engelstad, and I. Lindblom). Odense. 21–39.

Thirsk, J. 1961 Industries in the Countryside. In F. J. Fisher (ed.) *Essays in the economic and social history of Tudor and Stuart England in honour of R. H. Tawey*. Cambridge. 70–88.

Thirsk. J. (ed), 2000 *Rural England An Illustrated History of the Landscape*. Oxford.

Thomas, J. 2001 Archaeologies of Place and Landscape. In *Archaeological Theory Today* (ed. I. Hodder). Cambridge. 165–186

Thorn, F. and Thorn, C. 1980 *Domesday Book: Devon*. Chichester

Tilley, C. 1995 Rocks and Resources: landscapes and power. *Cornish Archaeology No. 34*. 5–57.

Tilley, C. 1994 *A Phenomenology of Landscape Places, Paths and Monuments*. Oxford.

Timms, S, 1994 'Deep Breathing to Grimspound': Archaeologists Discover Dartmoor. *Devon Archaeol Soc Proc* 52. 1–19

Todd, M. 1984 Excavations at Hembury (Devon), 1980–83: A Summary Report. *The Antiquities Journal* LXIV(2). 251–268

Tonkin, E. 1992 *Narrating our Pasts The Social Constructions of Oral History*. Cambridge.

Toulson, S. 1999 *The Blackdown Hills of Somerset and Devon*. Bradford on Avon.

Turner, S. 2006 Historic Landscape Characterisation: A landscape archaeology for research, management and planning, *Landscape Research* 31: 4, 385–398

Tuan, Yi-Fu, 1977 *Space and Place, The Perspective of Experience*. London.

Ucko, P. J. 1994 Forward. In *Sacred Sites, Scared Places* (eds D. L. Carmichael, J. Hubert, B. Reeves, and A. Schanche). One World Archaeology 23. London. xiii–xxiii.

Uhlig, H. 1961 Old Hamlets with Infield and Outfield Systems in Western and Central Europe *Geografiska Annaler*, 43(1/2). 285–312.

Vancouver, C. 1808 (1969) *General View of the Agriculture of the County of Devon*. Newton Abbot.

Van Bath, S. 1963 *The agrarian history of Western Europe, A.D. 500–1850*, London.

Vidal de la Blache, P. 1903 *Tableau de la Géographie de la France*. Paris.

Wakeling, K. 1999 Introduction. In *Clayhidon A Parish on the Blackdowns* (eds CLHG). Clayhidon.

Walls, S. 2004 Enclosure Awards, an igmored landscape: A case study of the Blackdown Hills. Unpub rep for the Community Landscapes Project, Univ of Exeter.

Warden Page, J. L. 1895 *The Coast of Devon and Lundy Island. Their Towns, Villages, Scenes, Antiquities, and legends*. London.

Watts, M. 2002 *The Archaeology of Mills and Milling*. Stroud.

Webber, R. 1976 *The Devon and Somerset Blackdowns*. London.

Weldon Finn, R. 1967 Devonshire. In *The Domesday Geography of South-West England* (eds H. C. Darby and R. Weldon Finn). Cambridge. 223–295.

West, S. E. and McLaughlin, A. 1998 *Towards a Landscape History of Walsham le Willows, Suffolk. East Anglian Archaeology Report no.* 85. Ipswich.

Wheatley, D. and Gillings, M. 2002 *Spatial Technology and Archaeology. The archaeological applications of GIS*. London.

Whitlock, R. 1977 *The Folklore of Devon*. London.

Wiecken, J. 2004 Iron working in the Blackdown Hills – A report on two slag mounds (features 3 and 4) on Bywood Farm/Dunkeswell and a general discussion of the distribution of iron working. Unpub rep for the Community Landscapes Project, Univ of Exeter.

Witcher, R. 1999 GIS and Landscapes of Perception. In *Geographical Information Systems and Landscape Archaeology* (eds M. Gillings, D. Mattingly, and J. van Dalen). Oxford. 13–22.

Wilkes, E. 2004 Survey and Excavation at Mount Folly, Bigbury-on-Sea. *Devon Archaeology Society Newsletter* (5).

Wilkinson, K. N. 1996 Of Sheep and Men: GIS and the development of medieval settlement in the Cotswolds. In *Imaging the Past. Electronic Imaging and Computer Graphics in Museums and Archaeology* (eds T. Higgins, P. Main, and J. Lang). British Museum Occas Paper No. 14. London. 271–282.

Williamson, T. 1987 Early Co-axial Field Systems on the East Anglian Boulder Clays. *Proc Prehist Soc* 53. 419–431.

Williamson, T. 2000 Understanding Enclosure. *Landscapes* 1(1). 56–79.

Wiliamson, T. 2002 *The Transformation of Rural England. Farming and the Landscape 1700 and 1870*. Exeter.

Williamson, T. 2003 *Shaping the Medieval Landscape: Settlement, Society, Environment*. Macclesfield.

Willy, M. 1955 *The South Hams*. London.

Woolgar, C. M. 1999 *The Great Medieval Household in Late Medieval England*. London.

Wyatt, P. and Stanes, R. (eds), 1997 *Uffculme: A Peculiar Parish. A Devon Town in Tudor Times*. Uffculme.

Yeats, W. B. 1888 *Fairy and Folk Tales of the Irish Peasantry*. London.

Youing, J. 1955 Devon and Cornwall Record Society Ns Volume 1. Devon Monastic Lands: Calendar of Particulars for Grants 1536–155.

Index of Place Names